THE CLASH

The CLASH!

A STUDY IN NATIONALITIES

BY

WILLIAM HENRY
MOORE

BRESCIA COLLEGE
LIBRARY

7020

1918

J. M. DENT & SONS, LIMITED
LONDON -- TORONTO
PARIS: J. M. DENT ET FILS

COPYRIGHT, CANADA, 1918
BY J. M. DENT & SONS, LIMITED
TORONTO

First Edition September, 1918.
Second Edition November, 1918.
Third Edition November, 1918.
Fourth Edition December, 1918.

PRINTED IN CANADA

TO MY FATHER
JAMES BEACH MOORE

CONTENTS

THE INTRODUCTION

THE last page of this book's manuscript had been placed in the printers' hands when the daily press announced that the army had been called upon to quell the violence of a mob protesting in the City of Quebec against the enforcement of the Military Service Act. The press emphasised the gravity of the situation by head-lines that reached half-way across the page. Bonnett and I read the news together as we hurried, as fast as a suburban train hurries these days, toward "Fairport Farm." Bonnett was intent upon repairing the ravages of winter, laid bare by spring temperature; and I, armed (literally) with a mass of pamphlets and reference books, upon complying with the publisher's request for an Introduction.

"It's a bad business," said Bonnett, referring to the mob's defiance of law.

"Shocking," I agreed.

"And yet it is an ill wind that blows no good," remarked Bonnett reflectively. "Now all English-Canadians will be at last united against the French. Those who have attempted to defend them will surely be convinced that they were in the wrong."

"But all French-Canadians are not opposed to

the enforcement of the Military Service Act,"
I expostulated. "The French-Canadian leaders
have said law must be obeyed, and the great body
of sentiment within French Canada is in favour
of its being obeyed."

" 'One language, one school, one flag': that's my
motto," said Bonnett.

Sincerely I admitted the necessity of having one
flag for all Canada, and as sincerely sought to convince Bonnett that neither in the happenings of
the past nor in the reasonings of the present, could
justification be found for the contention that "The
One Flag" was in danger by the existence of two
languages and two schools. "An English-Canadian Tory mob—presumably Protestant—once
burnt down the Canadian Parliament Buildings,"
I told him. "Yet it would be unfair, as a result
of that incident, to charge English-Canadian
Protestant Tories with disloyalty. As a result of
the withdrawal of a preference which the United
Kingdom had been giving to Canadian products,
many prominent English-speaking Canadians—
and Protestants—signed, in 1849, a manifesto for
annexation to the United States. They were not
insignificant men who thus strove to pull down
the Union Jack on Canadian soil. On the list
you will find the names of D. L. Macpherson,
who subsequently became Lieutenant-Governor
of Ontario; J. Rose, who afterwards, as Sir John
Rose, became Minister of Finance in the Cabinet
of Sir John A. Macdonald; and J. J. C. Abbot,

who, as Sir John Abbot, became Prime Minister of a Conservative Administration. It would be absurd to interpret their action as expressing the will of their co-religionists and compatriots."

These things and many other politically bad things, did I rake from the past in an effort to convince Bonnett that the makers of mistakes had not all been born to the French language and reared in Catholic schools.

"This country must remain British," said he.

"Few will question that statement. But surely a second language and a second school are not inconsistent with British principles. 'English Protestant' is not, as some would have us believe, a synonym for 'British.' None will doubt the plain truth that men may speak the English language and attend a Protestant Church without being British; while others may speak the French language, attend the Roman Catholic Church, and be stoutly British. Please remember that the English language and the Protestant religion are not the distinguishing jewels of the British Empire. There are far more of the English tongue, and far more of Protestant faiths in the United States than in all Greater Britain; and yet the United States is not British. If we are to believe our Whittaker, only one English-speaking man in three is a Britisher, and only one Britisher in six is a Protestant. We who live under the protection of the Union Jack are of no particular race: we are of all races; we are of

no particular language: we are born to all languages; nor are we of any particular Church: for
in Greater Britain, God is worshipped after the
manner of all Churches. The word 'British' in
the sense of nationality, expresses a 'super-nation-
ality,' incorporating without weakening the various nationalities which compose the humanity of
the British Empire. Therein lies the genius."

"This country must be English-speaking and
Protestant," doggedly maintained Bonnett.

"Perhaps you will admit that the English nationality and the Protestant Church are admirable—only to the extent of the virtues they represent. Further, you may admit—nay, Bonnett,
you may be willing to insist—that their crowning
excellence lies in their adherence to the principle
of *freedom*. While English-speaking people and
Protestants are actually only a small minority
within the heterogeneous British Empire, they are
in control of its destinies. Why? Is it not because men of other tongues and other religions
have believed in and relied upon their sense of
justice. The success of the Britannic Empire
has been only in proportion to the extent of the
good-will which has pervaded the peoples, who,
of different tongues and of different religions and
of different nationalities, constitute its population.
Destroy that spirit, *substitute for it the doctrine
that English Protestants are a ruling caste, or that
in each self-contained part of the Empire the
strong may compel the weak to surrender their*

individuality, then that which is British loses its essence—only an impermanent shell remains."

"Ordinarily you might be right," replied Bonnett. "But in these days men must protect their own. The priests are behind the troubles in Quebec and Ireland, the hierarchy is behind the priest and the Pope is behind the hierarchy. Whatever may have been involved at the commencement, the issue is now largely religious. The Pope is unfriendly to the Allies, and we must, in self-defence, curtail the power of his Church and schools in Canada."

"I am glad you have put the thing so bluntly, Bonnett. This is a day of plain speech. Having talked over the French-Canadian question with many people these past several months, I find there are others who think as you do, although for the most part expressing themselves by innuendoes and more or less indelicate insinuations. Now, let me ask you one or two pertinent questions. Why do you say the Pope is unfriendly to the Allies?"

"Because he is friendly to the Central Powers," answered Bonnett.

"And upon what do you make that statement?"

"It is to be expected," replied Bonnett; "since Austria has the last word in electing the Pope."

"It is true that at one time Austria had the power of vetoing the nomination of one cardinal, but that power no longer exists. In 1904, Pius X, as a result of the Rampolla affair, suppressed all right of veto or exclusion on the part of secular governments. Further, any cardinal accepting from his government the charge of proposing a veto, is, by that act, excommunicated."

Bonnett smiled incredulously, apparently believing me to be the misinformed dupe of some designing priest, probably a Jesuit.

"Mistrust not the source of my information, Bonnett; it is but the Encyclopedia Britannica."

"Austria is a Catholic country," asserted Bonnett defiantly.

"There are not nearly as many Catholics in Austria as there are in the Allied countries; and, for that matter, there are are not nearly as many Catholics in all the Central Countries as there are in the Allied Countries. If the Pope's sympathy is swayed by weight of numbers, then it is with the Allies, with a force of nearly two to one. However, let us proceed to another phase of the situation. I presume you, like most people, are of the opinion that Germany pushed the Hapsburg Government into the war, and has repeatedly intrigued and exerted influence to keep it there. Englishmen, until the verge of the war, were on friendly terms with Austrians, whereas we were bound some day to have a rupture with Germans."

To this Bonnett assented, and I continued: "Germany is Protestant; surely the Pope is not supporting its prestige!"

INTRODUCTION xv

"But Germany has a large number of Roman Catholics," suggested Bonnett.

"Let us be exact; the 'Statesmen's Annual' (1916) gives Germany's population as 61.6 per cent. Protestant, and 36.7 per cent. Roman Catholic. But let me ask another question. Are you not of the opinion that the most virulent part of Germany is—"

"Prussia," said Bonnett, as I paused for an answer.

"And Prussia is overwhelmingly Protestant," I added. "If you really are anxious for the truth, do not stop with remembering that Austria has more Roman Catholics than the British Isles. Remember also that Germany has more Protestants than England, Scotland, and Wales, combined. Now mistake me not, Bonnett, I am not attempting anything beyond an analysis of the reasons why the Pope could not possibly be supporting the Central Powers."

"But he said nothing against the outrages in Belgium; made no protest against the destruction of life and property."

"That is simply untrue. The Pope publicly protested against the invasion of Belgium. Could he have done more? Do you know of Cardinal Mercier?" I asked.

"Yes," replied Bonnett. "He is the Churchman who stood boldly against the German atrocities."

"There can be no question of Mercier's information as to the real situation. He must know all there is to know. There can be no doubt as to his loyalty and integrity. Mercier has been, and is, the big cleric of the war. And if a cardinal can give a certificate of character to a Pope, Mercier gave one to Benedict XV in addressing his people after returning from the Vatican. He said: 'He' (the Pope), 'understands and shares our anxieties concerning our religious liberties and our patriotic feelings. He was good enough to sum up his profound thought on your behalf, which I received most eagerly, in the inscription traced by his own august hand beneath his portrait; I here transcribe it for you in all simplicity:

"'"To our revered brother, Cardinal Mercier, Archbishop of Mechlin. We give the Apostolic Blessing with all our heart, assuring him that We are always with him, and that We share his grief and his anguish, inasmuch as his cause is our cause."'"

Bonnett had no comment to make upon this statement which, by the way, I read from a pamphlet entitled "The Pope and the War," by Neil McNeil, the Archbishop of Toronto. I continued:

"Tell me, Bonnett—and I have asked others the same question—what you would have the Pope do that he has not done? He has no army. Catholics, like Protestants, are divided in their allegiance in the Great War. Would you have him instruct Catholics to oppose the Central Powers? Such an instruction would be tantamount to an order for the revolt of Catholics within, let us say, Austria. That might please us now, but if the Pope *could* cause a revolt in Austria, it would be equally within his power to cause a revolt in England or Canada, or in the United States. And that would be distressing. We, who are not of the Roman Catholic Church, upon the success of a Catholic revolt in the Central Powers, would insist, for our own future protection, upon the curtailment of the Pope's power to repeat the performance."

"Do you mean to say there is no significance to be attached to the fact that Roman Catholic Quebec and Roman Catholic Ireland have both protested against conscription and both have shown an unwillingness to provide volunteers for the army?"

"The farmers of Ontario have protested against conscription," I observed, "and they are, for the most part, Protestant."

Bonnett lighted his pipe unconcernedly. Plainly my answer was unsatisfying.

"Australia voted against conscription, and Australia is 75 per cent. Protestant," I added.

Bonnett puffed at his pipe apparently quite unshaken in his conclusion that the situations in Quebec and Ireland were identical and due to Papal direction. I turned to my paper thinking the conversation at its end.

"You must know that the priests are leading the people in Quebec and in Ireland," said Bonnett after a few minutes of silence. "Do you mean to say that they are acting without instructions to embarrass the Allies?"

"Have you followed the domestic situation in Poland and Roumania?" I asked. "There, hundreds of thousands—and I think I am right in saying millions—of Catholics, and many priests as well, are protesting against Germany and Austria. Is the Pope behind those protests? or are they due to local conditions? No! Bonnett, the facts are all in favour of the contention that the Catholics of Quebec and of Ireland, like Protestant farmers of Ontario and many Protestants of Australia, and the Catholic peasants of Poland and of Roumania, are acting upon other than religious motives. If there be in allied countries a division on religious grounds at all, it is because those of your way of thinking have insisted upon its existence. The gravest danger of the Allies is the expression of suspicion and the not infrequent reproach of disloyalty against Catholic people. I do not say that these things are inspired by German agents with the object of destroying the unity of the Allies, but I do say that an anti-Popery campaign must necessarily be pleasing to the war lords of Prussia."

"But the Pope might have protested against the outrages in Belgium, against the burning of Louvain, against the bombardment of Belgian and French cathedrals," insisted Bonnett.

"Louvain is a Catholic university. It does not require much knowledge of human nature to conclude that the Pope is more deeply affected at its loss than even you, my dear Bonnett. They were Catholic cathedrals that were bombarded; they were Catholic monasteries that were pillaged; they were Catholic clergy who were dispossessed and Catholic nuns who were maltreated. They were mainly a Catholic people who were despoiled, and driven from their homes in Flanders and France. No, Bonnett, it is incredible that the head of the Catholic Church should not sympathise deeply with the Catholic civilian population that has borne the brunt of atrocious Prussian brutality."

Bonnett simply smiled incredulously; and, in the hope of having him see things as they are I turned to another side of the question. "I presume you credit the Pope with a fair amount of intelligence and foresight, and a desire to maintain the existence of the papacy. Tell me, please, can you see any future for a Vatican under Teutonic World-Wide Dominion? Is Kaiserism consistent with papacy? Does the Kaiser himself not presume to be the Vicar of God, and, if we are to believe what we hear, sometimes proclaims himself a peer with God? 'The Statesmen's Annual', an English publication, is my authority for saying" (and I turned to a recent edition for confirmation) "that 'the Jesuit Order is interdicted in all parts of Germany, and all convents and religious orders, except those engaged in nursing the sick and purely contemplative orders, have been suppressed.' That is the Hun idea of 'entire liberty of conscience and complete equality among all religious confessions.' In the name of common sense, is it believable that the Pope is intriguing to have these conditions extended to England, to the United States, and to Canada?

"The real explanation of the Pope's attitude in the War, lies in the fact, apparently little understood, that his jurisdiction is limited. The truth is that it is beyond his power to direct Catholics to either the Central Powers or the Allies. The Archbishop of Toronto has put the matter very simply before the public in these words:

> "'The Pope never instructs us Catholics as to how we should vote at elections or how we should conduct military campaigns or what part we should take in wars. These things are all outside his sphere of action. His duties have reference to the moral and spiritual side of life.'"

The train, stopping and starting, finally stopped at our suburban destination. Do I need to add that Bonnett proceeded to his work convinced that the Pope is intriguing on behalf of the Central Powers, that the weight of his influence is against the Allies, and that Catholic schools and the French language, have no proper place under the Union Jack in Canada? His mind had been made on the subject, and it was not to be unmade by facts. While willing to discuss the subject—most Irishmen are willing to discuss a subject—he frankly confessed that in his opinion this particular matter was not to be determined by weight of evidence. Think not Bonnett a narrow sectarian, a fanatical supporter of the tenets of some particular Church. I am sure he would be willing to admit that religion with him is a negative rather than a positive force, a political rather than a spiritual influence. He professes the broadest principles of toleration; but, in his opinion, Roman Catholics ought not to have their schools, and French-Canadians ought not to speak their language in Ontario, or for that matter in any part of Canada.

There are many in this Province of Ontario who, with Bonnett, solidly and stubbornly refuse to have this "French-Canadian question" determined upon its merits. They know only what they *want* to do and refuse to deliberate upon what they *ought* to do. Only the other day a man, having read the proof-sheets of this book, remarked: "You have all the argument, but 'good, bad or indifferent,' the regulations restricting the use of the French language in Ontario must stand." And he was not a plumber. With many, race, national, and religious antagonisms, are regarded as natural. That there should be harmony in diversity, is regarded as impossible. For them, heaven will not be Heaven unless it be conducted in their one language, and according to the rights of their particular Church.

No! Bonnett is not an unfamiliar figure. You may meet him on the trains, in the lodge-rooms, and public corridors, wherever the clash of nationalities is discussed.

I would not have the stranger to this Canadian question conclude that it is in any way an aftermath of the war. The war only served to change (slightly) the argument of those who, like Bonnett, resist French-Canadian pretensions through fear of Roman Catholic aggression. Nor would I have the stranger conclude that the question is solely religious. As we shall see, many another element enters into it. But we ought not to anticipate the argument.

I do not believe that all Canadians who speak English and say prayers in Protestant Churches are of Bonnett's mind; are equally opposed to a decision of our difficulties upon the weight of evidence. And in this belief, confident in the fair reasoning of my compatriots, have set forth the facts which bid the major—and junior—nationality within Canada give to the minor—and senior—freedom. I am asking the reader to go with me farther than a suburban journey; am asking him to travel in lands with diverse nationalities, wherever civilisation is professed; am asking him to review the works of Toynbee, Muir, Rose, Burns, Buxton, Low, Zimmern, Acton, Robertson, Hazen, Hobhouse, and others, who, analysing nationality, have made it possible to study Canadian national problems in the light of the world's history.

I would not do Bonnett an injustice. He is as sound in plumbing science as he is weak in political. With experienced eyes, he ferreted out the exact spot from which our troubles emerged. Fascinated—as most men are at the sight of others working—I watched Bonnett saw his way through floors and reaching, wrench in hand, into the darkness, deftly uncouple and bring before my eyes a frost-blown elbow.

"No fault in the system?" I asked.

"None," replied Bonnett.

"No flaw in the elbow?"

"It was sound."

"An abnormal temperature has been created, and a part, perfectly capable of performing efficient service under natural conditions, broke when subjected to the ensuing strain," I suggested.

"That's it," said Bonnett.

"The rest of the system was rendered useless. Destruction spread throughout the house. And the fault; that is the thing we must determine if we would prevent trouble for the future. The fault rests with those who created the abnormal condition."

"Quite true," assented Bonnett.

I am sure he was thinking merely of the broken joint, of my ruined ceilings and stained walls and of my negligent caretaker. But I was thinking of the national troubles of Canada, and that sound part of our system of Confederation which is being subjected to abnormal strain and of the immutability of the consequences of the violation of the laws which ought to regulate man's relation to man.

"FAIRPORT FARM,"

Rouge, Ontario, *July 18, 1918.*

THE CLASH

CHAPTER I

NATIONALITY! What is it?

"When the scholar Casaubon was taken to the great hall of the Sorbonne and was told by his guide that on that spot discussions had been going on for several centuries, he asked 'Qu'a-t-on décidé?' An equally pertinent question may be asked in the present instance without it being possible to elicit an absolutely satisfactory reply. It is, indeed, no easy matter to explain in epigrammatic form an idea so complex as that of Nationality. *Definitio est negatio.*" So writes Lord Cromer in the introduction to Arnold Toynbee's "The New Europe."

Nationality is one of those strangely elusive mystic forces which men may discuss at length, and yet fail to define in succinct sentences. Like electricity, its force may be felt; its appearance described; its sources traced; but, when we attempt to pin it down with a definition, it escapes. And yet a clear knowledge of the subject is imperative, for the forces of nationality have always had an important part in establishing the fortunes of mankind and, besides, are inextricably bound up in the underlying causes of the war.

While we cannot satisfactorily define nationality,

3

we can set forth the factors that usually, but by no
means always, enter into it.

1. Ethnical identity,
2. Identity of language,
3. The unity of religion,
4. Common economic interests,
5. Habitation subject to common geographical
conditions,
6. Common history and traditions of the past,
7. A uniform theory of government.

Canadians have a special interest in nationality
and are under a special obligation to study it. Not
only as participants in the war is it our duty to
bear an intelligent part of the world's problem of
nationalities; but, in addition, we have to shoulder
responsibility for right thinking in a domestic
problem of nationality. Let us not refuse to acknowledge the gravity of our own situation.
There are within Canada two nationalities, squarely opposed on issues which men have always considered fundamental. Canadians who are descendants
of the men and women of the Old French Régime,
complain that they have been deprived of legitimate claims to national expression in a state domin-
ated by those who, mainly of English, Irish, and
Scotch parentage, speaking the English language,
may be called, although, of course, not quite correctly, English-Canadians. The issues have to be
fairly met. Peace is not obtainable so long as each
group adheres to its present temper of "My own
side, right or wrong." That is the highway

towards destruction. Prejudice must be cast away and things seen as they are, if the country is to have harmony instead of dissension—and worse. And, as the old proverb runs, "Spiders might make silk if they could live in harmony with each other." Fortunately, there is now a voluminous literature arising out of the war on the relations of nationalities, from which we may draw a light upon Canadian affairs, and obtain a much-needed perspective.

At first sight, allegiance to a common state, appears to be the test of nationality; and in that sense the word is probably most frequently used. But the word nationality should not be confused with the word nation in the sense of a state. The state is the casing; the nationalities are the encased. The distinction is vital to an understanding of our subject. "What is a nation?" the great Kossuth asked a Serb Member of the Hungarian Diet. "A race which possesses its own language, customs, and culture, and enough self-consciousness to preserve them," replied the Serb. "A nation must also have its own government," answered Kossuth. "We do not go so far," said the Serb, "one nation can live under several different governments, and again several nations can form a single state." "Both the Magyar and the Serb were right," comments the editor of "War and Democracy," who relates the conversation; "though the latter was speaking of 'nationality' and the former of 'nation'."

Have the French-Canadians then a nationality? That must be first decided. The existence of nationality must be established beyond the shadow of doubt; for the mechanism of State ought not to be burdened with the duty of recognising two nationalities without adequate cause. The case for dual nationality must be clear and sound; its claims are not to be acknowledged merely for the asking. Let us then submit, not the claims of the French-Canadians as they have been presented, but the facts, as revealed by history and common knowledge, to the tests which have been laid down in the literature of the subject.

Ethnical identity, the French-Canadians have, and an identity, rare in its solidarity. At the date of the Conquest, there were only some sixty thousand French in Canada—we may assume about thirty thousand of each sex—and mainly from their mating have been reared the nearly three million French-Canadians of to-day. Nor is that all: this ethnical identity goes back far beyond the settlement of Canada; for, as we shall see later on, the parent-stock came mainly from the same districts in Northwestern France. There has been comparatively little intermarriage with the other ethnical groups in Canada; we may regret the fact, but it has made for race solidarity. What peoples to-day have a better preserved ethnical identity? There is certainly nothing like it on this continent, and nothing more striking on the European Continent. France has within its boundaries three well-defined races, as has Germany. The population of the United Kingdom is made up of several races, and much of the mixture is of comparatively recent compounding. The Jews are frequently held up as an example of race identity, but not even they have kept their blood purer than have the French-Canadians during the last three hundred years.

The French-Canadians have also a complete identity of language—another thing rare in the experiences of nationalities. To-day all the citizens of France are Frenchmen, and yet there are thousands in Northwestern France who speak a language more Celtic than French; the Corsicans are of French nationality, but my friend, M. Santini, tells me their tongue is more that of Italy than of France. There are Alsatians and Lorrainers who, proclaiming themselves of French nationality, speak nothing but German, as did their fathers before the days of '71. There is a Swiss nationality, much of it in Switzerland; and yet there are French, German, and Italian languages in Switzerland, all of them recognised in law, and a fourth which is unrecognised. When the German-speaking Swiss comes to America, he is not a German, but on the contrary, always a Swiss and proud of it. The Jews are said to have a nationality, but have only the thread of a common language; they speak the polyglot tongues of commerce. To-day the subjects of King George inhabiting England, Scotland, and Wales, may be said to have a common dominating nationality, and yet one out of every ten Welshmen speaks no English, and thousands of Scotsmen tenaciously cling to Gaelic. There is a nationality in Ireland which, violently distinctive, is, curiously enough, compelled to denounce England, its arch-enemy, in England's language. There are Americans of the United States, and Canadians of the non-French districts who have not mastered the tongues common to the group to which they belong, and yet proclaim themselves of its nationality. Again, in our testing, have we found the French-Canadians distinctive in homogeneity?

This brings us to that great influence in the relations of mankind, religion. Mohammedanism has been called a nationality, as has Judaism, so closely are men bound together by the ties of church. Before the Reformation, religion was an even more important force than language; than race itself— in holding men together. National distinctions are modern, as compared with religious distinctions. Religion was once the distinguishing group characteristic everywhere, and remains such to-day in India and several Eastern countries. Religion is still the deciding group factor in some sections of the Western world, as in South America, where the natives, upon giving up their pagan religions for Christianity, are admitted into the fellowship of the dominant group.

A force for unity; religion is also a force for dissension. A brief survey will show that in few nationalities is there a common Church. The Germans claim for themselves a high degree of nationality, and yet 60 out of every 100 Germans are Protestants, and the remaining 40 are Roman Catholics, and bitter has been their opposition. France has a splendid nationality, and is hopelessly divided on the subject of religion. The same may be said for Italy and Portugal. England has its divisions, as have Belgium and the United States. Spain is mainly Roman Catholic, but contains a large dissenting population. In Ireland, religion is practically the dividing line between the nationalities. With the French-Canadians, there is practical unanimity, for almost to the last man, woman, and child, they worship God at a common altar. While most nationalities are surviving in spite of religious dissensions, the French-Canadian nationality has within itself the strength that comes from approaching things spiritual in a common way, has the *esprit de corps* that comes from the association of its members in the wide range of charitable and social activities which are in all communities and under all religions conducted under the direction of churches.

For three hundred years, the French-Canadians have had a common history and common traditions; for a hundred years and more they have been the exclusive guardians of those traditions. Theirs are the glorious voyages of Champlain, the discoveries of La Salle and La Vérendrye, the battles of Frontenac and Dollard and the martyrdoms of Bréboeuf and Lalement; theirs, the memory of free life in a wilderness and dangers

3 c.

from a savage foe. That cannot be forgotten—
and there are other things that are remembered:
the struggles of past and present to maintain the
French language and French culture on the North
American Continent: in early days against the
American colonists who revolted from Great Britain, and later against the English-Canadians who
would have all within the country welded in
homogeneity.

A few years after the Conquest, when the United
States had established its power in the New World,
the French of France gave up their fitful dreams
of prestige in the New World. France closed her
American book and opened a new one, and wrote
"Africa" on the title page. Deserted, the French-
Canadians grew up in the New World, accepting
the theory of government and the economic conditions of their neighbours; but otherwise remaining islanders in a sea of continental Anglo-Saxon-
Americanism. Insularity breeds stubbornness; it
gave the Englishman his bull-dog tenacity. Like
the Englishmen of England, forcing their nationality upon none, the French-Canadians are of one
mind to hold fast to common traditions, and
are inspired with common aspirations for the present and the future. That resolve is the stronger
because of the oppression to which they believe
they have been subjected, none the less oppression
because it has been not of massacres as in Russia,
but of slurs of inferiority, limitations in the schoolroom, the courts of justice and the halls of legislation, as in Germany.

Nationality has been called group personality, a group soul; in English it is "the spirit of England," in German "die Deutsche Seele," in France "l'âme de la France," in Belgium "l'âme Belge." Renan has called nationality "a soul and a spiritual principle, the resultant of a long historic past, of sacrifices and efforts made in common, and of a united will and aspiration in the present; to have done together great things in the past, to be minded to do great things in the present." The definition is good, and yet it leaves much unsaid of this strong, elusive, human force. In "Towards a Lasting Settlement," one of the interesting English war books, an attempt has been made to define nationality: "It stands for the cultivation of those national habits of life and thought which are dearer to us than others because they are in a fuller sense 'our own'—just as family customs and family words have a peculiar savour for us, creating, as they do, a whole atmosphere, and calling up, without any need of explanatory speech, a hundred common memories and familiar ties."

In these attempts at definition the united will to preserve is regarded as essential. That there is little French, and little Spanish nationality in the United States to-day—as we are so often reminded in Canada—is because there was no will to preserve. If there be no Scotch nationality in the United Kingdom to-day, or only a remnant, it is because of lack of will to preserve; if there be a Celtic nationality in Ireland, it is because there has been and is, a will to preserve. And in Quebec, in Ontario, and Manitoba, the French-Canadians have displayed a tenacious will to preserve. The will to preserve: that is the force which must be constantly borne in mind by the student who would unravel the skeins of nationality.

No matter the test to which it is submitted, the French-Canadian nationality emerges. It has a Church with sermons and services in a distinctive language, a literature, a daily press, in short, self-consciousness, and the means to preserve it. It may be fairly said to have attained the status of a national culture. The events of the war have made men keenly conscious of the importance of nationality, and precise in their analysis of it. Among those who have followed the subject close-ly, is Arnold Toynbee who, in "The New Europe," tells us: "National culture means the conscious will to enjoy and increase this heritage through the med-ium of some particular language. It follows that a national culture, whenever it manifests itself, is as elemental a force as a national democracy, and that to fight against it is to fight against God. No alien culture may dispute its title." Strong words these, and remember they are not mine; they are the words of an Englishman versed in the conflicting forces of nationality, and applied to conditions such as we shall find in Canada.

But in seeking to limit French-Canadian cul-ture in Ontario, in Manitoba, or in any other sec-tion of the country once French, we are not only fighting "against God," as Toynbee puts it—a pretty large order—but also against the principle of freedom which Great Britain has said should regulate the lives of a people made British by the fortunes of war.

BOOKS OF REFERENCE

Charles Roden Buxton and others, *Towards a Lasting Settlement*. Macmillan.
C. Delisle Burns, *The Morality of Nations*. Putnam.
J. Holland Rose, *Nationality in Modern History*. Macmillan.
Arnold Toynbee, *The New Europe*. Dent.
Arnold Toynbee, *Nationality and the War*. Dent.
Freidrich Nauman, *Central Europe*. Knopf.
Felix Adler, *The World Crisis and Its Meaning*. Appleton.
Ramsay Muir, *Nationalism and Internationalism*. Houghton, Mifflin & Co.
Sydney Low and Others, the Spirit of the Allied Nations. Black.
Hugo Münsterberg, *Tomorrow*. Appletons.

CHAPTER II

(Britain's)

THERE are English, French, Germans, Italians, Russians, Turks—and the census officials alone know how many other kinds of men in Canada. All cannot have their languages recognised in law. Multi-lingualism is impossible; we would be repeating the embarrassing experience of Babel. From that sound conclusion, the unsound deduction has been made that multi-lingualism is the natural consequence of bi-lingualism. Admitting the existence of French-Canadian nationality, men have argued that its culture and individuality cannot be recognised without creating chaos. With equal force it might be argued that if I pay interest to the man who has a lien on my land, I shall some day have to pay interest to men who have advanced nothing on my land; if I give up my one-horse buggy for a two-horse democrat, some day I shall, like the drivers in a circus procession, be handling a six-in-hand.

We have found the French-Canadians in possession of all the attributes of nationality, including the all-important "will to preserve." We shall now find that the French-Canadians, in addition, have the rights of a people conquered by Great

14

Britain; and under British ideals the national interests of the conquered are sacred. The French-
Canadians are not to be dealt with as immigrants
who come to a new country, ready and willing to
throw off the old and take on the new—not in
Ontario and Manitoba; for the country within
these provinces was once theirs. That is British
doctrine expressed in the often-used, much-abused
words, "national freedom." Only a few generations ago our ancestors—English and French—
disagreed over certain matters, principally the
claims of a lady named Maria Theresa to a European throne, and when the war was over, English
suzerainty had supplanted French in Canada. The
fortunes of Maria are inconsequential, as compared
with those of the French-Canadians who had, as
a result of the dispute, come under a state organisation new and strange.

Much of our argument will surround the question which naturally arises: "To what rights are a
conquered people entitled?" No one will suggest
that they are not entitled, as individuals, to life.
Not even barbarians will attempt to justify the
wholesale slaughter of those who lose out in the
fortunes of war; but are a conquered people entitled to continue life as a people in the land which
has been ceded?—are they entitled to continue the
culture of their forefathers?—entitled to maintain,
in fact, a national existence?

There are two distinct views on the subject
which, for want of better nomenclature, we may

call "Britain's Way" and "The Other." I name the one Britain's way, because Britain has stood for it more than any other nation. Within it has lain her genius for empire. "Its 433 million inhabitants from Great Britain to Polynesia, from India and Egypt to Central Africa, are drawn from every division of the human race. Cut a section through mankind, and in every layer there will be a British citizen, living under the jurisdiction of British law." So writes Alfred E. Zimmern, one of England's foremost students of politics. Britain's success of Empire has been in proportion to Britain's preservation of the freedom of the nationalities within the Empire. Britain's treatment of the Canadians after the conquest, will serve to illustrate the application of this doctrine, and besides, it has a specific bearing upon the case in hand.

The Quebec Act and the debates in the Imperial Parliament in the days of its passing, set forth many of the principles which the British Government declared ought to prevail in the government of Canada. Sir Edward Thurlow was the Attorney-General of Great Britain at the passing of the Quebec Act, and upon his words we may safely— but need not solely—rely as to Britain's intention towards the French-Canadians after the Conquest. "You ought to change those laws only which relate to the French sovereignty, and in their place substitute laws which should relate to the new sovereign," he said from his place in Parliament; "but with respect to all other laws, all other customs

and institutions whatever, which are indifferent to
the state of subjects and sovereign, humanity, justice and wisdom equally conspire to advise you to
leave to the people just as they were." These are
plain words which should leave no misunderstanding in the minds of men. And they ought to remain
fixed in the memories of men who believe that
national understandings ought to be kept.

There was no question about the legal right of
Great Britain to limit the use of the French
language and French culture in the colony that
had become British, and if it be possible for a conqueror to force an alien tongue upon a conquered
people, there was little doubt as to Great Britain's
ability, since the French-Canadians had been abandoned by the then decrepit government at Ver-
sailles. The issue was a moral one, and as such it
was decided. "I consider the right of conquest so
little, and the right of human nature so much, that
the former has little consideration with me," said
the great Edmund Burke debating the Quebec Bill.
"I look upon the people of Canada as coming, by
the dispensation of God, under the British Government. I would have us govern it in the same manner as the all-wise disposition of Providence would
govern it." No piece of Canadian legislation received the care of greater statesmen than the Quebec Act, and throughout the debate over its provi-
sions, the constant thought expressed was care for
the interests of the French-Canadians. That was
the first consideration.

Two ways in the Canadian question were open to Great Britain at the time: freedom for a continuance of French culture and all that is implied in nationality; or a suppression—at least an attempt at it—and in its place a substitution of Anglicism. The way towards suppression lay ready at hand, namely, incorporation of the newly-acquired territory in one of the longer-held, nearby, American colonies. They were all English-speaking and it was only reasonable to assume that in time the French would learn not only to speak English, but would acquire an English mentality. And Britain did not take that course. After reciting what might have been done, A. Wyatt Tilby, an English historian, tells us what actually was done. "Happily for the Empire, the British Government decided to act generously," he says. "They made no attempt to overwhelm the French by planting British settlers in Quebec; on the contrary, the absurd arrogance displayed by the few hundred English immigrants who entered the colony of their own accord was frequently restrained by the Imperial authorities. . . Nor were the old French customs and laws of the province changed or interfered with more than was absolutely necessary; and the advice of those enthusiasts who believed that every British institution was of inestimable benefit and of universal application was sensibly rejected."

Sentences were not incorporated into the Quebec Bill specifically granting the freedom of the

French language; nor, for that matter, were there specific sentences granting the freedom of air. Without air, there could have been no continued life for the individual, and without language no continued life for the nationality.

For several years after the Conquest all Canada remained French. The old inhabitants retained throughout the country, in what is now Quebec, Ontario, and Manitoba, which were practically the Quebec of that day, their language, and all that went to make up their nationality. They paid allegiance to a British sovereign, instead of to a French sovereign; that was the principal change wrought in their condition by the Conquest. Britain secured sovereignty; the French retained cultural freedom; and the two were compatible.

Such was Britain's spirit in the days of the Quebec Act; such her application of it to an alien nationality. Has Britain grown less generous in her maturity? Can English-Canadians afford to be less generous in these days when freedom has become the watchword of civilisation? The answer to these questions brings us plumb against the underlying causes of the war.

In 1918 Canada is fighting for freedom. All the doing, dying, suffering, mourning, all the soul-stirring tragedies of the war, the Great War itself, are only means to an end—freedom. "Win the War," has become the spiritual injunction of Canadians, but winning the war merely for the sake of a win, would be poor consolation. It is the cause

for which the war is being fought that alone makes
the sacrifices endurable, makes winning worth
while. It is the idea behind the war, which makes
a decisive issue imperative, which makes peace
upon compromise equivalent to defeat. As well
might men have talked of peace parleys in the days
of the American Civil War, while men and women
were still slave-bound in the cotton-fields of the
South. Great Britain seeks not territorial expansion, nor commercial advantage, nor military prestige in the war; her stand is for freedom, unequivocally for freedom, and it is the definiteness of the
position which makes plain the path of British
duty. But we are told by the Germans, by the Austrians, by the whole group of Central Powers, that
they, too, are fighting for freedom, which reminds
us that seldom, if ever, have men consciously fought
against freedom. Even the Confederate States
were fighting for freedom—their own—in the
Civil War.

Clearly this word, freedom, needs to be defined;
its application to the war issues requires analysis
and explanation. We must know the nature of the
freedom that has been denied, must know to whom
and by what right it belongs; otherwise, it is a mere
catch-word which does not grip reality. There
has been a sad lack of education in Canada as to
the underlying causes of the war. Our publicists
seem to have assumed that Canadians would in-
tuitively understand. But we Canadians cannot be
expected to possess greater powers of intuition than

Englishmen, and in England scores of books have been written because it was found that large sections of the community failed to realize "the true inner significance of the struggle."

"The political causes of the present war," say the editors of "The War and Democracy," (the most influential of English war books) "and of the half century of Armed Peace which preceded it are to be found, not in the particular schemes and ambitions of any of the governments of Europe, nor in their secret diplomacy, nor in the machinations of the great armament interests allied to them, sinister though all these may have been, but in the nature of some of those governments themselves, and in their relation to the people over whom they rule." Thus we are told to look for the main cause of the war in the relations which some of the warring governments bear "to the people over whom they rule." To bring the matter squarely before the British people, the editors of "War and Democracy" quote the following paragraph from "Imperial Germany," a book written by Prince Bernhard von Bülow, who directed German policy as Imperial Chancellor from 1900 to 1909:

"If it were possible for members of different nationalities, with different language and customs, and an intellectual life of a different kind, to live side by side in one and the same State, without succumbing to the temptation of each trying to force his own nationality on the other, things on earth would look a good deal more peaceful. But it is a law of life and development in history that where two national civilisations meet they fight for ascendancy. In the struggle between nationalities one nation is the hammer and the other the anvil; one is the victor, and the other the vanquished."

Here we have the pith of the issue. It is the opinion of the editors of "War and Democracy" that *"no words could indicate more clearly the cause that is at stake in the present war"* than those which Prince von Bülow has written in this paragraph. Many reasons—most of them very good ones—have been given why Great Britain is in the war. But this is the central idea. Prince von Bülow's words, say the editors of "War and Democracy," show us that there are still governments in Europe so ignorant as to believe that the different nationalities of mankind are necessarily hostile to one another, and so foolish and brutal as to think that national civilisation, or, as the German Professors call it, 'kultur,' can and indeed must be propagated by the sword."

Great Britain is fighting to stay the hand that wields the hammer—and necessarily Canada, too, is fighting to stay the hand that wields the hammer upon the minor nationalities within the Central Powers. That, then, is the freedom for which we sacrifice.

It must be remembered that "War and Democracy" is not merely one author's view. It is the well-thought-out opinion of a group of England's best educationists—R. W. Seton-Watson, J. Dover

Wilson, Alfred E. Zimmern, Arthur Greenwood; it was written for the use of the Education Workers' Association of the United Kingdom. In other words, the book is authoritative.

Let us seek further clarity on this important question, let us attempt to have the principle which it outlines definitely fixed in our minds—surely there is nothing in Canada worth more pains! By force of circumstances, usually conquest, groups of people, once freely developing towards common ideals, have come under the government of an alien nationality. That is true of the Slavs in Poland, the Danes in Holstein, and the French in Alsace-Lorraine. Germany maintains that these minor nationalities must be made subject to her culture and may at her will be limited in their own. Great Britain declares that to be a violation of the legitimate freedom of nationality, and asserts that this, the most prolific source of wars, shall be ended once for all. With true pacifism, she sees in armaments only the means of war, in the clashing of nationalities a potent cause, which must be uprooted. To quote again from "War and Democracy": "So long as there are peoples in Europe under alien governments, curtailed in the use of their own language, in the propagation of their literature and ideas, in their social intercourse, in their corporate life, in all that we in Great Britain understand by civil liberty, so long will there be men who will mock at the very idea of international peace, and look forward to war, not as an out-worn instrument of a barbarous age, but as a means to national freedom and self-expression."

It is a splendid cause; but—surely we cannot refuse to apply to ourselves the principles which we seek by arms to force upon others. There is, in the Province of Ontario, a minor nationality the people of which say to the dominant English-Canadian nationality: You have curtailed us in the use of our language; you have restricted us in the education which is necessary for the propagation of our literature and ideas; you have taken away our national freedom and self-expression; and this in a land which was ours before it was yours and ours.

That accusation cannot be dismissed with the simple denial that the parallel between the minor nationalities of Germany and the minor nationality of Ontario does not run true. For we shall find the comparisons startlingly true, and we must squarely face the evidence. We can no longer use the old arguments of the "necessities of the State," "commercial advantages of homogeneity," "handiwork of agitators," "superiority of culture"; we can no longer appeal to the essentialness of the common school crucible; for as we shall find, Germany has advanced all these things in her self-defence, and they have been rejected as insufficient, rejected by Greater Britain, rejected by what we believe to be best in civilisation. We simply cannot be Germanlike, we must, as Britain's ally, as an integral part of Great Britain itself, be

unequivocally and splendidly unlike the Germans.
We believe in freedom; for that matter we
believe in generosity. But we may talk of generosity as much as we please, extol it to the skies, and
yet if we give not generously we merely prate. We
may extol the cause of freedom, we may shed our
blood for it; but the true measure of our adherence
to its cause is the extent to which we give freedom.
As Lord Acton has said: "The most certain test by
which we judge whether a country is really free,
is the amount of security enjoyed by minorities."

It is not denied by the English publicists who
have laid bare the relations of nationalities, that in
the past France and Great Britain have been guilty
of fighting in causes which were not essentially on
behalf of freedom—security for minorities. But it
is argued that while men cannot be held responsible
for all the acts of their ancestors, they can and
must be held responsible for their own acts. Mr.
J. M. Robertson, writing of France and Britain,
puts it this way: "Simple common sense, priming
common honesty, has dictated the avowal by ra-
tional men that the honors are substantially even,
that folly and sin played their part in both polities,
and that the sane course is for the self-governing
communities of to-day to live a better life, whatever their forefathers may have done."

We as Canadians must live that better life. But
—and I have in mind the words of a friend, the
head of an Ontario College—the minor nationality within Canada has not contributed its share

4 c.

of men and support to the present war; has not
shouldered its full part of Canada's responsibility;
in a word, "the French-Canadians have not been
patriotic." My friend's opinion may be taken as
illustrative of a large section of English-Canadian
sentiment. It is DeTocqueville who points out
that there are two kinds of patriotism, that of
instinct and that of reason; the former, which is
disinterested, indefinable, but associating the affections with the place of birth, the French-Canadians
have lavished wholly upon this country; but the
latter, that of reason, which is due to the personal
interest of the citizen, and depends on his having a
sense of security under the State, the French-
Canadians have not in full measure. Let us frankly
accept that many French-Canadians have not felt
their responsibility to the State as have most English-Canadians in this war. Let us agree that their
attitude is a disease of the body politic and then—
what shall we do? It is vain to regret the disease,
a waste of precious time to speculate on its serious
outcome. Our prime duty is to get at the cause,
to diagnose the seat of the trouble. And if we English-Canadians find the disease is mainly of our
own making, then it naturally follows it ought to
be of our own curing.

In our diagnosis we may again turn with advantage to "War and Democracy"; for this clashing of nationalities and its causes are of a common
origin the world over. The editors say: "There
are governments in Europe so foolish as to think

that men and women deprived of their national institutions, humiliated in their deepest feelings, and forced into an alien mould, can make good citizens, trustworthy soldiers, or even obedient subjects."

Have we been violating the principles which British men say ought to regulate the relations of nationalities within a common state? Have we been out of harmony with the essence of national freedom, and foolish enough to think that we could escape the consequence?

BOOKS OF REFERENCE

H. E. Egerton and W. L. Grant, *Canadian Constitutional Development*. Musson.

Alfred E. Zimmern and Others, *War and Democracy*. MacMillan.

Lord Acton, *The History of Freedom*. Macmillan.

A. Wyatt Tilby, *British North America, 1763-1867*. Constable.

CHAPTER III

(*The Other*)

THOSE who seek to limit or suppress the national lives of others, have not done so through mere love of cruelty; on the contrary, they believe themselves actuated by exceedingly creditable motives. Into that peculiar position they have been led by wrong doctrines preached since the days of nationality, and in modern times fashioned into an ingenuous philosophy by Teutonic brains. That philosophy we must study if we would understand the situation in Ontario and Manitoba or, for that matter, wherever one national group is trying to break or bend another to its way of thinking. Everywhere the reasonings which urge the use of force as a means to homogeneity, are remarkably alike, and all built upon several cardinal errors which in due time we shall discover.

Since the war we have incorporated the words Prussian, Hun, and Boche, into our vocabulary of bad men's names, and habitually fling them—sometimes without much reason—at our opponents. But a bad name will not stick unless it is deserved; there must be adhesiveness in the object against which it is thrown. My unbacked assertion is not likely to go very far in convincing the world that German and Ontario minds have run through similar grooves in working out the problem of dual nationalities within a single State. The evidence must speak for itself. We have seen Britain's way of dealing with a conquered nationality. From the exact words of Prussia and the exact words of Ontario, the reader may for himself determine whether Canada's national problem is now being treated Britain's way or the other.

The reasoning of the dominant nationality which would restrain by force the self-expression of a minor nationality, invariably begins with an effort to eliminate the moral factor. With morality out of the way, the arguments proceed rapidly and smoothly enough, until near the end, when another, and this time a supreme, difficulty arises in the shape of futility. In other words, the two things most wrong with Ontario's reasoning—and Prussia's—in forcing the culture of the dominant nationality upon the minor, are that it is morally wrong to try it, and impossible to do it. One would think that enough. But I am anticipating the argument; let us proceed by easier stages.

It is argued that since the State makes laws which define right and wrong for individuals, then the State, being the source of right and wrong, is above both. There are men who regard the State —the casing—as the highest human entity, and as a consequence of this reasoning the interests of nationalities—the encased—become of minor importance. Applying that principle to the Canadian situation, there was neither right nor wrong involved in the treatment to be accorded the French-Canadians at the Conquest: there was only political expediency; what was thought to be best for the State. And it has been contended time and time again by English-Canadians, and now and then by an Englishman of England—that such should have been the guiding spirit of the settlement.

Bismarck is supposed to have said: "Might before right." Max Nordau, denying that Bismarck ever said it, stated that the principle "is perfectly accurate, not as a principle, according to which action should proceed, but as a statement as to the manner in which it does proceed." The same doctrine is laid down in other words by the German philosopher Treitschke, whose teachings had a wide influence with the German people. "The State is Might. To maintain its power is the highest duty of the State; of all political shortcomings, weakness is the most abominable and most contemptible. It is the sin against the Holy Ghost of Politics."

The pernicious doctrine of the divine right of might has extended beyond Germany and the Germans, has crossed the Atlantic, undermining our own sense of morality as applied to the State. The doctrine is the more pernicious because there is no one to protect the victims that fall within its path. Of course, in the New World we do not expound the doctrine as bluntly as did Treitschke, nor as frankly—for there is something to be said for the German's claim that his race is Frank by origin. But there are men in Germany who preached it, as we do, in softer words. Nordau many years ago said: "Nowadays, of course, the cry of the common good is always raised, when the power of the State overrides the rights of subject or of neighbour weaker than itself. The method is the familiar one of identifying a supreme power in the State with the country, and the advantages of the ruler or ruling class with that of the people as a whole."

The logical wind-up of the doctrine that the State is above both right and wrong, is an end to civilization; and doctrines sooner or later reach their logical ends, just as water reaches its level.

The subjection of one individual to another, is obviously immoral. The dictates of conscience tell the individual that it is wrong to rob his neighbor of property, of personality, wrong to rob him at all. But the State, having no conscience—or at the best, one which is very irresponsible—no fear of hell or any of the other things that usually restrain individuals, has only to consider the interests of the majority under democracy, and the ambitions or whims of dictators under autocracy. Nor has the State, as organized to-day, a capacity for seeking right merely for the sake of righteousness. Great Britain and France were the first to define the meaning and consequences of what we

may call the Treitschke doctrine, and the first to
repudiate it, and they were not without personal
interest; for, obviously, if the State were right,
always right, then the rights of nationalities became wrongs when they conflicted with the will
of the State; if national interests within the State
were not to be considered sacred by the State, were
to be respected only so long as they did not conflict
with the desires—invariably called necessities
—of the State, then national interests without the
State were equally unsafe. Reasoning thus, Germany became intolerable to civilization.

We have seen in Lord Thurlow's words, the intention of the British statesman towards the conquered of Quebec, and in Mr. Tilby's words the
interpretation of the historian of what was actually
done. Now let us have a concrete application of
the Teutonic principle to a nationality incorporated into the German Empire by conquest. "We
certainly do not wish to deprive the Pole of his
mother-tongue," said Prince von Bülow, "but we
must try to bring it to pass that, by means of the
German language, he comes to understand the
German spirit. In our policy of settlement we
fight for German nationality in the East; in our
policy with regard to the schools we are really
fighting for Polish nationality which we wish to
incorporate in German intellectual life. Here,
again, we cannot proceed without severity, and
this will increase or be mitigated as the Poles
increase or diminish their opposition."

Which doctrine, the British or the German, has been applied by English-Canadians to the minor nationality in Ontario and Manitoba? With the introduction of self-government in this country, English-Canadians became the legatees of Britain's responsibility. Have the English-Canadians of Ontario and Manitoba argued with Thurlow that humanity, justice, and wisdom, compel them to give the French-Canadians possession of all "customs and institutions" that do not relate to French sovereignty, or have they argued, in practically von Bülow's words, that in their policy with regard to the schools, they are really fighting for the French-Canadian nationality which they wish to incorporate in English-Canadian intellectual life? Have the English-Canadians of Ontario and Manitoba accepted the British view that there is a morality above the written law, above the State, above their necessities or their desires, which protects the minor nationality in a land which was once theirs—or have they accepted the German view that, as a dominant majority possessing the State machinery, they may do as they please?

Human memory is short, and although the newspapers have been filled with explanations of Ontario's position, it may be as well to have before our eyes the exact words in which they are expressed. I take them from a "Toronto Globe" editorial, May 27, 1916. "The Globe" says: "The people of Ontario do not seek to abolish the teaching of French in the schools in districts where

French is either the prevailing language or the language of a large minority, as it is in the City of Ottawa. What they do insist upon is that, no matter what other language is given a place in the public-school course of study, English, the official language of the Province, shall be efficiently taught in all the schools of Ontario. More than that, they do not desire; with less the English-speaking majority—twelve times as numerous as the French-speaking minority—will not be satisfied."

"We certainly do not wish to deprive the Pole of his mother-tongue," Prince von Bülow said; "the people of Ontario do not seek to abolish the teaching of French," said the editor of "The Globe"; and yet, on writing these words both must have known that the regulations were designed to abolish not only the Polish and French languages, but the Polish and French-Canadian peoples as well, since under the regulations of both countries it was forbidden to use Polish and French as languages of instruction, except under limitations which amount practically to prohibition. All geography, all mathematics, all the subjects on the school curriculum, are to be taught solely in German and English, and the Teuton mind would follow in one country and the English-Canadian in the other. The effect of Regulation 17 of Ontario's Department of Education, is denationalisation; the object of Regulation 17, as expressed by its creators, is "to rescue this province from bi-lingualism" and dual nationality; and yet the "Globe" argues in words that might have been borrowed from von Bülow that the lingual rights of the minor nationality are preserved. As to the virtue of the business, it is mathematical: there are twelve English-Canadians and one French-Canadian; that settles the business, for, as the Germans put it, Might is Right. The application of mathematics as a test of national conduct, reminds me of a comment made on the subject by the Professor of History in Columbia, Charles D. Hazen, who in "Alsace and Lorraine Under German Rule," says: "The spectacle of a nation which prides itself upon its exceptional enlightenment, waging war in the twentieth century upon a language which is the mother-tongue of twenty per cent. of the population of Alsace, is unworthy, as well as intolerable." It must be remembered that Ontario and Alsace are alike in having once belonged to the men of the minority; although relatively to total population, there are slightly more French in Alsace than in Ontario, actually in numbers there are more French in Ontario than in Alsace. There is nothing in the atmosphere which makes the spectacle more tolerable in Canada.

The sovereign people, the English-speaking majority, know what is best for the French-Canadians, know the true interest of the French-Canadians, better than they know it themselves, it is argued. "Hands off Ontario," say the Ontarians; "Hands off Manitoba," cry the Manitobans. We

are not oppressing the French-Canadians, Manitobans and Ontarians will argue; and with strange
inconsistency add: It is for their own good that
their national culture be not allowed free play for
development. And the Germans have the same
spirit. To quote Treitschke: "We Germans, who
know both Germany and France, are better judges
than the Alsatians, of their true welfare; better
than the unfortunate folk who, by reason of their
intercourse with France have lived in ignorance of
the New Germany." Are these not all but the
identical words used by the press of Ontario in
protest of outside interference on behalf of the
French-Canadian minority? Writing of the bi-
lingual question, the "Toronto Star," of April 26,
1916, says: "We in Ontario are quite capable of
settling it. It does not worry us." The spring had
been taken out of the French-Canadian year; the
possession that mankind values most had been
taken from the minor nationality, and yet the English-Canadian—at least "The Star" editor—was
not worried. The English-Canadians were better
judges than the French-Canadians of their true
welfare. "We do not require any assistance from
the Dominion Government or Parliament," continues the editor. "We will do justice to all the
residents of Ontario, of all races, and religions, and
the less interference there is from outside, the better it will be for all concerned." While the paper
is before us, consider also this from the same
source: "Of course, everybody in Ontario must

know English. To deprive any child of the knowledge of English, would be like depriving it of the
use of its eyes or its legs or its arms. That is a
practical question. Why muddle it up with a lot
of racial, sectarian, and constitutional rubbish?"

Here you have the substance of Ontario's argument for limitation. Is there, I ask, anything of
the spirit of Thurlow, anything of the philosophy
of Toynbee, in this reasoning of the dominant
nationality? In these words which I have quoted,
and they are typical of Ontario's position, the British principle of freedom for the minor nationality
counts for nothing; the documents which set
it forth are as so much "constitutional rubbish,"
a forceful reminder of the "scrap of paper" phrase.
In the unreasoning of Ontario and Manitoba, I
can find only a clear-cut adherence to the German
principle, a supreme egoism of Teutonic sort in
exaggerating the necessity of the culture of the
majority and disregarding the value of the culture
of the minority, and above all the insistence that the
dominant nationality—the twelve-to-one superiority—shall alone decide as to what is right. Not
even Treitschke has phrased the doctrine of the
supreme power of the State in bolder words.

The desire for homogeneity in Germany, requires explanation—as it does in Ontario. Behind these attempts to deprive the Slavs, the Danes,
and the French, of their culture in Germany, and
the French-Canadians of their culture in Ontario,
will be found similar motives; and more than that,

we shall find the motives entering, at least in German opinion, into the war issues. Charles P. Steinmetz, in "America and the New Epoch," writing of Germany's political ideals, says: "Thus by effective and liberal government old-age insurance, sickness insurance, and unemployment insurance, the three great fears which hung over the masses in all other countries, were eliminated, extreme poverty vanished, slums disappeared, and the condition of the masses became superior to that in all other countries, even in America, where the neglect of social legislation is gradually making itself felt now." At first, one is at a loss to see what connection this program has to do with homogeneity, but, as Steinmetz explains: "co-operative industrial organisation presupposes racial unity."

Now for an Ontario parallel, which ties race homogeneity into socialists' ideals. There are several from which to select, but this one written while the grievances of the French-Canadians were discussed on the Lapointe resolution in the Dominion House of Commons, by the "Toronto Star," May 18th, 1916, will do well as any other: "If we are not trying to benefit our neighbour by legislation, we are apt to brood over some racial or religious difference which, as we fancy, divides us. If, on the other hand, we are devoting ourselves to plans for the improvement of the condition of working-men and working-women, we are not likely to be worried about the race or religious sect of these men and women. Social justice knows no racial or sectarian divisions. Justice is the same for all. It does not care whether the shop-girl is a Protestant or a Catholic, or to what race she belongs, so long as justice is done." We cannot overlook the hypocrisy of such an answer to a people crying out for their mother-tongue in the land which was once theirs—the double iniquity of refusing to hear the plea and covering the refusal with phrases of cant. "Of all men whom we know, the Lacedaemonians are the most notorious for identifying what is pleasant with what is honorable, and what is expedient with what is just." Not even a German —and in these days we regard him as the most heartless of men—would have given the "Star's" answer to a people petitioning for the right to have their children instructed by means of their mother's tongue. It is Prince von Bülow who says of the conflict between Teuton and Pole: "If the differences between the nationalities were thereby immediately intensified, it was certainly unfortunate, but it could not be avoided. In political life there are often hard necessities whose behests we obey with a heavy heart, but which must be obeyed in spite of sympathies and emotions. Politics is a rough trade, in which sentimental souls rarely bring even a simple piece of work to a successful issue." Ontario politicians have seldom given the French-Canadians even these inadequate words of sympathy.

But the real pith of "The Star's" reply—and it

is not an unusual one in the Capital of Ontario— is that the interests of the minor nationality must give way before social reforms desired by the major nationality. It is perhaps wrong to say, "desired by the major nationality," for it is not apparent that beyond Toronto there are many who believe that Canada, with millions of arable acres, unfarmed simply because men prefer town life, has reached the stage where measures for the relief of its self-constituted—and unduly large— industrial population are justifiable.

In both German and Ontario schools of social-istic thought, "racial homogeneity" is regarded as essential to their program. To get at the worth of this contention, English-Canadians have only to ask themselves this question: Would we sell our birthright of language, of mentality, for a mess of social reform pottage? The test is surely a fair one; and, unless the answer is in the affirmative, then those who offer social improvement argu-ments as a reason for refusing recognition of the dual nationality, stand self-convicted of seeking their own material ends, by the sacrifice of the deepest spiritual feelings of their fellowmen.

I have said that Steinmetz carries this question of socialism to the root of the war. England has been individualistic; Germany, co-operative. That is in effect the argument. He says: "The present world's war is the conflict between the passing era of individualistic industrialism and the coming era of co-operative organization, the former represented by England, the latter by Germany." And Steinmetz' statement is true—except his prophecy —in the sense that in England, the State exists for the man, and in Germany, man exists for the State; in England the thing most sought is the highest development of man, in Germany the highest development of the State. That is why, as we have seen, Germany regards human nationalities as so many hammers and anvils.

The Prussians, only a few hundred years removed from the armed camp into city, town, and civilisation, have the primary conception of the State as an army, and its citizens as soldiers. An impressionistic view of this conception is of men dressed alike in invisible grey uniforms, wearing identical helmets, moving with the same stiff, awkward but effective steps, and wheeling in identical manner at the State's word of command. Some years ago, I watched men feed a huge machine with steel rods of varying lengths, and saw an incessant stream of horse-shoe nails pour forth, all of the same length, all of the same bright steely polish, all with the same peculiarly shaped head, the same sharp point, the same weight to the minutest part of an ounce, the same resisting power and strength. Such is the product of the doctrine of homogeneity. It is a mechanical thing, but it is effective—and so are horse-shoe nails—for a purpose.

German modern achievements in peace and war are successes of a sort; but they are the successes of

5 c.

a State, not of humanity. They are the successes of a colony of ants. The single ant is a weak creature; but ants as a colony, pursuing their own selfish economic and social ways, battle with insects many times their size; countless numbers are destroyed; but ants as ants are preserved. Here is success, but is it the kind of success we would imitate? Germans, like ants, allow nothing to stand in the way of their kind. All are swept along in the crowd. Collective psychology is little understood, but as M. Grau points out, Eucken and many other German philosophers whom we admired—before the war—lost their critical faculties when surrounded by the collective mind. The Slav in Poland, the Dane in Holstein, the French in Alsace-Lorraine, the Walloon and the Fleming in Belgium, all must be hacked down in the triumphant march of the Germans, inspired by their fanatical, collective self-worship. It is essentially a Prussian idea, but not exclusively Prussian; for others, including many English-Canadians, have accepted it.

Books of Reference

Charles Downer Hazen, *Alsace-Lorraine Under German Rule*. Holt.

Prince Bernhard von Bülow, *Imperial Germany*. Cassel.

Charles P. Steinmetz, *America and the New Epoch*. Harpers.

Max Nordau, *Paradoxes*. Heinemann.

J. M. Robertson, *The Germans*. Putnam.

Emile Hovelaque, *The Deeper Causes of the War*. Dutton.

L. T. Hobhouse, *Questions of War and Peace*. T. Fisher Unwin.

CHAPTER IV

THE ONTARIO THAT WAS CARVED OUT OF QUEBEC

NONE will deny that the geography of the Province of Ontario was first put into scientific shape by men of the French tongue; that its most interesting and entertaining pages of history were written in the French language; that the Jesuit "Relations" set down before Ontario was carved out of Quebec, contain geographical and ethnological information of the land between the Ottawa and the Great Lakes, as necessary to the modern geographer and historian as foundation stones to the builder. They are in fact invaluable records of the province, often written, as Thwaites reminds us, "in the midst of a chaos of distractions, immersed in scenes of squalor and degradation by men overcome by fatigue and improper sustenance, suffering from wounds and disease and maltreated by their hosts, who were often their jailors." "I do not know," says one of the apostles—who, by the way, as we are reminded, was writing from Canada an epistle to the Romans—"whether your Paternity will recognise the letter of a poor cripple who formerly, when in perfect health, was well-known to you. The letter is badly written, and quite soiled because, in addition to other inconveniences, he who writes it has only one whole finger on his right

hand; and it is difficult to avoid staining the paper
with blood which flows from his wounds, not yet
healed: he uses arquebus powder for ink, and the
earth for a table."

While Roundheads and Cavaliers were fighting
it out in England, Frenchmen were mapping the
Great Lakes of Canada. According to Parkman,
the map of Galinée was made nearly a hundred
years before the British conquered Canada, and it
"gives the course of the Upper St. Lawrence and
the shores of Lake Ontario, the River Niagara, the
north shore of Lake Erie, the Strait of Detroit, and
the Eastern and Northern shores of Lake Huron."
This map professed only to represent the country
actually visited by the Sulpician missionaries, Dol-
ier and Galinée. Three years later, according to
the same authority, another map "indicating a
greatly increased knowledge of the country, was
made by some person whose name does not appear. This map, which is somewhat more than
four feet long and about two feet and a half wide,
has no title. All the Great Lakes, through their
entire extent, are laid down on it with considerable
accuracy."

The Ottawa River was traced to its source, and
travelled over and over again; the French River,
[Rivière-des-François] and Lake Nipissing, the
Kaministikiwa River, Rainy River [Rivière-à-la
Pluie], the Lake-of-the-Woods [Lac des Bois], and
the great chain of waterways that just missed con-
necting the plains of the West with the Inland Seas,

were put on the map by French-Canadian geographers. During the days of the French Régime, Canadians paddled the Winnipeg River to Lake Winnipeg. They had explored the Red River and the Assiniboine. They had discovered Lakes Manitoba, Winnipegosis, and Dauphin, and travelled the Saskatchewan as well; tracing its branches to the foothills of the Rocky Mountains. The Ontario that lies between James Bay and the Great Lakes they knew as well, almost better than it is known to-day; and, to the pride of Canada, the greatest name in Canadian exploration is that of the native-born Pierre La Vérendrye, born at Three Rivers in the year 1685. Lawrence Burpee in his "Search for the Western Sea," pays this tribute to the "natural rights" of Canadians who speak French:

"The cause of North American exploration owes much to the men of New France and to none does it owe more than to Pierre Gaultier de La Vérendrye. No explorer ever accomplished so much under such extraordinary difficulties. His story is the story of a man who having set himself a gigantic task, not for his own profit but for the glory of his native land, followed it unflinchingly in spite of obstacles of every kind, in spite of wearing discouragements, in spite of misrepresentation and calumny, until at last death intervened, the task incomplete, but notable in its incompleteness. His name must always remain one of the most honored names in Canadian exploration."

Before me lies a map of the Province of Upper Canada, made in the days when His Excellency, John Graves Simcoe was Lieutenant-Governor, and over it French names are thickly strewn. Let me mention some of them at random: River Petite Nation, Lesmilles Roch, Long Sault, Rapid Rolat, River Rideau, Gannanocui, Frontenac, Pt. Travers, Presque Isle de Quinté, River Trent, River Tonty, Point aux Pins, Pt. Pelé, Cedre River, River Canard, Isle au Bois, Lac St. Clair, River aux Sables, Maisonvilles Mill, Chenaile Escarté, and—but why continue? The extent of the French hand is not recognisable in the map of to-day, for in later years many of the early French names have been replaced by those of English construction. In the plan which I am reading, Toronto's summer playground is named Lac la Clie; but the name was afterwards changed to Simcoe, in honour of a lieutenant-governor, who also gave to three of its bordering townships the names of Tiny, Tay, and Floss, names borrowed, it is said, I think, by John Ross Robertson, from Lady Simcoe's pet poodle dogs.

The failure to concentrate population along the shores of the St. Lawrence, has been set down by historians as a fatal weakness of French colonial policy. Weakness then, it is strength to-day. The plain truth is that the Government was unable to restrain the Canadians from moving up the waters of the Ottawa and up the waters of the St. Lawrence, out into the land that lay beside the

Great Lakes. Nor was the policy of the home government consistent as to the desirability of concentration; there were governors who saw clearly that if the claims to the vast territories within New France were to be recognised by the Powers, occupation of a sort was necessary, and efforts were made to plant settlements in various parts of the country, even at the cost of the safety of the first and main colony on the St. Lawrence. But no matter what the Government's policy, the Canadians were carried by a spirit of *wanderlust* into the wilderness.

As a result of an impression that there were no French-Canadian settlements at the coming of the British in the lands which are now called Ontario, some have refused to acknowledge the lien of French culture upon this province. The force of the argument is lost in the fact that the Quebec Act was applied to certain definite tracts of land, the boundaries of which were set forth. The direct and implied promises contained in the Quebec Act and given in the British Parliament at its passing, had essentially a regional basis. There was then no Ontario, no Manitoba, only Quebec. But the records show that the French-Canadians have also a sound claim based on settlement; for there was settlement—considerable for the period—in what is now Ontario, before the division into provinces. Lacking an exact basic figure, we cannot make an exact mathematical calculation; but all the knowledge available shows that there was then a sufficient population west of the Ottawa to account for the present number of French-Canadians in Ontario. Of course, there has been migration into Ontario from Quebec, but there has been a balancing migration from Ontario to Quebec, to other parts of Canada and to the United States. We know that the sixty odd thousand French who were in Canada at the time of the British Conquest, with a few thousand Acadians, have grown to something like three million French-Canadians in Canada and the United States to-day. Accepting these figures as the natural rate of increase by birth, only a few thousand men and women would be required then to account for the 250 thousand French-Canadians now in Ontario.

It is significant that in the sections where there were settlements before the British Conquest, there are French-Canadian settlements to-day. In Northern Ontario there are French-Canadians at the various points where the missionaries built their first churches and cleared the land for the agricultural support of the community. There are French-Canadians to-day wherever voyageurs made their trading-posts and French soldiers built their log fortresses. Settlers have come and gone, but the stream of population has for several centuries constantly flowed into the Hinterland. After Upper Canada, and later Ontario, had been taken from the side of Quebec, the English-Canadians for many years neglected the north country—they had what seemed to them fairer fields in the western prairies—and, as a result, the population on the Lower Ottawa was left free to move into unoccupied lands on the tributaries of the Upper Ottawa and the waters that, rising on the divide, flow into Hudson Bay.

In South Western Ontario, Essex was first settled by the French. Early in the eighteenth century, a colony of French-Canadians was planted along the banks of the Detroit River—the colonists being soldiers from a disbanded French regiment. "In 1752 was born the first white child in the future county, Jean Dufour, by name." The country appealed to the French. Says the historian: "Every farmer had his yoke of oxen for ploughing, his calash for summer, and his cariole for winter driving, whilst everywhere were to be seen blossoming shrubs and fine fruit-trees. In fact,

> " 'Many a thrifty Mission pear
> Yet o'erlooks the blue St. Clair,
> Like a veteran faithful warden;
> On their branches gnarled and olden,
> Still each year the blossoms dance,
> Scent and bloom of sunny France.' "

It was not until 1788, when the French settlement had grown strong in numbers, that English-speaking men and women came from the United States to the Detroit River settlement.

In Eastern Ontario it was natural that there should have been settlement. It came up the St. Lawrence by easy stages in the centuries of French occupation; and, in the subsequent division of the country into provinces, the eastern boundary of Ontario was to be fixed scarcely more than 30 miles from the heart of the old St. Lawrence settlement at Montreal, and necessarily left many old French-Canadian families on the Ontario side. For more than three decades of British government, the lands in what is now Ontario were held under the French system of tenure, and the people's rights regulated by the French code of laws, and during those years the French-Canadians, knowing no boundary lines, continued to settle where they pleased east or west of the Ottawa River. And they carried with them, under Britain's principle of freedom, their cultural rights.

The extent of the numbers of the minor nationality, cannot always be gauged by parliamentary representation—as a rule they are proportionately greater than the number of members they are able to elect. In 1796, just after a boundary-line had been fixed at the Ottawa River, fourteen members constituted the House of Assembly of Upper Canada—and the French-Canadians had one-fourteenth of the representation, comparable with what they have to-day in the Ontario Legislature. The French-Canadian member was Francis Baby, whom the late Dr. C. C. James has identified as the Francis Baby who "lived on the east side of the Detroit River in, or on the borders of, the present town of Sandwich." The Baby family was prominent in the West, and its name is continuously appearing in the early history of the country. When General Hull invaded Canada, he established his headquarters in the partially completed house of Francis Baby. When Quebec was taken in 1759, and Montreal capitulated in 1760, Major Rogers was sent by General Amherst to proceed westward and take over the posts of Michigan. The negotiations between Rogers and Bellestre, Commander of Detroit, were carried on through M. "Babée" for the French, and Mr. Brehme for the British. This member of the family is identified by Dr. James as "Jacques Duperon Baby, the son of Raymond Baby and grandson of Jacques Baby de Rainville, who came to Canada from Guienne, France, with the Carignan Regiment." Another member of the Baby family, Jean Baptiste, represented Kent County in the Fifth Parliament (1809-12).

That the influence of the old French Régime in the early life of the country now called Ontario, is not fully realised by the present generation, is easily explained. *The truth is that much of the evidence was destroyed.* A paragraph from the Proclamation dividing the Province of Upper Canada into counties, shows the means, and indicates the extent of destruction:

"That the seventh of the said counties be hereafter called by the name of County of Ontario, which county is to consist of the following islands, an Island at present known by the name of Isle Tonti (to be called Amherst Island) an island known by the name of Isle au Fôret (to

be called Gage Island), an island known by the name of
Grande Isle (to be called Wolfe Island) and an island
known by the name of Isle Chuchois (to be called Howe
Island), and to comprehend all the islands between the
mouth of the Garanoque [a misprint for Gananoque] to
the Eastermost extremity of the late Township of Marys-
burg, called Point Pleasant."

I complain not of the change of names, but of
the conclusion that is drawn: that the French had
not much to do with the geography of the Province,
and little to do with its settlement, since its
names are now so largely English, instead of
French. Such reasoning is unsportsmanlike.

As I write, Le Petit Côté Creek flows at my feet
—at least it would if its bed were not dry—and
when the drouth is over this autumn it will flow
into Outer Frenchman's Bay, marked Baie des
Français on the old maps. If I rise in time to
catch the morning train for town, I shall take it at
a station a stone's throw from the mouth of the
River Rouge—and for miles around there are no
French families! There is more than a tradition
that years before the days of the United Empire Loyalists, a little French school was planted
on the shores of the Inner Bay. What a stirring
tragedy of clerical intrigue and racial extermination could be written if only the names were English and the country-side in the Eastern Townships
of Quebec, instead of in the County of Ontario
scarcely twenty miles from the City of Toronto!
But then, as John Ross Robertson reminds us in

his interesting "Landmarks of Toronto," "the dawn of civilised life on the shores of Toronto Bay" came when Frenchmen erected old Fort Rouille, and "made the rough clearance in the primitive forest of an area of about 300 acres immediately around its palisades." But, for that matter, practically all the old French trading-posts have been converted into cities and towns, and the old trails and portages of the voyageurs made over into highways.

Before the English came, the means of navigation had all but run their course,—the canoes were followed by the flat-bottom bateaux, and they in their turn by sailing craft of the schooner type. Men of the French tongue built the first ship on the Great Lakes; men of the French tongue first sailed across Lake Erie, up through the Detroit and St. Clair Rivers into Lake Huron, through the Straits of Michipotcoten to Lake Michigan; and when the "Griffon," with her cargo of valuable furs, was wrecked on the return voyage, men of the French tongue paid with their lives the first toll exacted of those who carry commerce by vessel on the great inland seas of Canada.

The missionaries who went forth into the wilderness carrying the story of the Gethsemane to the savages along the shores of the Georgian Bay and up into the Hinterland, gave to the world an imperishable example of devotion and sacrifice. Some will find fault with the way the message was delivered; but, after all, the criticism is of details, the

mere manner of telling, not the story itself; and in
these days the emphasis is being placed on the like-
nesses, not the differences, of the several phases of
the Christian belief. Men of all religions, and
men of none, are forced into a whole-hearted
admiration for the unselfish devotion of the early
Canadian missionaries. Between 1615, when
Leçaron first visited the Georgian Bay, and 1650,
when the dispersion of the Hurons was complete, twenty-nine missionaries had laboured
among the Hurons; and of these, seven had
suffered violent deaths.

The mangled, charred bodies of Bréboeuf and
Lalement were buried at Ste. Marie beside the
waters of the Georgian Bay. The memory of their
heroism is the treasured possession of all men who
admire sacrifice for conscience's sake.

Of Bréboeuf, the historian tells us: "All forms of
torture were devised—his flesh was cut out bit by
bit, they lifted the skin of his head in the form of a
crown, and bored his eyes out with hot irons. Then
they mocked him, saying: 'You told us the more we
suffered here the greater would be our reward in
Heaven. So you see we are preparing you for a
happy home!' They surrounded the priest's body
with bark covered with resin and set it on fire.
Throughout all this monstrous, horrible ordeal
Bréboeuf stood impassive. He could not speak, he
could not see, but his face showed no twinge of
pain and his giant form towered erect and unfalter-
ing."

And of Lalement, "weak from childhood and slender almost to emaciation," we are told, "he was unequal to a display of fortitude like that of his colleague. When Bréboeuf died, he was led back to the house whence he had been taken, and tortured there all night, until, in the morning, one of the Iroquois, growing tired of the protracted entertainment, killed him with a hatchet. It was said that, at times, he seemed beside himself; then, rallying, with hands uplifted, he offered his suffering to Heaven as a sacrifice."

The safety of their converts was the first consideration of these pioneer ministers; their own, a matter of inconsequence, compared with duty. "Fly!" screamed the priest, as the hostile legions broke into the palisades, driving his flock before him. "I will stay here. We shall meet again in Heaven."

The ashes of French-Canadian martyrs mingle with the earth of Old Ontario; yet there are men who wantonly scoff at the "natural rights" of the descendants of the Old Régime within the Province! The soil of Ontario is a veritable sanctuary to the French-Canadian people.

The exploits of the coureurs-des-bois extended over the vast land between the Ottawa River and the Great Lakes and beyond to the foothills of the Rocky Mountains. Their wanderings have impressed the imagination of every race; many who know nothing of Canada's mundane wheat crops and railways, admire its coureurs-des-bois. Their

memoirs of travel serve as guide-books to engi-
neers who nearly three hundred years later were to
follow their practically undisturbed footsteps and
lay out railways for the opening-up of the country
to a new civilisation. "Not all paths have evolved
into railways," writes John Finley, President of
the University of the State of New York, "but the
railroads have followed practically all of these
natural paths—paths of the coureurs-des-bois,
instinctively searching for mountain passes, the
low portages from valley to valley, the shortest
ways and the easiest grades."

The names of these frontiersmen of civilisation
are too little known within the land of their
achievements. It is not only prophets that are
denied fame in their own land. Etienne Brulé, the
guide of missionaries, ventured into streams and
forests against the advice of his neighbours and,
in the end, paid the usual penalty of the men who
wrested Canada for civilization—death at the stake.
Jean Nicolet was taken half way across the Continent by the spirit of *wanderlust*. Dulutte and
his cousin, the intrepid Tonty, spent practically a
lifetime in the outposts which the most hardy
visited only after consigning their souls to God.
Hennepin, the first white man to see and describe
Niagara Falls and tell of the buffalo, although
wearing the frock of a priest and writing with the
pen of a Fenimore Cooper, possessed the soul of a
coureur-des-bois, and his name will live in their
annals. La Salle was more than a coureur-des-bois,

although intimately associated with their travels;
he was an explorer, and his achievements are
among the world's greatest records of exploration.

The shores of Lake Huron and the Georgian
Bay are marked with many an historic battle-field,
witnesses to the bravery and perseverance of
French-Canadians. The wars which raged between
the French and the Indians from the banks of the
St. Lawrence to the plains of the Great West,
their sieges and, unhappily, their massacres, are
indelible pages of heroism and tragedy, which
cannot be erased from the records of the Province
of Ontario. It is impossible, as it is unnecessary, to
describe even the more important battles which the
French-Canadians fought with the Indians to make
this country "safe for civilisation." No greater
heroism is recorded in the wonderful pages of
Greek history than the action in which Dollard and
his handful of French-Canadians went at the Long
Sault to certain destruction by a horde of savages, that the colony might be saved. But that is
only one of the many instances of self-sacrifice in
the days of the Old Régime. Professor Colby,
referring to Wellington's boast, that during the
Peninsular War the English captured more than
one strong place in Spain without any provision of
bullets, save those fired at them by their enemies,
having trusted to this chance when they formed
the siege, says that while "this is a good story, one
could undertake to match it from the exploits of
the Canadians who followed François Hertel,

6 c.

Hertel de Rouville, Le Moyne de Sainte-Hélène, and Pierre Le Moyne d'Iberville."

When I was a boy, the history of Canada before the coming of the English, was dismissed with a few cursory lessons. I admired the patient toil of the English pioneers who hewed their farms out of the forest, but down in my heart I envied the boys of Scotch, English, and Irish descent who could repeat tales of the days when knighthood was in flower in the shires of their forefathers. Childish? Of course it was; I was a child. Foolish? Perhaps; but we must remember the words of Byron:

> "Parent of golden dreams, Romance!
> Auspicious queen of childish joys,
> Who leads't along, in airy dance,
> The votive train of girls and boys."

And then I read Parkman—and later "Les Relations," page after page, book after book, the wonderful tales in which knights, voyageurs, missionaries, and soldiers, lived again their lives of adventure in this country of my birth. Their exploits rivalled those of the Iliad and the Odyssey; and, having been performed in my homeland, stimulated my youthful patriotism.

The French-Canadians are justly proud of the achievements of their forefathers, for they bespeak the soundness of the national foundation stock; and bitter is their regret that these things may no longer be told in school to their children and their children's children in the French language; for they are either geography or history, and Regulation 17 proscribes French as the language of instruction.

"Ontario is not a bi-lingual province" said a Minister of the Crown from the hustings, and his words are echoed in the press of the province, "Ontario is not a bi-lingual province." Well, there are men foolish enough to say the world is not round; but their say-so does not make it flat.

Books of Reference

C. W. Colby, *Canadian Types of the Old Régime.* Holt.

Francis Parkman, *The Jesuits in North America,* and other books of the series. Little, Brown Company.

H. E. Egerton and W. L. Grant, *Canadian Constitutional Documents.* Musson.

C. C. James, *The First Legislation of Upper Canada,* (pamphlet) Hope, Ottawa.

Edward Channing and Marion Lansing, *The Story of the Great Lakes.* Macmillan.

Lawrence J. Burpee, *The Search for the Western Sea.* Musson.

John Ross Robertson, *The Landmarks of Toronto.* Robertson.

Emily P. Weaver, *The Counties of Ontario.* Bell & Cockburn.

John Finley, *The French in the Heart of America.* Scribners.

CHAPTER V

RACE SUPERIORITY

SOME years ago I sat at a restaurant table with two Canadians, one of English and the other of French extraction. In the course of conversation, the English-Canadian made a remark which was decidedly uncomplimentary to the French-Canadian race. Afterwards I reproached him for the unfairness of what he had said, and for the rank indecency of having said it in the presence of a man of the race. "Tut, tut!" he expostulated. "Henri doesn't mind. Down in his heart he knows that the Latin race is not as good as the Anglo-Saxon." That was news to me, and upon meeting Henri, I gently sought confirmation. I have not forgotten the reply. "Heaven grant that I may never cease resenting unjust reflections upon my race," adding, after a pause, "and keep my mouth shut." "Why keep silent?" I remonstrated. "Our position as a race would become untenable in Canada were we to resent everything that is said against us," was the reply.

The average English-Canadian believes not merely in the worth of the Anglo-Saxon race, but in its inherent superiority. Naturally, wherever there is a superior, there is an inferior; and, the French-Canadian being nearest at hand, it is with his race comparison is usually made. Herein lies the well of Canada's national trouble. To fix the badge of inferiority upon a race is the unpardonable sin of nationalities. Regulation 17 is in reality only an incident, a manifestation of the spirit.

For all I know, the Englishman of England also believes in the superiority of Anglo-Saxon blood; but, if he does, he seldom says so. It isn't good form. Ripe old experience has taught him that by deeds, not by boasts, are relative race values determined. To-day the Englishman of England is standing upon what he has done and is doing. There was a time when the Englishman of England gloated over his superiorities, and paraded other people's supposed inferiorities; and in those days the Englishman of England was anything but an international favourite. Significantly enough, when he changed his tune from "Rule Britannia" to "Keep the Home Fires Burning," other races more clearly recognised Anglo-Saxon virtues, and more readily paid tribute to them. After all, there is a lot of human nature in group psychology.

But the English-Canadian still shouts the virtues of Anglo-Saxonism from press and hustings; it is his favourite stock in the political trade; and then, always, is there an object of comparison. In 1917, it was the French-Canadian who was inferior; in 1911, the American of the United States. The comparison is the unhappy part of the business, and so far as the French-Canadian is concerned, a disastrous part. The American does not mind; he is used to bragging, and looks upon the English-Canadian's proclamation of superiority with the lofty, benignant smile of the man in the moon. But the French-Canadian is too close, and too sensitive, to pass it lightly off. His racial hide is not as thick as that of the American. He is wounded to the quick by the reflections cast upon his race so freely and persistently by English-Canadians.

It is important that the reader should have in mind a clear distinction between race and nationality; the two words are often used interchangeably, whereas, of course, the former means "community of blood," and the latter community in those several factors, sometimes including blood and bones, which were analysed in the first chapter. Men may be of the same race and of different nationalities; and, for that matter, of the same nationality and different races. A man may throw off the nationality of his parents and accept another, as many are doing to-day in the New World. But a man cannot change his race; the blood which courses his veins is the product of his uncountable ancestors. A man may, by thought, increase the contents of his skull, but he cannot, by thought, change either its size or shape, nor can he add a "cubit to his stature." According to the man on the street, "blood will tell"; and according to the man of the laboratory, like Professor Osborne, the learned author of "The Men of the Old Stone Age," "heredity has a deep, subtle, and per-

manent influence on the actions of men." Therefore, we are forced to turn the pages of science
in an attempt to determine how much of our national clash is due to immutable ethnical differences.

Here, as elsewhere, we shall find changing
views. Not so long ago, we were dependent upon
the philologist for our knowledge of the men who
lived and did things in the far-away eras before
contemporary historians chronicled conditions for
future generations. As a result of philological investigations, we had an Aryan race, from which
sprung most European races, and we spoke of an
Anglo-Saxon race, a Celtic race, and a Latin race.
But reflection should have told us that we were
then treading uncertain ground. We were trying
to determine men's blood, bones, stature, and
brains; to decide in fact what kind of animals men
were by the way they had manipulated consonants
and vowels. The fallacy of this reasoning may, perhaps, be best understood by a supposition. If the
philologists of a thousand years from now were to
write of the American race that had lived in the
United States in 1918, proving its existence and
outlining its character by the language that had
been preserved, the people of 2918 would be wholly misled. A mere examination of the formation of
words used in the United States in 1918, as our
philologists have examined the languages of people
that are gone by, would not reveal the fact that ten
out of every hundred Americans were then de-

scended from the several races of the African Continent, and that the other ninety were from several separate and sharply different race groups. Clearly, the work of tracing race history beyond the era of chronicled pages is more that of the ethnologist than that of the philologist.

To-day the European peoples are divided by ethnologists into three stock race groups. Although a common nomenclature has not been everywhere accepted, all are in substantial agreement as to the number and distribution of the groupings. We may accept the classification made by Madison Grant in the "Passing of the Great Race," the latest work on the subject, and accept it the more readily because it has the approval of Dr. Osborne.

First. The Nordic or Baltic race. The Nordic race developed around the shores of the Baltic and North Sea, its original home being in the Scandinavian Peninsula, and "is, therefore, the *Homo-europeus,* the white man par excellence," says Mr. Grant. The race is known by its "blondness, wavy hair, blue eyes, fair skin, high, narrow and straight nose, which are associated with great stature, and a long skull, as well as with abundant head and body hair."

Second. The Alpine race. This race is of Asiatic origin, and in all probability its centre of original evolution was the Western Himalayas. The Alpines are of stocky build and moderately short stature, and distinguished "by a round face and correspondingly round skull, which, in the true

Armenians, has a peculiar sugar-loaf shape, a characteristic which can be easily recognized.

Third. The Mediterranean race. "Throughout Neolithic times, and possibly still earlier," says Mr. Grant, "it seems to have occupied, just as it does to-day, all the shores of the Mediterranean, including the coast of Africa, from Morocco on the west, to Egypt on the east. The Mediterraneans are the western members of a sub-species of man which forms a substantial part of the population of Persia, Afghanistan, Baluchistan, and Hindustan, with perhaps a southward extension into Ceylon." The Mediterranean is a relatively small, light-boned race, of brunette color, becoming even swarthy in certain portions of its range. This race has a long skull, like the Nordic, but the absolute size of the skull is less.

This opening up of old tombs has an interest for those of us who are investigating the relation of races in Canada, for it is the bones of our ancestors that have been uncovered, measured and classified. The ethnological classification corresponds roughly to that of the philologist. We have been calling the Mediterranean, Latin; the Alpine (in a most general way), Celt; the Nordic, Teuton; and our branch of the family, Anglo-Saxon, when discussing our ancestral business. Before pressing a claim of English-Canadian race superiority, we ought to examine the evidence as to Anglo-Saxon superiority upon which it rests.

Having come mainly from the British Isles, we English-Canadians must return to them for evidence of our race ancestry. We have been accustomed (such is the force of popular nomenclature) to regard ourselves as all Anglo-Saxon. Had we been right in this supposition, we would be of the Nordic race, for the Angles (probably) came from Jutland and the Saxons from the base of the Danish peninsula; districts in which the Nordic race was cradled. But as time runs in the life of races, the Angles and the Saxons, and kindred Nordic tribes, invaded England in recent years. We must of necessity go behind their invasions, if we would determine the entire nature of our own ancestral stock. And, when the historian's hand raised the veil of obscurity from the British Islands, *the country was inhabited by Mediterraneans.* "When the Teutonic tribes entered Britain, they found there peoples all speaking Celtic of some form, either Goidelic or Cyrmic," writes Mr. Grant, "and promptly called them all Welsh (foreigners). These Welsh were preponderantly of Mediterranean type, with some mixture of a blond Goidel strain and a much stronger blond strain of Cymric origin, and these same elements exist to-day in England."

Of course these early Britishers who were disturbed in their occupation by the marauding Teutons, were not "Latins" in the sense that they spoke in Latin tongues, but they were and their descendants are to-day Latins in the sense that they were and are of the same race as the Spaniards, Portuguese, Italians, and South country Frenchmen, who, subsequently speaking in Latin tongues, were called of the Latin race.

In the Bronze Age, [roughly from 3000 to 1800 B.C.,] the Mediterranean race prevailed over all France and the British Islands, although the Alpines had even then succeeded in forcing their way from Central Asia across Europe through Central France to the North Atlantic. In neither France nor Britain had the Nordic race then obtained a foothold; in the Bronze Age it was still hugging the cold glaciers of Scandinavia.

In the next era, extending from 1800 B.C. almost to the birth of Jesus, the distribution of races was altered. The Nordics sailed westward along the shores of the Baltic and North Sea, and drove the Mediterraneans and Alpines away, establishing a chain of colonies that reached from Scandinavia westward and covered all Northern France, with the exception of Brittany. The Nordics crossed the Channel into Britain, but did not succeed in expelling or exterminating the Mediterraneans, who remained and handed down in the present generation of Englishmen (according to ethnological measurements) unmistakable evidence of having continued in the capacity of ancestors.

Nor was "the original" race the only source from which we derive Mediterranean blood. If we do not forget that for 350 years Britain was occupied by the Romans, we often fail to estimate the race effect which it had upon the inhabitants—our ancestors. It is true few Romans brought their Roman wives with them to Britain; but it is impossible that they should have occupied the country for 35 decades without leaving descendants who were of their blood and their race. It is also true that the Roman armies were not purely Mediterranean; were in fact gathered from all portions of the great Roman Empire; but that they were preponderantly of Mediterranean blood, is beyond question. Let us turn from the ethnologist to the philologist for evidence in support of this contention. Thomas Wright, who examined the period closely, concludes that as a result of the Roman occupation all except the peasantry "became obedient to Roman laws and institutions, used the Latin tongue, and had indeed become entirely Romanised." Sir Arthur Quiller-Couch, Professor of English Literature at Cambridge, in a recently published volume of lectures, says: "I see a people which for four hundred years was permeated by Rome. If you insist on its being a Teutonic people (which I flatly deny), then you have one, which alone of Teutonic peoples, has inherited the Roman gift of consolidating conquest, of colonising in the wake of its armies; of driving the road, bridging the ford, bringing the lawless under its sense of law."

Then the reader may remind me there was the later influence of the Norman invasion. We

know from general history its effect upon nationality.   It is Lord Lyttleton, the historian of
Henry II, who says : "It must also be confessed that
so long as the Anglo-Saxons were masters of England, that kingdom was of no account in the system
of Europe; but grew to have weight and authority
on the Continent under the government of the Normans, both from the dominions which the princes
of that race possessed in France, and from their
active ambition which, seconded by the enterprising and warlike disposition of all their nobility,
rendered the English name respected and illus-
trious abroad."

But the effect of the Norman invasion was to
strengthen the Nordic strain rather than that of
the Mediterranean, *for the Normans were Nordics.* Mr. Grant tells us: "The Normans landed in
Normandy in the year 911 A.D. They were
heathen Danish barbarians, speaking a Teutonic
language. The religion, culture and language of
the old Romanised populations worked a miracle
on the transformation of everything except blood
in one short century. So quick was the change that
155 years later the descendants of the same Normans landed in England as Christian Frenchmen,
armed with all the culture of their period. The
change was startling, but the blood of the Norman
brood remained unchanged and entered England
as a purely Nordic type."

Thus the inhabitants of the British Isles,
originally of Mediterranean blood, were crossed

by the Nordic blood of Danish tribes, then by the
Mediterranean blood of Romans, again by Nordic
blood from the shores of Scandinavia and Germany, and finally by Nordic blood by way of Normandy. This latest, and in some ways strongest
blood infusion, is of double interest to Canadians;
for in it *English- and French-Canadians have common ancestry*. Mr. Grant says that the French-
Canadians are of the Alpine race, because they are
"largely from Brittany." But Mr. Grant should
stick to ethnology; he is out of his province in the
history of Canada's colonisation. The French did
not come to Canada largely from Brittany, the
North-West corner of France into which the Alpines had been crowded. Nor did they come
largely from Southern France, in which the Mediterranean race continued to prevail after the Alpine and Nordic invasions had subsided. We know
whence almost every Frenchman came who entered Canada between 1615-1700. There is no
people in the world whose geneology has been
more clearly traced than that of the French-Canadians. Most of them came from those very provinces whose inhabitants Mr. Grant and ethnologists
say were almost purely of Nordic or Baltic blood.
The births and migrations of the French-Canadians have been preserved with remarkable fidelity
in parish "régistres."

Very recently the excellent work done by Mgr.
Tanguay, l'abbé Ferland, M. E. Rameau and M.
Benjamin Sulte in tracing the source of French

migration to this country has been carried further towards completion by M. l'abbé S. A. Lortie, a professor of Laval University. In view of the importance of the subject and the controversies which have waged around it, I make no apologies for reproducing the results of Professor Lortie's labors in the table (on the following page), which indicates the number and origin of French emigrants arriving in Canada from 1608 to 1700.

It will be seen that within Normandy—not Brittany, as stated by Mr. Grant—lies the secret of the ethnology of the French-Canadian population. It was from Normandy the first settlers came, and naturally it was the first settlers who left the strongest blood strain within the colony. Many of them were great grand-sires and grand-dams with numerous progeny when the later colonists began to climb the banks of the St. Lawrence. An official statement in 1680, estimated that four-fifths of the Canadian population were either "Normans by birth or by parentage, or had married Norman wives." The settlers who came from Paris, were, for the most part, officials, priests and merchants; the men who went on the land were mainly from Normandy and adjoining provinces—and of Nordic blood.

What an upsetting of tables when the works of ethnologist and of historian are fitted together! The French-Canadians can no longer reproach us with what is now a rather unpopular Teutonic ancestry —although Heaven knows it is virile enough—

ORIGIN OF MIGRANTS, BY PROVINCES	NUMBER OF MIGRANTS				Totals from 1608 to 1700
	Periods of Migration				
	1608 to 1640	1640 to 1660	1660 to 1680	1680 to 1700	
Angoumois	....	13	54	26	93
Anjou	2	56	60	21	139
Artois	....	2	9	3	14
Aunis, Ile de Rhé, Ile d'Oléron	23	115	293	93	524
Auvergne	....	3	18	14	35
Béarn	....	1	1	8	10
Beauce	14	22	46	23	105
Berry	1	5	32	11	49
Bourgogne	1	6	36	21	64
Bourbonnais	....	1	2	5	8
Bretagne	4	9	108	54	175
Brie	2	7	25	2	36
Champagne	7	23	76	23	129
Comté de Foix	....	1	1	....	2
Dauphiné	....	4	14	6	24
Flandre, Hainaut	....	1	11	3	15
Franche-Comté	....	....	1	5	6
Gascogne	....	5	22	24	51
Guyenne	....	8	61	55	124
Ile-de-France	36	76	378	131	621
Languedoc	....	1	26	23	50
Limousin	....	5	26	44	75
Lorraine	1	6	7	2	16
Lyonnais	1	3	13	16	33
Maine	1	66	31	15	113
Marche	....	1	1	4	6
Nivernais	....	2	4	1	7
Normandie	89	270	481	118	958
Orléanais	4	7	33	19	63
Perche	89	122	24	3	238
Périgord	....	1	28	16	45
Picardie	11	7	60	18	96
Poitou		54	357	158	569
Provence	...	3	13	6	22
Roussillon	....	...	2	....	2
Saintonge	10	37	140	87	274
Savoie	....	....	6	6	12
Touraine	....	21	42	28	91
TOTALS	296	964	2542	1092	4894

without reflecting upon their own blood; and we can no longer sneer at Mediterranean "lack of virility" in their blood without reflecting upon ours.

"These latter day Normans," says Mr. Grant, referring to the descendants of the "Latinised Vikings," who once conquered England, "are natural rulers and administrators, and it is to this type that England largely owes her extraordinary ability to govern justly and firmly the lower races."

It is probably true, the ancestors of the French-Canadians taught the Angles and Saxons and the Welsh (when they could get hold of them) to cut their hair, shave their faces, and be better mannered over their plates and less intemperate in their cups; but there is no evidence, as Mr. Grant intimates, that they became a superior caste. As we shall find, they introduced learning into England, of which there was, apparently, sad need, since before they had obtained "possession of England, learning and religion were brought to so low a state in that kingdom that most of the clergy could hardly read divine service; and, if, happily, any one of them understood grammar, he was admired and wondered at by the rest as a prodigy," but neither grammar nor manners, nor ability to rule, remained the exclusive possessions of the Normans who became Englishmen. The "original" Mediterraneans, the Angles, and the Saxons, who

7 c.

inhabited the kingdom, acquiring these things, have taken their full share in British administration.

For reasons over which we had no control, neither all French-Canadian nor all English-Canadian skulls measure uniformly according to Nordic or Mediterranean or Alpine types. If, as we are told, "it is to the Mediterranean race in the British Isles that the English, Scotch, and Americans owe whatever brunet characters they possess," then innumerable thousands have been mistaken in imagining themselves pure-bred descendants of the Angles and Saxons. History will have it, and ethnology, too, that neither of us is pure-bred, and that both of us are mainly of the same cross-breeding. He who would attempt to assign to one a greater proportion of Nordic skulls and to the other a greater proportion of Mediterranean skulls, or attempt to arrive at racial difference by finding a few Alpine skulls in one, and none in the other, would be counting hairs, if not actually splitting them.

Ethnologists are not working merely to satisfy curiosity. They seek to show, by their investigations, that races have special aptitudes for certain pursuits. "The Alpine race," says Mr. Grant, "is always and everywhere a race of peasants, an agricultural, and never a maritime people," while the "Nordics are, all over the world, a race of soldiers, sailors, adventurers, and explorers, but above all, of rulers, organisers, and aristocrats."

The Mediterranean race, "while inferior in bodily stamina to both the Nordic and the Alpine, is probably the superior of both, certainly of the Alpines, in intellectual attainments. In the field of art its superiority to both the other European races is unquestioned." This grouping is not altogether new to us. We have been accustomed to speak of the Anglo-Saxon, as a soldier, a sailor, an explorer, and a ruler of men; and of the Latin as the Anglo-Saxon's inferior in bodily stamina,—and, sometimes—his superior in the intellectual arts. Of course, Latins put the thing somewhat differently; but men who thought themselves Anglo-Saxons have written most of the English books on the subject. It is a significant fact that it is for "good red blood" we admire our ancestors, rather than for their sense of justice and benevolent disposition. We never tire of boasting that the blood of Vikings courses our veins, in spite of the fact that they spitted children on their spears and brutally maltreated the women of the coasts they ravaged. I have several friends who swell with pride in relating the sheep-stealing exploits of their Scottish Highland ancestors. All is forgiven in the memory of the "good red blood" which made them first in war and first in discovery. But since science has established that a fair portion of Englishmen—and Irishmen, too—are of the Mediterranean race, is it not time that we revised our ideas of race characteristics? Does history bear out these generalisations of racial aptitudes?

The two Polos, who, first of Europeans, made their way "through barren wildernesses, across burning deserts, in the face of hardships indescribable," who showed the way from Europe to the Far East, were merchants of Venice, and presumably of the Mediterranean race; and, of course, the famous Marco Polo, the son of one and nephew of the other, the favourite and mendacious messenger of Kublai Khan, was also a Venetian. Bartholomew Diaz, who first beat a way round the Cape of Storms, afterwards called Cape of Good Hope, was a Mediterranean, working for the Mediterranean King of Portugal. Christopher Columbus, who, more than any other man, may be said to have "turned the world upside down," was an Italian, born in Genoa; and Amerigo Vespucci, who wished his name upon the New World, was also a Mediterranean, as were most of the sailors who sailed with them across the Atlantic to the New World. There is a tradition that the Nordic Lief had sailed from nearby Iceland to North America, and named it Vineland, nearly 500 years before Columbus "discovered America." But if we are to credit the Nordic race with that achievement, we must also debit it with lack of courage or lack of enterprise in failing to make another trip. The Scandinavians, the progenitors of the Nordic race, have been established in Greenland

and Iceland since the ninth century; and, apparently, did not discover the inhabitants of the Western Continent—and, strangely enough, were not discovered by them. They were content to keep on sailing the North and Baltic Seas.

> "Our sea-steed through the foam goes prancing,
> While shields and spears and helms are glancing;
>   From Fjord to sea
>   Our ships ride free,
> And down the wind, with swelling sail,
> We scud before the gathering gale."

The ballads and tales of the old Viking days fairly snort with virility; but, as one of their supposed descendants, some day I am going to ask—when I meet them in the next world—why they allowed the world's great prizes in overseas' discovery to go to the farther away, "less virile," Mediterraneans.

The red-blooded Nordic, Sir Francis Drake, sailed around the world in 1557; but he was half a century too late to make the voyage a race achievement; he was fifty years behind the Mediterranean Ferdinand Magellan, backed by the Mediterranean State of Spain. The indomitable Magellan lost his life before the voyage was completed, but his ship was brought to port by the Mediterranean Captain del Cano. Balboa of the Mediterranean race, was the first to see the Pacific Ocean. The Mediterranean Vasco da Gama was the first European to reach India by water. Eng-

land's great discovery of Newfoundland was conducted under the leadership of the Italian Cabot,
although the Portuguese declared that one of their
countrymen, Cortereal, also a Mediterranean, had
"discovered the land of the codfish in 1463."
There is little doubt that Portuguese and Spanish
discovered "the Island Continent," and significantly named it Terra Australis.   And so runs
the story of Mediterranean discovery on through
the South Sea Islands, along the coasts of Africa
and Asia to the Island Kingdom of Japan.   Even
the heroic old Anglo-Saxon, Captain Cook, was
constantly discovering things in the South Seas
that had been already visited by Mediterranean
men.

In spite of our preconceived ideas, and in spite
of the race aptitudes set down by ethnologists, the
pages of history show that the Mediterraneans (the
Latins), despised as "inferior in bodily stamina,"
did the big things that are only done by strong
men.   If anything be required to make the situation more unconsoling, we have but to remember
there was usually a priest in the offing.

"And then the great Laudamus rose to heaven."

Was it by accident that Mediterraneans lead the
Nordics in discovery?   Since ethnologists tell us
they came to Europe from "foreign parts," it may
have been a sort of homing instinct which carried
them back to "new lands," which, after all, were

only new in the sense that they were unknown to Europeans.

And, the Alpines—we must not forget them, although the controversy in Canada has been mainly over the merits of Northern and Southern blood. Mr. Grant, erroneously naming the Alpines of Brittany as the chief French-Canadian ancestors, concludes that they are an "indigestible" part of the population. But why should men who came from the British Islands find in Bretons a race with which it is impossible, or even difficult, to coalesce? Dr. Beddoe, in his learned essay on "The Races of Britain," points out that in the period when England was subject to invasion, "Bretons came over in large numbers;" and further intimates that in some measure the Bretons are descended from Britons who, in the fifth century, made a part of Brittany's sea coast their own. While both English- and French-Canadians are more indebted to the Normans for ancestry than to other groups from Old France, both are to a lesser, but still an appreciable extent, obliged to recognize Picards, Mainards, Angevins—and Bretons—also as ancestors. Nor need those who, speaking French or English, with broad skulls, and having reason to suspect themselves (especially Cornishmen) of Breton descent, worry over Mr. Grant's conclusion that the Alpines are "a race of peasants, and never a maritime people," for our encyclopedias describes the Breton as "a bold seaman and a steady soldier." Remembering the glorious achievements of the men of St. Malo they will probably prefer to believe the encyclopedias.

The English-Canadian has been claiming for his race superior merit in colonising, and is usually unwilling to admit his first cousin, the French-Canadian, to equal credit. "It is true that one often hears the Frenchman called a poor colonist. But when Canadians say this, I wonder what they mean," writes McGill's Professor of History. "Obviously the first merit of a colonist is power to take root and hold his own, whether against the aborigines or the forces of nature. If we judge by this criterion, the French in Canada are among the best colonists of whom we have any record. Left with an axe in his hand amid the solitudes of a primeval forest, the French settler knows what to do, even though, like Louis Hébert, he is a Parisian apothecary. And as for initiative, where can more enterprising explorers be found than the whole line of those who, from Champlain to La Vérendrye, lay bare the recesses of North America, while the English were content to linger between the Atlantic and the Alleghanies?"

The Nordics are "above all, rulers, organisers, and aristocrats," according to Mr. Grant. But what of Napoleon, who, coming from the Island of Corsica, was of the Mediterranean race? He was both soldier and ruler par excellence. It is true that he came to an end untimely for his years, —and so have many of our great statesmen in modern parliamentary times. What of Lloyd-George, who, as a Welshman, according to Mr. Grant's generalisation, ought surely to have Mediterranean blood in his veins? What of Cortes, who, with a little army of 450 men, bullied and butchered his way to conquest in Central America? Surely he was soldier, ruler, and aristocrat of the right blood! And his achievements could be almost duplicated by a further turning of the pages of Spanish and Portuguese history. If history will have it that we English-Canadians are originally and copiously of Latin blood, let us make the best of it. Sir Arthur Quiller-Couch goes the full distance, and in a lecture on the Lineage of English Literature, says: "I hazard that the most important thing in our blood is that purple drop of the imperial murex we derive from Rome."

The field is inviting, and one is disposed to follow the men of the Mediterranean race as "rulers, soldiers, and aristocrats"; but it is necessary to go back to our unravelling of the Canadian race garment, remembering that the French-Canadians are none the better for their share of Anglo-Saxon blood, and we are none the worse for our share of "Latin" blood.

There are race differences, it is true, and these differences affect nationalities: but the doctrine that God gave one race an inherent superiority over another, is the nostrum of those who want something for nothing; the consolation of those, who, finding little commended by others in their own lives, fall back upon the achievements of race as a source of pride. The doctrine of race superiority is particularly out of place in Canada, since it is without a scintilla of support. It is "important to get rid of the old notion that there is a fundamental physical difference between the average English-man and the average North Frenchman," writes Dr. Holland Rose of Christ's College, Cambridge, a deep student of matters affecting race and nationality. It naturally follows that it is equally important to get rid of the old notion that there is a fundamental physical difference between their descendants, the average English-Canadian and the average French-Canadian; it is more than ordinarily important, it is essential, to rid ourselves of that notion, if we are to deal with Canadian national problems in the light of the truth that is alone worth while.

The theory of inherent race superiority has been time and time again blown up, and yet as often revived by a race which seeks to dominate, which pursuing its own advantage at the expense of another, seeks to ease its conscience by the pleasing idea that it is the will of God that the fittest should dominate. To those who persist in still believing in race superiority, I commend this sentence from Mills' "Principles of Political Economy": "I cordially subscribe to the remark of one of the greatest thinkers of our time, who says of the supposed differences of race, 'of all vulgar modes of escaping from the consideration of the effect of social and moral influence on the human mind, the most vulgar is that of attributing the diversities of conduct and character to inherent natural differences.' "

BOOKS OF REFERENCE

Madison Grant, *The Passing of the Great Race*. Scribner.

M. l'abbé S.-A. Lortie, *Origine des Premiers Colons canadiens-français* (Premier Congrés de la Langue française du Canada). L'Action Sociale Limitée.

Sir Arthur Quiller-Couch, *On the Art of Writing*. Cambridge University Press, Dent.

J. Holland Rose, *Nationality in Modern History*. Macmillan.

William Bennett Munro, *The Seigniorial System in Canada*. Harvard University Press.

Dr. Beddoe, *The Races of Britain*. London.

CHAPTER VI

THE TRADE ARGUMENT

WHILE the conviction of ethnical superiority is shaken by the hard figures of the measuring stick, when read in the light of history, and its last refuge is crumbling upon the battle-fields of Europe and Asia, the belief in the superiority of nationality—the result of language, education, tradition, religion, and the like—persists. A precise distinction between race and national characteristics, that which men have inherited and that which they have themselves acquired under group influences, cannot be always maintanied. Nor have I sought to maintain it, since the object of our investigation is to be accomplished by remembering the existence of the difference.

It seems to be inevitable that men will call the achievements of their own nationality best.

> "What strange infatuations rule mankind!
> How narrow are our prospects, how confined!
> With universal vanity possessed,
> We fondly think our own ideas best."

While there is no harm, and often a great good, in the conviction of the worth of one's own nationality, even when it is only a pleasant deception, there is grievous harm in the comparisons that inevitably follow. The average English-Canadian is convinced that he is a superior man. He does not appear to realise that belief in superiority is universal, and only its manner of expression local. This belief is closely associated with patriotism, and might be helpful rather than harmful, were it not persistently accompanied by an overweening desire to make over the inferior nationality. Then the belief becomes dangerous; it amounts to an hallucination, which candid opinion has diagnosed as megalomania; it is dangerous, because force rather than persuasion is its means of assertion.

Mohammed's crusade was primarily that of a megalomaniac, since it contained the element of belief in divine direction, a characteristic sign of the disease. "There is one God; and through me, Mohammed, that God summons you to submit to Him." That was the teaching of Mohammed which pushed a smaller world into pretty much the same trouble that we are in to-day. Mohammedans were superior to the rest of mankind; by the will of God, the rest of mankind should be raised to the level of Mohammedans.

The Germans argue pretty much the same way. They are not merely wicked in promulgating Teutonism. "Deutschland über alles!" has become a divine command. They have seen their virtues reflected in the mirror of their own ideals, and have been struck with collective egoism. They have measured men by their own accomplishments and found them inferior, failing to recognise that the rest of mankind may not have done what they have done simply because the rest of mankind did not want to. That is true of most men who proclaim national superiority. We can clearly see the megalomania of the Germans; but the Germans cannot see it; nor can we see our own. That is a typical symptom of the disease.

There is this to be said for the Germans: they have been, according to their lights, really great. They argue, with some force, that the Slavs of Poland are their inferiors in achievement; that is why the German philosopher places so much emphasis upon the necessity of the Slav accepting the Teutonic mind. It was the late Herr Althoff who is reported by Prince Von Bülow to have said: "We Germans are the most learned nation in the world, and the best soldiers. We have achieved great things in all the sciences and arts; the greatest philosophers, the greatest poets and musicians are Germans. Of late we have occupied the foremost place in the natural sciences and in almost all technical spheres, and, in addition to that, we have accomplished an enormous industrial development." Then added the candid, knowing, Althoff, "How can you wonder that we are political asses? There must be a weak point somewhere."

The Slavonic German is not as good a business man as the Teutonic German. Therefore, Slavism ought to be abandoned and all men within the German Empire merged in Teutonism—argue the Teutons. And there is some force in the argument.

Likewise, English-Canadians argue with some force that if French-Canadians were to accept the English-Canadian mind, they would be keener traders. Probably both Poles and French-Canadians—many of them at any rate—would admit so much of the argument, and yet tenaciously cling to their national birth-right, especially when in danger of losing it by compulsion.

How often I have heard men figure on the wonderful commercial strides this country would make if its population were all Anglo-Saxon. It may be true, but only a megalomaniac would urge it as a reason for forcing the English-Canadian mind upon the French-Canadian. While statistics are not available, it may be accepted that French-Canadians are not in big business, as are the English-Canadians. Of course, there are exceptions —anyone can think of them—but the French-Canadians have 28 per cent. of the country's population and have not 28 per cent. of the country's interest in railways, manufacturing, commerce and finance. But the difference between the two nationalities in trade importance, is not to be accounted for solely by difference in mentality.

All things were changed for the old inhabitants after the Conquest, as they would be for the present inhabitants, if Germany were to win the war. There were new trade channels; the old way to Paris was closed, and the new ways led to New York and London. There was a new credit system, with which the French-Canadian was unfamiliar, and in which he was unknown. The French-Canadian importer closed his shop doors and withdrew from the country, or remained open only to start over again in the retail trade. There was, then, no manufacturing, and when its era opened, under the shelter of the protective tariff, some years later, the French-Canadian was still handicapped by lack of credit. France has done little or nothing for her American sons who became British. The French-Canadian has proved himself an industrious, capable, quick-handed artisan, and in a number of industries—the boot and shoe industry, for example —has more than held his own in ownership, management and workmanship.

In measuring what the French-Canadians have done and left undone in commerce and finance, we have habitually made a comparison with what has been accomplished in Canada, not only by English-Canadians, but by the Englishmen of England and the Americans of the United States, as well. In the comparison, we must not forget that our railways and our industries generally have been built up by money largely obtained from the United Kingdom and the United States. England has taken the lead in advancing funds for the railways, and the United States for industrials. It is surprising how many large manufacturing houses in Canada are but branches of larger houses across the boundary-line, and how many others, com-

THE TRADE ARGUMENT 89

menced as Canadian and remaining under Canadian management, have been expanded by the aid of New York and Chicago finance.

The extent and sources of our financial operations in recent years for industrial and railway purposes, are shown in the following tables, recently compiled by the Dominion Securities Corporation. Here is the table in reference to the railways:

Year.	Canada.	United States.	Gt. Britain	Total.
1911	$549,500	$4,249,500	$95,673,700	$100,472,700
1912	150,000	13,290,000	56,532,320	69,972,320
1913	......	11,475,000	97,053,044	108,528,044
1914	......	12,690,000	46,715,666	59,405,666
1915	......	17,500,000	20,415,665	37,915,665
1916	......	15,920,000	....	15,920,000
1917	200,000	17,500,000	4,866,666	22,566,666
Total	$899,500	$92,624,500	$321,257,061	$414,781,061

And here is the table in reference to industrials and miscellaneous undertakings:

Year.	Canada.	United States.	Gt. Britain.	Total.
1911	$26,814,000	$10,970,000	$75,722,000	$113,506,000
1912	22,484,000	13,700,000	82,727,000	118,911,000
1913	18,832,800	13,360,000	64,245,976	96,438,776
1914	4,744,540	11,395,000	27,586,100	43,725,640
1915	5,775,000	13,140,000	3,740,000	22,655,000
1916	5,430,999	32,185,000	4,866,666	42,482,665
1917	11,097,800	21,340,000	55,000	32,492,800
Total	$95,179,139	$116,090,000	$258,942,742	$470,211,881

Mr. Fred. W. Field, of the "Monetary Times," is my authority for saying that there are not less

8 c.

than 2,914 million dollars of British money, and 637 million dollars of American money, invested in this country.   Naturally, these funds and the things which they represent are largely under the control of English-speaking men.   According to Mr. Field, the Americans of the United States have 81 million dollars in Canadian lumber mills and standing timber; have as much, if not more, in Canadian mines; and, further, have large investments in the meat-packing industries, the manufacture of agricultural implements, and manufacturing generally.   The progress of these industries is generally regarded as indistinguishable from that of Canada.   But there is a difference.   For since the investments have come from the United Kingdom or the United States, the profits must naturally go back to the United Kingdom or the United States.   A few moments' work with pencil and paper will show that each year an astonishing sum must be exported from Canada to satisfy these obligations.   Since the French-Canadians have borrowed less from abroad, the profits from the industries under their control remain more within the country.

These things must be taken into account in comparing what the two nationalities are doing to sustain the economic life of the country.

No! the French-Canadian failure to hold a place in the country's trade and finance, comparable to its population, is not all explainable by difference in mentality.   And yet I am inclined to think that mentality, has something to do with the English-Canadian's more important position in trade.

Recently I was discussing these national issues with a Member of the Canadian Parliament—he is not a back-bencher—when he remarked that all Protestant countries were richer than Roman Catholic countries. Scotland's wealth, wrung from Scotland's barren hills, was compared with Italy's poverty, in striking contrast with the fertility of Italy's soil. After a little while I found that the illustration was advanced as evidence of the greater aptitude of the Protestant mind for trade, an argument for the crucible of the public school in Ontario, and the religious and national conversion of the French-Canadians. The argument is not new; you may hear it wherever race and religious controversies are discussed. The evidence is too exhaustive for our present analysis. But if it be true that the Protestant serves mammon more industriously than the Roman Catholic, and with greater rewards, then it is equally true that the Jew serves mammon still more industriously; yet none but a jester would urge, on that account, Protestants and Catholics should be delivered into the rabbi's hands.

I am not now asserting that in business the Roman Catholic is inferior to the Protestant, that the Protestant is inferior to the Jew; but such assertions have been made so often that they are generally believed. Yet Jews do not parade their business acumen as a bait for proselytes; nor do any number of Protestants accept Judaism on that account. Neither religious nor national ideas are tangible matters to be weighed like wool and salt on commercial scales. While success in trade is not to be despised, as it is by some, neither is it to be exalted, as it is by others, out of its due proportion in the achievements of mankind. The argument for general acceptance of the English-Canadian mind and general use of the English language, is strongest when expressed in dollars and cents, but would English-Canadians sell their national birthright for the same consideration?

The situation of the two nationalities in Canada is not without precedent. The Germans have built a huge net-work of railways in Alsace and Lorraine; the provinces conquered in 1871 have been converted into "hives of industry" by German talent for practical things. But the Alsatians and Lorrainers, sharing in the prosperity, have not accepted the Teutonic Lutheran mind, which is generally credited as its creator. Jacques Preiss, of Colmar, in Alsace, as a member of the Reichstag, forcibly expressed the limitation of the influence of materialism over nationalism, in these words: "History will say: The German Empire succeeded in conquering Alsace and Lorraine materially, but its administration did not know how to conquer her morally, did not know how to win the heart and soul of the people." There is a vital something lacking in the argument of trade advantage, when applied to nationality.

Again at the risk of being blamed for repetition. I would have the reader bear in mind that I am referring only to national tendencies and national emphases. Of course, there are many English-Canadians who have neither inclination nor aptitude for trade, while there are many French-Canadians who have both. It is only in a general sense that one nationality sets more store than the other upon commerce, and has a greater aptitude for it.

Canada is ambitious for an export trade in manufactured products, and already several organisations are in existence to promote the country's commercial interest when peace has restored the safety of the seas. The government even now is supposed to be engaged busily in surveying the country's natural resources, out of which foreign commerce can be created; and in a class with our iron ores, our timber, our hydraulic power, our waterways and railways, our factory buildings and machinery, we should include our ability to use as working tools the two great languages in which the world's commerce is conducted.

The Englishman has never excelled in the use of languages, and has largely depended upon the services of others as interpreters. It appears that before the war Germans were employed by the British Government as interpreters in commercial and other matters. With the knowledge we now have of the character and extent of German espionage, the nature of these services becomes apparent,

as well as the identity of their real employers.
Before the war the British public had been warned
that many of the Germans, who, by reason of linguistic attainments, had secured employment in
governments and export businesses overseas, were
but the paid officials of the German government
and German trade associations; but without avail.
How much of the phenomenal and apparently in-
explicable success of German foreign trade has
been built upon information derived by those
agents who penetrated into the secret places of official trade information of the British Government,
is only a matter of interesting speculation; the
important fact is that the weakness of the old system has been acknowledged, and Great Britain is
making preparations to render herself and her subjects self-contained in the matter of languages affecting foreign commerce.

The Canadian Government, through the Department of Trade and Commerce, publishes weekly a
bulletin, providing commercial information for the
guidance of the trade interests of Canada, and in
an issue of February, 1916, states that:

"A special committee of the Aberdeen Chamber of
Commerce, appointed to consider the question of trade
after the war, has drawn up a series of resolutions. These
recommend that a Ministry of Commerce be formed; the
British consuls should be of British origin, with fuller
powers for the development of British trade; that our
system of education be revised, with particular reference
to modern languages, which should be made compulsory
subjects in all universities."

Sir Charles Wakefield, the Lord Mayor of London, speaking about the same time of the new alliance with France, referred to the importance of this matter in the following words:

"However necessary a knowledge of the French language and literature was before the war, it is obvious that the most sacred alliance in which the two nations are now united make such a knowledge absolutely essential. We have been great friends in the past, and our friendship will be infinitely increased by our fighting shoulder to shoulder in this terrible conflict. In future a mutual study of each other's languages should be a compulsory part of the curriculum of every college and school in the respective countries."

The French language a compulsory part of the curriculum of every college and school in England! And why not? There is nothing that would more advance British trade throughout the world. Yet French is taught in the High Schools of Ontario, in the University of Toronto, and—I speak from experience—few are the graduates who can use it in life's work. I can remember my own silly astonishment—and envy—at first hearing the newsboys of Montreal glibly speak the French that had cost me so many hours of labour. The command of languages does not come easily to the youth trained in Ontario's English schools. The French-Canadian may not have the English-Canadian's aptitude for the practical sciences, but he has a greater aptitude for modern languages. If, as we are told, the French-Canadian is not as quick at mathematics as the English-Canadian, then is the Ontario Government going to make him quicker by insisting that he be mathematically instructed solely in a language in which he necessarily thinks with greater difficulty? Is Ontario serving the national interest any better by limiting instruction in the French language to an hour a day? Having in mind our foreign trade aspiration, such restriction appears to be a deliberate destruction of one of the country's "natural" resources. We might, with equal advantage, set fire to our forests. Our great advantage over other countries in the competition for foreign trade that is to be after the war, will lie in our command of the language required for successful international salesmanship.

Hitherto it has not required much effort to dispose of such products as we had for export. Our trade has been principally in cereals, cheese, pork, and lumber; and the two great English-speaking countries, Great Britain and the United States, have been our principal customers. But war commerce has opened up visions of new foreign trade. In the twelve months prior to the declaration of war, Canada exported manufactured goods to the value of sixty-three million dollars, and for the twelve months ending November, 1917, these exports reached the astonishing total of 703 million dollars in value. Although built up, for the most part, by war munitions, manufacturers will not, at the close of the war, yield without a struggle their new footing in foreign markets. Taught economy and efficiency by war conditions, and con-

fidence through initial success, Canadian manufacturers will do their best to maintain a permanent
overseas demand for goods made in the land of the
industrious beaver. There will be bridges to be
built in Flanders, Poland, and France; railways
to be constructed; huge structures of steel and concrete to be erected. Our entrepreneurs think they
ought to have a share of this business. And with
reason. They have men trained in this work, from
the skilled foreman, to the clerk in charge of finance, who are conversant with the two great languages of commerce. Without delay, they can submit tenders and specifications in the accepted language of the buyer, and can carry the work
through, minus the inevitable misunderstandings
that arise through a lack of knowledge of the language of the buying country. Nor are our oppor-
tunities limited to the building trades. In the
paper and pulp industries, in the making of agricultural implements and a number of other commodities, we possess the necessary raw materials,
cheap power, and experience; we can turn out our
goods at a factory cost as low or lower than any
other country; the turning point in advantage may
well lie in the salesmanship that depends on being
able to speak the language and understand the
mind of the buyer.

Already Canada has a respectable beginning in
foreign industries. There are in Mexico important
public utilities (tramway, light, power, and water
services) mainly owned by Canadians and managed

by them. These undertakings naturally involve frequent communications with Government and municipal officials. If the Company's representative has command of the Spanish language, there is no difficulty, for it is the mother tongue of the country. If he be conversant with only the English language, then the interests he represents must suffer all the disabilities of communication by means of an interpreter. If, however, he speaks French, the interpreter is unnecessary, as French is the language of official life in Mexico. There are important public utilities controlled and managed by Canadians in South America; and if the Canadians in charge cannot speak Portuguese, they are usually compelled to resort to the unsatisfactory services of an interpreter, unless they know French, for French is known and spoken in official circles of the Latin Republics. So it runs the world over.

There is no intention to belittle the importance of the English language; through it a large portion of the world's commerce is conducted. But the English language is not all prevailing. That we must remember if we are to break through the shell of our present trade boundaries. The all-knowing Whittaker tells us that while 160 millions people speak English, 70 millions speak French, and 125 millions more speak in tongues kindred to French. Our advantage in salesmanship is evident; our success ought to be limited only by our capacity to assemble materials and the means of transport.

CHAPTER VII

EDUCATION

THERE was evidence in the last chapter that some of the difference between the material achievements of the two nationalities is due to differences in mentality, presumably the result of differences in education. If our conclusions had been formed upon the speeches made from certain hustings, we should have believed that it was almost the sole cause of differences in achievement. It is impossible, in this investigation, to go thoroughly into the subject of education, and the reader may well say: "Then, better left alone." But it is, also, impossible to escape reference to a subject which affects vitally the business in hand. The French-Canadians, almost solidly Roman Catholic, have been educated mainly in Church schools; and English-speaking Canadians, almost overwhelmingly Protestant, have been instructed mainly in State schools. We are, therefore, compelled to consider education, in spite of our hesitation to attempt the survey of such a controversial and comprehensive subject in a single chapter.

Education and nationality are as closely and as confusedly related as the hen and the egg. Which came first, a hen or an egg, was a conundrum of my early youth, and if there be an answer I have

not yet heard it. The school makes the man, but
the man makes the school that makes the man;
schools are accountable for much of the French-
Canadian character, and the French-Canadian
character is accountable for the schools.   And
there we are, headed on our way round and round,
until we remember that both school and man have
evolved out of the traditions and ideals of the past.

The man on the street too often sees only the product, and not the factory or field in which it was
made or grown. He too seldom stops to ask Why?
—and there is no particular reason why he should;
unless, not being pleased with the product, he seeks
to destroy it. Then, if he is depriving someone else
of a pleasing something, as a reasonable man, he
ought to stop and ask, Why? That is the position we are in to-day in regard to the French-English schools of Ontario.

The average man in Ontario sees first—and
sometimes last and always—the hand of a French
priest intriguing to wrest the school from the
legitimate authority of the State. He regards the
common school as a unit produced by the State,
upon which have been built the high school and
the university, and believes that the Church is attempting to usurp the legitimate ownership of the
State; but, of course, such a conception, in the light
of history, is wholly erroneous. It was French
priests who brought education first to Canada, and,
curiously enough, it was French priests, who, if
not responsible for introducing the school into

England, were at least responsible for reviving it to such an extent that it became permanent in the country's life. Peter of Blois has given us an account of the early days of Cambridge in these quaint words: "Abbot Joffred sent over to his manor of Cotenham, nigh Cambridge, Gislebert, his fellow-monk and divinity professor, with three other monks, who followed him into England; and, being well furnished with philosophical learning and other ancient sciences, they daily repaired to Cambridge, where they hired a publick barn, made open profession of the sciences, and in a little time drew a great number of scholars together. In less than two years their number encreased so much, out of all that country as well as the town, that there was not a house, barn, or church, big enough to hold them all. Upon which they dispersed themselves into several parts of the town, imitating the university of Orleans. Betimes in the morning Frier Odo, an ex-grammarian and satyric poet, read grammar to the boys and younger sort, who were assigned him, according to the doctrine of Priscian and Remigius upon him. At one o'clock, Terricus, a subtle sophist, read Aristotle's logick to the elder sort, according to Porphyry's and Averroe's introductions and comments. At three of the clock Frier William read lectures in Tully's rhetorick, and Quintilian's institutions. And Gislebert, the principal master, preached to the people upon all Sundays and holidays. From this small fountain we see large flowing streams, making glad the city of God, and enriching the whole kingdom with many masters and teachers, who came out of Cambridge, as from the holy paradise."

The common schools came after the university. They were the outcome of the university; not the university the outcome of the common schools. Education works its way downwards, not upwards. In their inception, the common schools were also regarded as "flowing streams making glad the city of God." Not so many years ago that was a universal conception. There was a Laval in French-speaking Canada before there was a Harvard in English-speaking America; and both were Church institutions. From these seats of learning went forth the missionaries who founded what became the common schools of to-day. The Canadian schools were, in their inception, purely missions for teaching His Christian Majesty's language to little savages. Nor was the conception of the common schools, as "flowing streams making glad the city of God," changed at the Reformation. The object of the stream remained the same; there was change only in the channels. After a while, the channels that were made when the Reformation first began, became more numerous, and, with the increasing number of sects, became divided and subdivided into big and little streams. But if history is right, it was not on that account that the State assumed jurisdiction over education. It was because the State wished to turn the direction of the streams from the city of God to something else.

It was Napoleon, says J. W. Headlam of Cambridge, in a chapter contributed to the "Unity of Western Civilisation," who first deliberately attempted "to convert the whole fabric of French schools and the university into an instrument for the organised propaganda of the cult of the Empire. Since then there is scarcely a government (always except that of England, which alone has been strong enough to rest on the native and undisciplined political sense of the people) which has not followed in his path. In particular, when the State is founded on the nation, the school is used to develop in the children the full consciousness of nationality. That institution, that was for so long the home of European unity, has become the most useful agent for the perpetuation and exaggeration of national differences." "In Trieste and in Poland," says Mr. Headlam, "in Alsace and in Macedonia, we find kings and politicians contending for the minds and souls of children, and it is in the school, the college, and the university that has been prepared the conflict that is now devastating Europe."

It was only natural that, under the State, the whole idea of the school should become changed; for the school could not very well continue to be a stream making glad the city of God, since making glad the city of God was not always a plank in the program of the party in power. The school became secular, and in France, the home of the

State school, it sometimes (depending on the Government of the day) became not only non-religious but anti-religious. "It is said," declared an official appointed by the French Government to address the scholars, "that we have expelled God from the schools. It is an error; one can only expel that which exists, and God does not exist."

The gospel preached in the school thus became identical with the gospel preached by the dominant political party, and varied according to its or the State's exigencies. Where the country was pushing its way to power, it was military greatness; where the country was suspicious of aggression, it was very often, chauvinism instead of patriotism; where the country was seeking to be wealthy, it was production. Germany used its schools to foster the idea that the thing most worth while was the wealth and military power of Germany. The United States, teaching loyalty to the Stars and Stripes, designed its school curriculum for the commercial greatness of the United States. And English Canada followed all the example of the Americans of the United States, with the exception of the design of the flag.

In Canada and the United States, the education mills are designed and equipped to turn out products tongued to fit the country's industrial grooves. Misunderstand me not, the subjects taught in these schools spread over a wide range; but the emphasis is upon that which makes for efficiency in factory and shrewdness in office. That is the plank of the party in power, and probably the plank of the party that wants to be in power. Some of us think that the principal economic function of this country is agriculture, and that the country's agricultural interests are being sacrificed by the State school for industrialism. To that phase of the subject we shall return in another chapter, for it is of more than passing interest. Certain it is that the efficiency of our schools is too often measured by the industrial needs of our cities and towns, and too seldom by the needs of the country as a whole. What passes for public opinion, let us not forget, is very often merely town opinion. It is more readily organised and more often appears in print, and thus becomes more generally accepted as the voice of the people.

The reports made by Dr. Merchant and others on the rural French-English schools of the province revealed bad conditions. The public was shocked. But there were no equally searching investigations into the rural schools where English is the sole language. It was only the other day that an official of high rank in the Department of Education informed me that these schools are not as good as they were thirty years ago. As evidence of their unsatisfactory condition, he stated that in the average county, there are each year changes of teachers in seventy out of a hundred rural school districts. It may well be that searching investigations into the affairs of the English rural schools of the province would be—at least interesting.

9 c.

Nor is the condition of our city schools entirely satisfactory. Many have interpreted the growing attendance at schools that are not under State direction, as a growing desire for exclusiveness, whereas, in reality, it is a desire of parents that their children "should be taught to form tastes," as Goethe expressed it, "rather than have knowledge communicated to them." They want their children to be educated, not merely instructed. And the plain truth is, that the State schools have shown a limited capacity for education; they have entirely failed to do the work in character building that is being done by preparatory schools under private and Church (Protestant and Roman Catholic) direction in the Province. The State schools of Ontario are probably at their best in Toronto, and yet there are thousands of parents (Protestant) who find them unacceptable streams of education, as shown by the innumerable private schools in the city. Some day, we may conclude, in spite of the present current of opinion, that the State can only instruct. It certainly has not succeeded in filling the place of the old Scotch dominie, who may not have instructed as well, but educated better.

The French-Canadian is not ground to so fine a business edge in the Church school as the English-Canadian in the State school. But he is taught a philosophy of life. We may not all agree with that philosophy, but are we mending matters by leaving the explanation of the whys of life to the precarious home training, and the inadequate one-hour-a-week education of the Sunday school? In the Church schools everywhere, the object of education is the same: it is the student's realisation of his or her place in the scheme of the universe. The schools are "flowing streams making glad the city of God." The Church has seen no reason to change its mind. It continues to reason—in 1918 as in 1418—that life here, being only a stage preparatory for life hereafter, becomes a period of schooldays. Earthly life is not an end in itself; it is only a means to an end. "To-day we are weaving the structure we are henceforth to inhabit." Since man has been placed on earth that he may make himself ready for God's kingdom and acquire a capacity for God's righteousness, that then becomes the real business of life; all other things are comparatively insignificant. Anyway, treasures accumulated on earth will become moth-eaten, corroded by rust, or stolen by thieves. Since men cannot count, at the most, on more than three score years and ten, no day in the week may be safely lost in looking after the only thing that is worth while, the only thing that is permanent. There is no sharp distinction to be made of what is man's and what is God's, for all should be—and, in fact, all is—God's. I assume thus far this reasoning is that of the Protestant and Roman Catholic Churches alike. But if so, we are then at the parting of the ways, for the Roman Catholic Church carries the argument to what seems from the premises a logical conclusion, that the school and the Church are inseparable. With that the average Protestant does not agree. The Church and the school, reasons the Roman Catholic, are, in fact, an indivisible institution, designed to conduct the human being from infant years, through maturity and old age, until consciousness flickers out and earthly school-days are over, to "the city of God."

The State schools of Ontario have never been, as in France, anti-religious; nor are they non-religious. God is admitted to the school room, but only as a "neutral." He is a formal and formless visitor. He is not, as in the Church school, regarded as the indispensable spirit of school work. But there are signs of change, for philosophers— and non-Catholic philosophers at that—are "discovering," as Mr. Brierly says in "Ourselves and the Universe," "that God is not only the source and object of the religious feelings, but that He is also a musician, an artist, a mathematician, the Creator and Giver of all beauty, and that in seeking perfection in these directions we are seeking Him." Surely that view is a "discovery" only in a limited sense! It is simply a return to the old idea of a "flowing stream making glad the city of God."

We have seen it generally asserted that the Protestant mind is superior to the Roman Catholic mind in business; and if it be true, then surely an explanation lies in the system of Roman Catholic education, which lays so much daily stress upon an understanding of things spiritual. While men may go on believing that they can serve both God and mammon, it is only common honesty to recognise that the direction of the training largely determines the direction of the service. Mind you, I am not asserting that Roman Catholics understand spiritual things better than Protestants, but I do assert that they devote more time in attempting to understand them. There are men who will think that the Roman Catholics are laying aside the substance for the shadow, and others who will think, having been badly trained in the political economy of the material world, Roman Catholics are being as badly trained in the science which has to do with production, distribution, and consumption of the wealth of the spiritual world. But into that unfathomable question I will not go.

Probably nothing will illustrate the difference between the two nationalities in education better than an outline of the ways in which they have separately shaped their organisations for its administration. In Ontario, when the Premier of the Province is picking his Ministers for roads, lands, farms, and finance, he also picks one for education—and that is the general practice in the other English-speaking provinces. Education is regarded as an ordinary subject of government. There is no pretence that the people are given an opportunity of selecting the ablest man to direct the training of their children. The Premier cannot be blamed if he does not select the ablest, since his choice is limited to one of the sixty or

more men who have been returned as his supporters. The Province has varied interests, agricultural and industrial, which ought to be protected
in the schools; and yet it is not by the combined
voice of those interests that the choice is made.
The Province, as a whole, has no voice in the
matter. The member who, as Minister, has charge
of the educational affairs of the Province, may
represent a city constituency, and have no knowledge of rural needs; or he may represent a rural
constituency, and be equally ignorant of city needs.
Of course, the Province may resent the Premier's
choice, and punish the government at the next
election—that is the safetly-valve of our constitution—but in doing so it has to punish a government which may have done very good work in
other directions. As in all games of hazard, there
is a chance of success. Now and then it may hap-
pen that a constituency has sent to the Legislature
a man who happens to have the qualifications and
happens to have supported the platform of the
Prime Minister. But if such things do not hap-
pen, then great harm is inevitable. If there be no
member with qualifications supporting the government, then a member without qualification has
to be picked; for a Minister of Education we must
have. In each of the nine provinces a lawyer with
papers duly signed and sealed must be (Attorney
General) Minister of Laws. But it is not regarded
as essential that the man who presides over education be an educationist, and sometimes not consid-

ered necessary that he be educated. If the unqualified Minister happens to realise his lack of qualification and leans upon the bureaucracy which presides over the education of the province, we are in the practical position of having no Minister. That is unfortunate. Still it would have been more unfortunate if, not realising his lack of qualification, he had attempted to administer the technical side of the schools. Realising his limitations or not, the Minister is always at hand when party politics are involved; and, having a Minister, party politics are frequently involved. That is wholly unfortunate.

In Quebec there is no Minister of education. Education is removed from party politics. The minister's place is taken by two committees, one a Roman Catholic committee, consisting of 36 members, and the other a Protestant committee, consisting of 22 members. Each committee contains representatives of clergy and laity. Each committee has home-rule over the affairs of its own side of the house. The committees bear the same relation to the bureaucracy that the Minister bears to the bureaucracy in the other provinces. Their regulations must be approved by Orders-in-Council, but approval is a matter of course. The politicians stand aside; the government simply lends it machinery to carry out the wishes of the committees. Obviously the committees are the real factor, and the government which names their members takes pride in appointing the most distinguished educationists and public men within Quebec. But there is many a slip between theory and practice in government. Here, however, if we may judge from the names on the Protestant committee, the deed is as good as the theory. The following are members of the committee: Sir William Peterson, K.C.M.G., LL.D., Chairman; Prof. A. W. Kneeland, M.A., B.C.L. (Macdonald College); Rev. A. T. Love, B.A., D.D., Quebec; Sir Herbert Ames, K.B., LL.D., M.P.; Gavin J. Walker, Lachute; Hon. Sydney Fisher, B.A., Knowlton; W. M. Rowat, M.D., Athelstan; Hon. Justice McCorkill, D.C.L., LL.D.; Prof. J. A. Dale, M.A. (McGill); Principal Rev. R. A. Parrock, M.A., D.C.L., Bishop's College, Lennoxville; Howard Murray, Esq., Montreal; R. Bickerdike; W. S. Bullock, M.L.A.; Rt. Rev. Lennox Williams, D.D., Bishop of Quebec; Hon. W. G. Mitchell; Rev. E. I. Rexford, D.C.L., LL.D.; W. L. Shurtleff, K.C., LL.D.; Hon. George Bryson, M.L.C.; Chas. McBurney, B.A. (Principal of the Academy, Lachute); Marcus G. Crombie, Richmond; Miss I. E. Brittain, M.A.

These have been appointed for life, with the exception of a member who is elected annually by the teachers. They are what "unprogressive" Quebec has in place of a political Minister of Education; no, they are only half of it; for there is another body of distinguished clergymen, educationists, and public men which presides over the Catholic schools. The committees do not change with the government. They do not change by reason of the government's malfeasance or misfeasance in crown lands or in road-building. Governments may come and governments may go; but the training of children remains in the hands of men selected by reason of their academic standing and their aptitude for educational administration. Recognising the existence of difference, there has ceased to be dissension. There are no cross-currents. There are narrow men in Quebec who delight to throw mud in the other stream, who try to dam it with barriers, but they are measured at their true value. There is criticism; but in Quebec the Catholic (generally) reserves his criticism for the Catholic schools, and the Protestant (generally) for the Protestant schools. Both Protestants and Roman Catholics are in free possession of "flowing streams making glad the city of God."

Since education has come down to the common schools from the universities, we may well go to them in our further quest for the difference in the educational turn of the two national minds. I have no desire to undertake an analysis of what is taught at the Universities of Toronto and Laval; there is something more conclusive in what has been learned there. Upon twenty years of intimate acquaintance with the college men of both nationalities, I venture to assert that the French-Canadian is generally better versed in the Classics. He is not only more familiar with Plato, Aristotle,

Cicero, and the rest of the men who have inflicted pains upon youth; but has more often retained the ability to express himself in Greek and Latin prose, especially in Latin. Men may differ as to the value of classical training; by many it is now-a-days regarded as labour lost; but we must not forget that it was the sort of education that gave to England Fox, Pitt, Acton, Gladstone, Balfour and many of her best, and the world's best, men. In his inaugural address as chancellor of the University of Bristol, Mr. Haldane, now Lord Haldane, said: "After a good deal of observation, both while I was at the Bar and while I was in charge of an administrative department, I have come to the conclusion that, as a general rule, the most stimulating and useful preparation for the general work of the higher Civil Service is a literary training, and that of this a classical education is, for most men, the best form, though not exclusively so." Lord Haldane's opinion will carry weight with all who are not wholly immersed in materialism.

We may call the classical course old-fashioned, if we will, and in truth, as we have seen from Peter of Blois, it is the oldest-fashioned way of education. "No doubt men vary," continues Lord Haldane, "and science or modern literature may develop the mind, in the case of those who have aptitude for them, better than Latin or Greek literature." But a knowledge of the dead languages is, by no means, the French-Canadian's sole claim to education. He has had also the better instruction in the

living languages, or perhaps—more correctly—
has been more successful in acquiring a knowledge
of them. The reader may think I have been
fortunate in the French-Canadians I know, and
unfortunate in the English-Canadians I know; but
I am the more confident in my conclusion, since it
is corroborated by others who know the two nationalities equally well. The English-Canadian may
have passed through the Collegiate Institute and
through the State University, but only now and
then is he able to use French in general conversation; rarely has he more than a laboured acquaintance with the French classics, and seldom is he able
to keep abreast with the current French thought.

Is it not probable that the French-Canadian's
advantage in moderns is derived from his advantage in classics? That so far from being lost
labour, knowledge of the classics is indispensable
to knowledge of English? We sometimes wonder at the nicety with which the French-Canadian
picks his way in the English language. Even his
apparent mistakes are often found to have a foundation in etymology. We have been attributing
his success in languages—with our usual careless-
ness—to race aptitude, but it is in reality due to
careful work already done in the ground from
which the material has been taken for the English language. We may persist—if we will—in
speaking of ourselves as of the Anglo-Saxon race,
but we can continue to talk of an Anglo-Saxon language only by defying the opinion of the masters

of English. For three hundred years there was bilingualism in Great Britain. For those who will persist in believing that the French of French Canada is impure: it was mainly a Norman-French dialect that lived side by side with Anglo-Saxon, and became fused into what is now our national tongue. In truth we owe much to the ancestors of these French-Canadians and—let us not forget— to their priests as well. For from the latter we obtained the Latin words which make up "the bulk of our literary language." The machinery—the inflexions, numerals, pronouns, prepositions and conjunctions—is Anglo-Saxon; the words are mainly Latin and French; and the spirit, the thing which gives it life, that is from Continental parts that paid cultural tribute to Rome. Consider the following passage from "the much admired opening of Piers Plowman," which Sir Arthur Quiller-Couch, Professor of English Literature at Cambridge, considers the very best of Anglo-Saxon:

"Bote in a Mayes Morwnynge—on Malverne hulles
Me bi-fel a ferly—a Feyrie me thouhte;
I was weori of wandringe—and wente me to reste
Under a brod banke—bi a Bourne syde,
And as I lay and leonede—and lokede on the watres,
I slumberde in a slepynge—hit sownede so murie."

"That is good, solid stuff, no doubt: but tame, inert, if not actually lifeless," comments Sir Arthur. "As M. Jusserand says of Anglo-Saxon poetry in general, it is like the river Saône—one doubts which way it flows. How tame in comparison with this, for example:—

"In somer, when the shawes be sheyne,
  And leves be large and long,
Hit is full mery in feyre foreste
  To here the foulys song:

To se the dere draw to the dale
  And leve the hilles hee,
And shadow hem in the leves grene
  Under the grene-wode tre.

Hit befel on Whitsontide,
  Erly in a May mornyng,
The Son up feyre can shyne,
  And the briddis mery can syng.

'This is a mery mornyng,' said litell John,
  'Be Hym that dyed on tre;
A more mery man than I am one
  Lyves not in Cristianté.

'Pluck up thi hert, my dere mayster,'
  Litull John can sey,
'And thynk hit is a full fayre tyme
  In a mornyng of May.'"

"There is no doubting which way *that* flows!"
continues Sir Arthur. "And this vivacity, this new
beat of the heart of poetry, is common to Chaucer
and the humblest ballad-maker; it pulses through
any book of lyrics printed yesterday, and it came
straight to us out of Provence, the Roman Province. It was the Provençal Troubadour who, like
the Prince in the fairy tale, broke through the
hedge of briers and kissed Beauty awake again."

The French-Canadians, Nordics like most of us
(for if we persist in our claim of descent from
Northmen, we cannot refuse to accept the French-

Canadians as first cousins), have been brought up at the source; they may become entangled in the complicated Anglo-Saxon machinery, but they commence the study of the English language with an enviable knowledge of the whys of English words. It is an old proverb that says: "He who knows only one language knows none." It is a rare old bull in its way, but has lived many years by virtue of its intrinsic worth.

The neglect of any State to train its high school students in the use of the "accepted neutral language of all nations," is bad enough; but the neglect of English Canada is indefensible. It is explainable only on the theory that, having imported our scheme of education from the United States, along with our shaving soap and talcum powder, we have neglected to adapt it to conditions which are peculiar to this country. Nothing has contributed more to our national misunderstandings than the English-Canadians' plain disposition not to understand the French tongue; it has been accepted (and not unnaturally) as a disposition not to understand the French-Canadian. The man who tries to understand us and fails, we can forgive— even if we be in violent disagreement; but the man who ignores us is hardly to be forgiven. There are Cabinet Ministers responsible for the administration of the affairs of all the people, who cannot understand the language that for three hundred years has had a fixed place in the country, and that is now the native tongue of three-tenths of the

people. There are men high in the civil service
—the public's service—who can neither read nor
write the language spoken and written by three-
tenths of the public. They are not our exceptionally ignorant English-Canadians; they are our
exceptionally well-educated. Several of them are
outstanding products of Provincial colleges and
universities. There are, as a matter of fact, few
English-Canadians in public life—and I include
newspaper editors—who ever know, except upon
interpretation, what more than seven-tenths of the
Canadian people are writing and thinking about.
On the contrary, there are many French-Canadians
who follow the workings of the Canadian mind
as a whole.

If a school object be to prepare men for public
service, then the State higher school is at least a
partial failure. If an object in education be to
make man a more social being, more capable of
rendering service to his fellows—and particularly
his countrymen—then the French-Canadian university graduate is educationally the better-built
man. If the school be essentially a place in which
youth is to be given access to learning, the French-
Canadian Church university has better succeeded,
since it presents its graduates with keys that will
turn the locks of the world's two greatest storehouses of knowledge. The State universities of
English Canada pretend to do the same; but one
of the keys which they present on diploma day
rarely fits; and there is nothing more useless than

a key that won't unlock. The French-Canadian
makes use of his advantage. He is a good reader.
As a rule, he does not write enough in English,
but that is because he believes the English-Canadian is not interested in his point of view. He has
ready access to the transactions of all meetings of
international science, for they are, of course, conducted solely in French, the world's neutral language. He is able to follow (at least in the sense
of knowing what they are) the great strides which
France has made and will continue to make in
the sciences and arts, while the English-Canadian
must helplessly await the usually unsatisfactory
translations.

There is more of mathematics in these French-
Canadian universities than the counting of beads;
more of the classics than the recital of Latin prayers. At Ottawa, the seat of Federal Government,
the graduates of the two systems meet upon common ground, and comparison is inevitable. The
French-Canadian is not the man with the inferior
education. On the floor of Parliament, where in
an exceptional debate keen analysis and quick wit
are required, and a knowledge of history and
philosophy is useful, the French-Canadian, educated in the Church school, can hold his own with
or against the English-Canadian instructed in the
State school. For all precedents in British law,
exceeding 400 years in age—and it was, then that
the corner-stones of our constitution were set—the
French-Canadian has an obvious advantage since

it was not until about the commencement of the
sixteenth century that the British Parliament expressed its laws in English instead of French.

But as Herr Althoff said of the Germans, "there
must be a weak point somewhere." And the weakness of the French-Canadian Church higher school
lies in the laboratory. The teaching of the Church
higher school excels in the political, historical, and
mental sciences; falls down in the "dismals" but,
curiosuly enough, excels in the "gays." The State
is generally conceded to have excelled in the applied sciences. In short, the Church has done its
best work in the sciences which are pursued for
the love of knowledge; and the State in the sciences
that yield financial returns. That was to be
expected in the light of our knowledge of the difference in approach. The State has put the emphasis in its school on the tangible things of the
outside world; the Church has put the emphasis
in its school on the intangible things of the inside
world. The State is instructing us to control
nature and the Church is educating us to control
ourselves.

The Church regards the school as "a stream
making glad the city of God," and the State regards the school as an instrument which will con-
tribute to the material prosperity of the community. Laval has departments of polytechnics, medicine, dentistry, pharmacy, and agriculture, but it
is not there its best work is done. There was
a time when the arts course of University College

was the strongest link in the chain of the University of Toronto; but it is not to-day. At McGill, medicine and practical science have always had greater prestige than arts. But because we prefer apron and overalls to cap and gown (forceful reminders of the universal influence of the Church in education), we should not regard one as a substitute for the other. The best specialists cannot be produced without a sound foundation in general knowledge. Perhaps that is why, specialising in the applied sciences, we have signally failed to make more than two or three outstanding contributions to the world's achievements in the applied sciences. If there be a something in our country's life which prevents our combining the two, let us at least amicably agree to leave the French-Canadians to pursue the humanities, while we follow the practical sciences. Agreeing, we will cease to wrangle over the childish question as to which is superior.

There is always danger in generalisation; and especially in so controversial a subject as education. I am writing of national differences in education in only a general sense. It must not be thought that the French-Canadian despises instruction in the practical things. Within recent years emphasis is being placed on the necessity of special training for artisans; *and Quebec led Ontario in providing modern facilities for technical instruction.* I find in the report (1913) of a Royal Commission appointed by the Federal Government to investigate this subject that in 1911 Montreal had a technical school "which owes its foundation to Sir Lomer Gouin," and which "for its size, the building and equipment are amongst the finest in either America or Europe." The Quebec Government, under French-Canadian direction, had also established a technical school in the City of Quebec, which "is three-fifths of the size of the one in Montreal," and "constructed on practically the same lines." Ontario was then (upon the same authority) *only discussing* the advisability of introducing technical instruction on a scale equal to its importance, and only in Hamilton had it a school with anything approaching suitable accommodation and equipment. Quebec's "progress" in technical education, stirred Ontario to action. Toronto now boasts of its excellent technical school; but it followed, it did not lead, Montreal.

My friend, the Member of Parliament, whom we found in the last chapter, maintaining that the Protestant mind was superior in business, was right only in a qualified sense. The Roman Catholic no more neglects business than the Protestant neglects religion.

Books of Reference

Viscount Haldane, *The Conduct of Life*. Musson.

Sir Arthur Quiller-Couch, *On the Art of Writing*. Putᵻam.

J. M. Brierly, *Ourselves and the Universe*.

J. W. Headlam and Others, *The Unity of Western Civilisation*. Milford.

Reports of the Royal Commission on Industrial and Technical Education. The King's Printer, Ottawa.

Ernest Weekley, *The Romance of Words*. Musson.

CHAPTER VIII

NOT INFERIOR—DIFFERENT

"THE French-Canadians are illiterate," said an Ontario high functionary one night when Regulation 17 was being discussed at the dinner table. And illiteracy has been so often charged that it cannot be passed by with a mere denial.

"I have not found them so," I replied.

"Quebec is the most illiterate province in the Dominion," he said.

"Not according to the census," I answered.

"That statement has been made by a Member of Parliament."

"A French Member?" I asked.

"Don't be facetious," he replied. "What are the figures, if you know them?"

We sent to the library for a Canadian Year Book and found—to his surprise—that, although Ontario has compulsory education, there is an attendance at school of only 51 per cent. of its boys and 52 per cent. of its girls between 5 and 20 years of age; and, while Quebec has voluntary education, 50 per cent. of its boys and 51 per cent. of its girls, between the same ages, are at school. Evidently, voluntaryism in Quebec is almost as efficacious as conscription in Ontario—in securing school attendance. There are more grown up illiterates in Quebec, where only 86 per cent. can read and write, than in Ontario, where 92 per cent. can read and write. But it is only fair to add, that Quebec stands fourth in literacy, not last, among the nine provinces.

"The French-Canadians of Northern Ontario are very stupid," continued my friend, apparently not at all abashed that the official statistics failed to back up his dogmatic assertion.

"You have much business with them?" I suggested.

"Most of my business is with them," was the answer. "Besides, I have lived with them since I was a boy, and know what I am talking about when I say they are stupid. Their mentality is not as good as that of English-Canadians."

"And in what language do they talk to you,"

"In bastard English," he replied, in tones of contempt. "I don't understand French," he added, as if submitting evidence of his own superiority.

I have related this bit of conversation, because it illustrates the attitude of mind in which English-Canadians frequently approach this much discussed question of comparative literacy and intelligence. Surely there are evidences of megalomania here. The average English-Canadian of Ontario does not understand French, and yet presumes to judge the quickness and soundness of the French-Canadian mind. I make no pretensions to superior mentality, but if what I have were put through the sieve of the French language, it would appear even less than it is; and, of course, it would be even more unfair to judge the mentality of all English-Canadians by the spectacle of my unfortunate results.   Yet, in a similar way, we often appraise and condemn the mentality of the French-Canadian.   Strange as it may seem, I have heard men of intelligence assert dogmatic opinions of French-Canadian character upon no better authority than a summer's experience with the farmers of St. Agathe or Murray Bay.   It is significant of the whole controversy, that those English-Canadians who know French and also know the French-Canadians, have for them the highest respect.

Having heard so much of the "patois" charge, and realising my own inability to try it, I was pleased when, some years ago, M. Shotland, one of the editors of the great Parisian daily, "Le Figaro," told me that he was on his way to Montreal, for the purpose of studying the French-Canadian "patois."   It required only a suggestion that my company would be welcome, to take me along.

After breakfast, we set out on our task with becoming earnestness, and in the early morning visited the docks.   The Parisian journalist industriously questioned the labourers and the stragglers that frequent that quarter of the city.   At a more decent hour we visited the mercantile section of Montreal, and I introduced the editor to several of my French-Canadian business friends.   In the afternoon, we called upon the lawyers and the doctors, and spent the evening at "Le Club Canadien." There we met many of the younger professional group. As we returned to the hotel, I anxiously asked for my friend's opinion of the French, spoken in Montreal. "It is good," he replied, "excellent. I could have well imagined myself in a club at home. It is true your friends have not all our latest slang, but their speech is the better for that. The professional men, the financiers, the business men, have been educated by competent teachers, for they have acquired not only the grammatical construction, but the accent of the language, as spoken to-day in Paris. It is sheer nonsense to talk of French-Canadian "patois." The labourers speak as do the labourers in the larger towns of France, although there are traces here of more contact with English. But at home we are still borrowing from the English, and they from us. Nor in this country is the taking of words all on one side. I assume that you do not consider your tongue corrupted because it contains such words as lacrosse and canoe, plainly taken from French Canada."

Of course, all French-Canadians are no more infallible in the use of French than all English-Canadians are infallible in the use of English. A country in which each word is dropped with its proper accent into its precise setting is only the Utopian dream of a well-fed school-master.

Old words and old phrases, old proverbs and old constructions, forgotten in France, have lived in

Canada. But they are no more reprehensible than the quaint folk-songs and the quaint villages in which they have been preserved. In fact, all three have won the admiration of intelligent American tourists. These old forms are being collected and put into dictionary form, of which M. Adjutor Rivard says: "Monument solide, qui prouverait aussi que notre langue est un véritable français, où se rencontrent sans doute des archaismes et des formes dialectales, mais absolument respectables." They are not of modern vagabond creation, these archaic and dialectic words and phrases which are being collected; they are perfectly respectable members of linguistic society.

Quoting M. Rameau de Saint Père, Professor Rivard writes: "Nos armes portent cette devise: Je me souviens. Et cela veut dire, non seulement: 'Je me souviens de la France, de la grande patrie et de sa langue,' mais aussi: 'Je me souviens de la Normandie, du Perche et de la Bretagne, de la Picardie, du Maine et de l'Anjou, du Poitou, de l'Aunis et de la Saintonge, du Berry, de la Champagne et de l'Angoumois. . . . Je me souviens des petites patries et de leurs parlers.'

There are also "corruptions" which have crept into the language—words taken from the English and sometimes malformations of English—but they are the exception, not the rule as some would have us believe. French-Canada is being subjected to a grilling attack; no respect for the intimate feelings of men and women has spared her; all her faults—and something more—have been laid bare to the world. One of two results was inevitable: the people, humiliated in their deepest feelings would either lose their self-respect and abandon that which others held so cheaply; or, humiliated, would defy their critics and resolve by achievement to vindicate themselves before the world. French-Canadians chose the latter course. While violation of the law of grammar is not punished by the State in Quebec; it is punished, after the manner of Judge Lynch, by society. Through the influence of "La Société du Parler français au Canada," men and women that do not assist in the conservation of the purity of language, are regarded as unpatriotic, the natural subjects for condemnation. This society, formed 16 years ago under the auspices of Laval, at Quebec, has extended its organisation wherever French is spoken in Canada and the United States. "Sans tenter de proscrire l'usage d'aucun autre idiome, reconnaissant au contraire que c'est aujourd'hui, et chez nous, une supériorité que de pouvoir parler deux langues, la Société veut entretenir chez les Canadiens français le culte du parler maternel, les engager à l'étudier, à le perfectionner, à le conserver pur de tout alliage, et à le défendre de toute corruption. Elle prétend faire par là oeuvre nationale."

Nowhere is there a stronger public sentiment for an undefiled tongue than in French-Canada, and

English-Canadians may safely leave the guardianship of the French language in Canada to its jealous care.

While there will always be disputes as to what constitutes purity in language, and while changes in the mode of life make for changes in vocabulary and expression, the French-Canadian, clinging to certain old forms, as M. Rameau has said, through attachment for the "little mother countries," has accepted the modern national language of France as a standard. They speak the French of France and speak it well. How can it be otherwise? As M. Théophile Hudon has said:

"C'est bien le français que nous parlons.   Et pourquoi pas?

"Les enfants l'étudient dans les livres français, dans des auteurs français, des grammaires françaises, des manuels français, tout comme les Anglo-Canadiens étudient l'anglais dans des auteurs anglais.

"Pourquoi les gens étrangers à la langue française parviennent-ils à maîtriser le français, tandis que nous ne saurions y réussir, bien que la langue française soit notre langue maternelle?

"Nos enfants lisent et comprennent les contes de Perrault, les récits de madame de Ségur, les fables de La Fontaine et tant d'autres qui font les délices des enfants de France. Ce serait folie de prétendre que des enfants lisent des choses qu'ils ne comprennent point!

"Les jeuns gens se passionnent pour Bossuet et Lacordaire; ils savourent la finesse de La Bruyère et de Veuillot; ils savent par coeur les tirades de Racine, de Corneille et de Boileau.

"Enfin, universités françaises, collèges classiques français, écoles françaises de toute sorte, couvents français, journaux quotidiens et hebdomadaires français, revues et périodiques français, nous avons tout cela; que veut-on de plus?"

It will be remembered that when M. Viviani, the representative of the French Government to the United States, addressed the Canadian Parliament from the floor of the Commons Chamber at Ottawa, he complimented the descendants of the French settlers of Canada in "having maintained, in all its purity and perfection, the French language which is to be heard throughout the whole world." Continuously the French of France and the English of England have complimented the French-Canadians upon their mastery of the two great languages. Yet the "patois" charge still lingers. But that was to be expected. It is another symptom of the disease. "They speak a patois," the Flemings said of the Walloons; "they speak a garbled tongue," the Germans say of the Slavs in Poland; and across the Atlantic, "patois" is flung at the French-speaking people in Canada. Everywhere the charge is the same against the minor nationality. If these charges had been true, then, surely, they were only a very good reason to have the tongues improved by better education, rather than degraded by restricting the hours in which they may be taught.

In recent years the English press of Ontario has had far more to say of the impurity of French in Canada than of the necessity for purity in English, although one would naturally have thought the latter their greater and more direct concern. English-Canadians do not speak English as it is spoken in England. They apparently prefer the pronunciation of the Americans of New York State, and both often reproach the Englishman for affectation in the use of his own language. Nor is there uniformity of speech in English Canada. There are Canadians, in the sections of the country bordering Vermont, that speak with that twang we always think of as peculiar to the "down-east Yankee," well-exemplified in the play, "The Old Homestead." Nor are we purists in written English. The learned judges of Britain's Privy Council, in interpreting the circular containing Regulation 17, found that "unfortunately it" (the circular) "is couched in obscure language" (English), "and it is not easy to ascertain its true effect." Since the circular was written by those who preside over Ontario's Department of Education, and promulgated for the better instruction of French-Canadian children in English, it may be taken for granted that even a grave court sometimes indulges in humour. There are many words in general use in England that are seldom spoken or written in Canada or the United States, and in North America English words are in common use that are practically unknown in England. Nor do Englishmen and Canadians always use the same word in the same sense. If we English-Canadians do not write English that is readily understood by Englishmen of England, it may be that the emphasis of reform is being put on the wrong school.

In literature the French-Canadians have had a struggle, as had the Flemings of Belgium. The buyers of their books were not numerous; and, after all, like the cobbler and the farmer, the author must pay for his food and clothes. Yet French Canada presents a reasonable list of authors. Sir John Bourinot has this to say of what the French-Canadians have done in the field of letters: "Their histories and poems have attracted much attention in literary circles in France; and one poet, Mr. Louis Fréchette, has won the highest prize of the French Institute for the best poem of the year. In history, we have the names of Garneau, Ferland, Sulte, Tassé, Casgrain; in poetry, Crémazie, Chauveau, Fréchette, Poisson, Lemay; in science, Hamel, LaFlamme, De Foville; besides many others famous as savants and littérateurs." The French-Canadians have not produced a Maeterlinck nor a Conscience—nor have the English-Canadians.

The Germans have a wealth in literature with which to attract minor nationalities within the

Empire, and it must be a deep-seated antagonism which bids the Slavonic German refuse the Teutonic heritage in letters. But the prestige of the dominating nationality in Canada, is not so strong. The French-Canadians have no heartaches in refusing to bask in the glory of English-Canadian literature. We have books, written by Englishmen and Scots; but the French-Canadians say they are not Canadian; the English classics are good, and so are the French. And, we have books —tons of them—by American authors. Significantly enough, many of our best books on Canada have been written by the Americans of the United States. Harvard has done more work and better work in Canadian history than Toronto. But neither books made in the United Kingdom, nor books made in the United States, contain a national appeal to the Canadian whose mother-tongue is French. National literature can alone make a national appeal; and the blunt truth is that our own English-Canadian literature is not appealing. I might have said, with little exaggeration, we have none; and, strangely enough, its absence does not seem to cause national concern. In the war lies our greatest interest, and yet, so far as I know, only one book has been written by an English-Canadian on its underlying causes, and that by Sir Gilbert Parker, who has become an Englishman. We are concerned with the cost of living, the tariff, the unrest of labour, technical education, the race question, colonisation, and yet may count on our fingers the books that have been written by English-Canadians on these subjects and others of equal national importance. In England and the United States one may buy a score of new books each month on current economic and social questions, and here not so many in ten years.

The daily press of French Canada is as good as our own; and the periodical literature, I must sadly confess, probably better. We English-Canadians prefer stories with the scene set in New York rather than in Toronto; we have little interest in Canadian heroes or heroines (when done into type); we prefer to buy magazines which relate the doings and sayings of Roosevelt and Wilson, rather than those of Laurier and Borden. Of course our preferences are our own business, but until we produce a literature worth while, and create national heroes, that we ourselves respect, we shall never draw the French-Canadians from their own.

The Germans have a splendid theatre and a national drama with which to attract the minor nationalities, and it has had an influence in that direction. The play, depicting the landscape of the country, the virtues, vices, follies, and humour of its people, has always been considered a mighty force upon national character. But we English-Canadians have no national drama. The best we have to offer the minor nationality is that we hire by the week from the United States. Theatrically—and truthfully—we are but spokes in a wheel hubbed in New York.

The major nationality in Germany has expressed itself in sculpture and painting; how well, we need not here discuss. But it is doubtful that the major nationality in Canada has done as much in art, in proportion to its numbers, as the minor nationality. We have not produced an artist who has done better work in the field than Suzor Coté; we have not produced a sculptor the superior of Philippe Hébert. We have had more artists, but some of those we claim as our own, are Canadians only by adoption. Wyly Grier was born in Australia, Bell-Smith was born in England, as were Fred Challoner and C. W. Jefferys. William Brymner is a Scot from Greenock.

Pursuing the comparison from letters and painting to music, we at once think of Albani. English-Canadians have done better in music than in any of the branches of non-material achievement, but no Canadian has had so much of the world's musical appreciation as Marie Louise Emma Cécile La Jeunesse, the French-Canadian Chambly girl, known as Albani. Making her appearance at the Royal Italian Opera in London, she sang acceptably in America, Russia, Germany, Australia, South Africa; in fact she sang the world over. It will be remembered by many that she appeared professionally at the funeral services of Queen Victoria; and, subsequently, at the Guild Hall reception given to King Edward and Queen Alexandra,

11 c.

and from King Edward received the Order of Merit for Art, Science, and Music. There are others of the French-Canadian school of music who have obtained more than national recognition.

To attempt here a detailed comparison of the achievements of the two nationalities in music is impossible. It may, however, be safely asserted that the French-Canadian is fonder of, and has greater aptitude for, melody than the English-Canadian. It is not everyone who may excel in music, but its appreciation is essentially the national possession of the French-Canadians. They have one of the best collections of folk-songs in the world— there is nothing more indicative of *esprit de corps* than the song which is peculiarly that of the group. As grave seniors and dignified professors gather round a piano, and, with emotion, sing the songs of their Alma Mater, so does the whole French-Canadian nationality with emotion—and usually with harmony—sing the hymns and ballads of Old and New France; the songs that take the mind back to days of the bateaux and the canoes, to running waters and moaning pines, to moonlit cariole drives over crunching snow, to courting days in log cabins, and all the sweet nothings and somethings of pioneer life. It is almost sacrilegious to suggest that this possession of song should be given up for the popular music we English-Canadians import from the United States.

"Has the French-Canadian proved his capacity for filling responsible positions under the Crown?

NOT INFERIOR—DIFFERENT   139

Read the life of Lafontaine, of Morin, of Cartier, of Dorion, of Joly, of Laurier, as to the Dominion; and Chauveau, De Boucherville, Marchand and Sir Lomer Gouin in the Quebec Legislature; and the answer will not be disappointing. In the House of Commons, in the Senate, in the Speaker's chair of both Houses, in Spencerwood, in the Supreme Court, he has taken a place side by side with men of the Saxon race, without any evidence of mental inequality or inferiority." These are the words of the late Sir George W. Ross, the opinion of a man who, as Member of Parliament, went "to Ottawa with certain preconceptions of the French-Canadians" which were found, "on wider acquaintance and investigation, to be neither complimentary nor just. These preconceptions were formed by the public press of the early sixties, when public opinion was agitated over Separate schools and Representation by Population, and when political speeches were rounded off by a vehement denunciation of priestcraft and French domination." These are the opinions of a man, who was not only a member of the Federal House, but was Minister of Education for Ontario, Prime Minister of Ontario, and a Leader in the Senate, expressed at the close of life, and with a rare intimate knowledge of the worth of public service.

We have previously concluded that, generally speaking, the English-Canadian has the greater aptitude for trade and finance; is it too much to conclude now that, in proportion to numbers—as

28 is to 72—the French-Canadians have a greater aptitude for the finer arts? Nationalities have well-defined natural aptitudes. Are our differences in aptitudes, in achievements, only natural? and is it, after all, not foolish to say, that because one excels in this and the other in that, that one is the other's superior? Dr. Sarolea tells us that "Civilisation is not based on unity, but on diversity and personality, on individuality and originality. And if there is one lesson which history preaches more emphatically than another, it is this: that small nations have, in proportion, contributed infinitely more than great empires to the spiritual inheritance of our race. Little Greece counts more than Imperial Rome; Weimar counts more than Berlin; Bruges and Antwerp and Venice count more than the world-wide monarchy of Spain; and the dust of the Campo Santo of Florence or Pisa is more sacred than a hundred thousand square miles of the black soil of the Russian Empire."

"Why callest thou me good?" might have been asked of the things of the world. Each of us will answer according to our personal tastes. That English-Canadians call trade good, and place a high valuation upon the output of factories and farms, is undoubtedly true. National progress is measured by the country's balance sheet. The country is going ahead or behind, not by what is being done in literature, music, painting, and philosophy, but by what is being done in trade. We may be bankrupt in the fine arts, but if our trade balance is right, all is well. If we were to search for reasons, one would be found in the influence of American thought in creating our national ideals. Consciously or unconsciously, we have accepted the American measuring-stick of achievement and the American method of securing it. We have been overcome by the collective thought of the hundred million people who live within the nearby American Republic. The Americans of the United States protest that they have been getting away from commercialism; but there was a time, not long ago, when, if not their dominant ideal, it was certainly their most conspicuously displayed characteristic. And the dominant note of our English-Canadian life is money-making—or shall we say, has been? Until the coming of the war, State honours, knighthoods, and titles, were bestowed mainly upon those who had succeeded in amassing wealth. Since the war the practice has not been wholly abandoned. Making money constituted, in the King's Canadian eyes, success. In nothing have the two stock nationalities of the country differed more than in this respect. The English-Canadians are constantly striving and straining for greater economic achievement; while French-Canadians look upon economics, not as an end in themselves, but merely as a means of supporting a life that is to be lived. When enough of this world's goods have been secured to satisfy the physical needs and comforts, the average French-

Canadian is ready for the great something else, Life; and the English-Canadian, with appetite whetted, is usually only ready for more goods that can be weighed or measured and sold.

We English-Canadians and English-Americans are fairly open to the charge of having mistaken the means of preserving and sustaining life for Life itself. The French-Canadians, as a people, do not go as far as we towards economic development, simply because they feel they can live very well without it; they do not regard civilisation as consisting of a mere increase in the complication of material wants, which can be satisfied only by further material production. That is not the end for which they maintain a national existence. Quebec has two or three public holidays to Ontario's one; and these days, set apart by Church custom, are invariably spent in enjoyment. The Church in Quebec teaches its people not only how to pray, but how to play as well. "They are always holidaying in Quebec," groaned a commercial traveller from Toronto to me in a French-Canadian town one day, as with stores and shops locked up, he impatiently kicked his heels on the hotel verandah. Selling goods and more goods, was his main aim in life, was, in fact, his life; and, unfortunately for him, he was in a community where buying and selling is only a minor—and, perhaps, a regretted—means to the appreciation and enjoyment of life.

Depending mainly upon the United States for

our prose and poetry, music and drama, sports and amusements, in short the things that make up national life, we English-Canadians maintain that we have a nationality that the French-Canadians ought to accept; and, with characteristic confidence in the value of our own judgment, regulate our school laws to make them accept it. It is true there are many reasons why we have not held on to cricket, have not been satisfied with lacrosse, and have given up both for baseball; or, in other words, have not retained the national spirit of the British Isles, have not developed a distinctive national life of our own, and have borrowed from the United States. But we cannot expect explanations to satisfy an alien nationality, that has a group personality so deeply-seated as that of the French-Canadians. With a growing knowledge of human nature, we may, some day, be willing to pardon them for being slow in giving up that which they have so largely created for that which we have so largely borrowed—even if we continue to believe that what we have is "best."

Contrast the little, steep-roofed, white houses snuggling companionably along the highways and waterways of the French settlements, with the stiff, red-brick, modern farmhouses so often set apart in the hundred-acre lot of the English settlements. Men and women from all parts of the United States visit Canada—French-Canada, not English-Canada—to view its villages. They are old-fashioned, but—in spite of current opinion—people do not admire fashions simply because they are old. French-Canadian villages and rural houses are "quaint," but they are above all beautiful in their quaintness. There is a harmony, a fitting of one building into another which speaks a community-sense of the beautiful. Nowhere in North America has this sense been preserved as in French Canada. If we are unwilling, or unable to accept that sense as a part of ourselves, let us at least preserve our appreciation of it in others.

Contrast the three-storeyed, thick-walled, grey-stone, business-houses of Montreal, with the white-tiled, twelve and twenty-storeyed office buildings of Toronto. The French-Canadians are "backward"; they are usually willing to admit it; but what they have is theirs, an unseverable part of themselves. The architecture of our farm-houses —or, rather, its lack—we have taken from New York, Michigan, and nearby States; and our business buildings are but feeble imitations of those that scrape the sky above Broadway. Where New York erects a forty-storey building, Toronto builds one half as high—and boasts of its performance.

The buildings which house the representatives who make the laws for Ontario and administer the affairs of the Province, were designed, not by Canadians, not by Englishmen, but by Americans of the United States; a significant fact when we remember the philosopher's conclusion that the soul of a people is expressed in its architecture.

Books of Reference

Canada Year Book, King's Printer.
Charles Sarolea, *The Anglo-German Problem.* Nelson
George W. Ross, *Getting into Parliament and After.*
Briggs.
Sir John Bourinot, *Canada.*   T. Fisher Unwin.

CHAPTER IX

THE SEAT OF TROUBLE

LURKING somewhere there is usually an economic motive which leads one nationality to attack another, and invariably the possession of land is involved. The clash in Ontario is not an exception. In Europe, lived in for centuries, the lands have become crowded and the conflict of nationalities has meant dispossession; but in Ontario the conflict is mainly over land occupied only by the animals of the wild forest. Map in hand, the reader will find a vast area of land lying north of the waters of the Ottawa, north of Lake Nipissing and the Great Lakes. Not all of it is capable of production, but there are within this Hinterland sixteen million acres of soil which, by knowing industry, may be turned into farms. Here lies the main seat of controversy between French and English in Canada.

The reader may picture a race for the possession of this great prize. For great it is. To use the Government's own words: "The great clay belt running from the Quebec boundary west through Nipissing and Algoma Districts and into the District of Thunder Bay comprises an area of at least 24,500 square miles, or 15,680,000 acres, nearly all of which is well-adapted for cultivation.

146

This almost unbroken stretch of good farming land is nearly three-quarters as great in extent as the whole settled portion of the Province south of Lake Nipissing and the French and Mattawa Rivers. It is larger than the States of Massachusetts, Connecticut, Rhode Island, New Jersey, and Delaware combined, and one-half the size of the State of New York." Further, it lies within a little more than twenty-four hours' run of tide water. A prize it is; but there is no race for its possession. Although the sixteen million acres within what is named New Ontario have been there since the province was formed—and thousands of years before—it was only in 1900 that the Province had this territory surveyed and its resources partially examined. That was eighteen years ago, and it is still "New Ontario," in the sense that it is not farm-worn. When the surveyers' reports became public, Ontario marvelled at the size of its Clay Belt, publicly discussed its potential wealth, voted money for its development—in fact, did everything but colonise it. Not that the importance of settlement was wholly unrealised! The man on the street knows that Canada's wealth is drawn mainly from Canada's land. He has been told that Canada must pay her huge foreign obligations mainly out of the proceeds from farm products. But, in spite of that knowledge, it is doubtful if the average citizen fully realises that Canada's national expansion depends upon the development of its timber, mineral, and agricultural wealth—and mainly upon agriculture.

Admitting the importance of agricultural expansion, why does Northern Ontario still remain uncultivated and unproductive? English-Canadians have lost their love for the land. That is the plain answer. By the census returns of 1910 Ontario's rural population was shown to have declined by 52,184 in the ten years under review. In these ten years, French-Canadians had come into the Province from Quebec and settled on the land; Englishmen from England had become Ontario farmers, as had Americans and Europeans; and, in spite of these accessions, there was a decline rather than an increase in the number of Ontario people classed as rural. Very apparently some one made way for these newcomers, and that some one was the English-Canadian. There is no mystery about where he went, and no mystery about the cause of his going. The same ten years showed an increase of 400 thousand in Ontario's urban population. English-Canadians prefer town rather than country life: that tells the story. And it has a bearing upon the national clash.

Nor are Ontario English-speaking people alone in preferring town life. There is a well-recognised tendency of the English-speaking population of all North America to settle in cities and towns. Mr. Grant finds in it a Nordic race characteristic. In "The Passing of the Great Race" he says: "The increase of urban communities at the expense of the countryside is also an important element in the fading of the Nordic type, because the energetic countryman of this blood is more apt to improve his fortunes by moving to the city than the less ambitious Mediterranean." And thus, since the city will not permanently reproduce itself, the "great race is passing." The case is interesting. But is Mr. Grant's theory of a race characteristic borne out by the facts? It is here necessary to remember again the distinction between race characteristics and national characteristics. The Dane is the purest Nordic of them all, the progenitor of the Baltic race, "the real *Homo-europeus*," and Denmark is one country in the world where agriculture has maintained the balance of power. In Canada and the United States, the Mediterraneans from Italy herd in cities, and when seeking work beyond them, seldom look for it on the farm; while in Argentina most farm work is done by Italian and Spanish labour.

Much has been written in attempted explanation of the growth of cities and towns, and the relative decline of the rural communities. Doubtless several influences are at work. But attentive ears will identify the call of the city as the ring of the dollar. The response is naturally to the extent of the attunement—and the tuning is done by the nationalities. It does not come from the blood: it is not of race. In so far as the school trains for aptitude in money-making, in so far as the national ideal is money-making, to that extent will the nationality seek money where money is to be found in amounts that constitute riches. There is a comfortable living to be made on the farm, but that was not enough to satisfy the ambition of Dick Whittington, nor is it enough to satisfy our national longings to-day.

If we were right in surmising in the chapter on Education, that the English-speaking youth are being educated off the land, evidence of the attitude of French-speaking Canadians towards the land, becomes interesting; for the French-Canadians have been educated in separate and different schools. Let us then compare the two nationalities in the only way that comparison is statistically possible, by comparing agriculture in Ontario with agriculture in Quebec. The results will not be exact, but near enough to form some interesting conclusions.

John Pratt of Ontario and Jean Pratte of Quebec, commence their spring plowing at practically the same time, cultivate their land, sow their seed, and harvest their crops, in much the same way; and from spring to autumn both minds run the same course of anxieties and hopes.

John Pratt is farming 98 acres in Ontario, valued at $52.59 per acre; while Jean Pratte is farming 97 acres in Quebec, valued at $52.13 per acre. Their holdings and values are strikingly alike. Pratt beats Pratte in making more cheese, and as if to return the compliment Pratte beats Pratt in making more butter. Neither Pratt nor Pratte is a grain grower of renown, and produces field crops mainly to turn them into animals and animal products; they are, in fact, factory farmers. Pratt excels as a cropper of grains, in 1916 having 16.25 bushels of spring wheat to Pratte's 15; having 25.50 bushels of oats to Pratte's 22.75; and about in these proportions did they run the cereal list; Pratte growing no fall wheat of account and having the advantage only in buckwheat. But when we look at the potato yields the honors are reversed, for while Pratt was digging 61 bushels from the acre in 1916, Pratte took 131 bushels, and both were disappointed, for in the previous year Pratt had 92.66 bushels and Pratte 149.66 bushels to the acre. They are both good cattle men; and, while Pratt has imported more pure-bred animals, Pratte has developed a strong, serviceable cow of his own— he is generally original—and it has been set down in the official live-stock registry as "Canadian." Only the names are of my own creation; the figures are from the records of the Census Department of the Dominion Government.

So far there is not much difference between the Ontario man on the land and the Quebec man on the land, but there is a difference, and a real one; for the Ontario man takes more from the soil than does the Quebec man. To what extent the English-Canadian's income is greater cannot be determined with mathematical accuracy. Estimates have been made and freely circulated, but since they are generally arrived at by adding the values of the field products to the values of the several animal products, regardless of the fact that the hay, roots, and some of the grain, went into the cows that produced the milk that was converted into butter or cheese that alone yielded a cash revenue, they are worthless. Accurate accounts are not kept on either Ontario or Quebec farms, and from personal experience, I can testify that farm book-keeping is not, in practice, as simple as it appears in theory. It is only from the study of all the basic figures that we conclude that the Quebec farmer derives a smaller gross revenue than the Ontario farmer.

We have habitually made comparisons by placing the totals of the various agricultural products of the two provinces side by side, an obviously incorrect procedure, since Ontario has the greater arable acreage, having in 1911 "under improvement" nearly 13½ million acres as against Quebec's 8 million acres "under improvement." Bearing these acreage figures in mind, the progress of live-stock in the two provinces, as revealed by the annual census returns, becomes significant.

Quebec:	1912	1917	Gain or Loss
Horses	367,402	379,276	+ 11,874
Milch Cows	755,770	911,023	+ 115,253
Other Cattle	695,906	958,010	+ 262,104
Sheep	620,881	849,148	+ 228,267
Swine	747,254	712,087	− 35,167

Ontario:	1912	1917	Gain or Loss
Horses	805,271	887,246	+ 81,975
Milch Cows	1,033,392	1,082,119	+ 48,727
Other Cattle	1,380,890	865,847	— 515,043
Sheep	677,462	595,477	— 81,985
Swine	1,693,594	1,236,064	— 457,530

From these figures Quebec is more than holding its own, while Ontario, the "progressive" province, with room for almost indefinite expansion, is going behind. That is one lesson, and the other is that, bearing in mind the size of the occupied lands— about as 8 is to 13—the average farmer in each province owns approximately the same number of animals.

A part of the Ontario man's greater revenue goes for hired labour, and a part as poor payment for a back bent over Ontario soil from sunrise until late at night, payment for working on the holidays which the French-Canadian enjoys and which are necessary to men engaged in every kind of labour. The Ontario farmer has for years been working under the light of the red lantern that signals danger.

In Quebec, although the farmer does not obtain as much from the soil, the rural population of that province increased 39,951 during the ten years that the rural population of Ontario decreased by 52 thousand. These figures are significant. Their significance is increased by the knowledge that in Ontario 82 per cent. of the farmers own their own places and in Quebec 92 per cent. of the farmers own the farms upon which they live.

If we had as much faith as some in ethnological race characteristics, we might have seen in inheritance an explanation for the French-Canadian's loyalty to the land. When the cat turns round and round before settling down for a nap, we are told she is following an instinct inherited from a tiger ancestor who thus packed the jungle grass into a sleeping bed. Wtih a little imagination, we could think back to early days in French Canada, when the farmer was forbidden the pleasures of town under penalties almost as severe as those then imposed in England for sheep-stealing. But possibly the mental impression created by the edicts of M. Bigot and other Intendents of the Old Régime, is too young to have displayed itself in the present generation.

Under conditions of economic freedom, a man stays at uncongenial work only until he can find something more to his liking. Working, as he does, from morning until late at night, the Eastern English-Canadian farmer cannot acquire more than a labourer's wages for himself and family, and less than the current industrial rate of interest on his investment. And he works fourteen hours a day against the city man's eight. In normal times most things that the Canadian farmer buys are bought at one of the world's dearest retail prices and most of the things he sells are sold for less than the world's wholesale prices,—a cramped course within which to acquire riches. But the English-Canadian farmer has imbibed the national idea of getting rich. What more reasonable than he should conclude that the thing of his heart's desire is not obtainable on the farm?

If the authorities who plan Ontario's policy of education have seen the danger, they have not wholly protected against it by adding "garden plots" and a smattering of agricultural instruction to the curriculum of the rural schools. These things are good, but they do not reach the vital spot, nor do the learned treatises of the press on "How to Keep the Boy on the Farm." Production and more production, is the English-Canadian slogan, and it is made to apply to farm as well as factory. Contentment is no longer a virtue; it is almost, if not quite, a vice. The French-Canadian farmer who is not inclined to exert himself to the breaking point, is considered "unprogressive." But significantly enough, taking less from an acre of land, leaving it oftener during the year for rest and enjoyment, he is less ready to desert it for something else; while the English-Canadian farmer, with his children, anxious to fall in line with "progress," drops the hoe, slams the barn-door, and treks for the city, where "progress" is conducted with shorter hours and less distressing physical fatigue.

Of course, we should not carry our reasoning too far. Only in a general sense are the English-Canadians leaving the land, and only in the same general sense are the French-Canadians staying on it. We have seen the extent of Ontario's decline and Quebec's increase in rural population in the ten years covered by the last census, and we have found that these figures only tell a part of the story. There were also English-Canadians who left Quebec farms for the city. Their places were taken mainly by French-Canadians, so that the French-Canadians' net gain of land in Quebec was probably much greater than the gain of the Province in rural population. That movement has been represented in Ontario as inspired by clerical direction, and in fact it is, to the extent that the Church schools have preached the gospel of contentment on the land. There is no evidence, as represented, that it has been a vulgar intrigue for Church prestige. The change in ownership of the farms of the Eastern Townships is fully accounted for by the well-marked inclination of the English-Canadians to seek, in Quebec, as in Ontario, their ideal in industrialism; as a matter of fact, they have had in French-Canadian money a welcome consideration for their farms.

The man who is surveying conditions in Canada, from a distance, may have found, as yet, little cause in these national tendencies out of which trouble could reasonably develop. He may say: Surely there should be happiness in Canada; the two nationalities have separate ideals, let each pursue its own course. But if the stranger has come to that conclusion, he has not considered the intricate and conflicting forces of religion, politics, and economics, that are inextricably bound up in the human life of this country. Before turning to the play of these forces upon our national and colonisation problems, let us again secure our geographical bearings by reference to the map, for tradition and geography have also had an influence upon the issues.

The reader will see that the Ottawa River stretches from the centre of French population near Montreal, north-westerly back into the Hinterland of Ontario. The French-Canadians have traditionally followed rivers; flowing water has had a strange fascination for them, possibly a race-instinct carried over from the days when river and lake were roadway and railway combined. The Ottawa is to them not a new route. Their forefathers put it on the maps of civilisation and, with pardonable pride, called it, "Le Grand." Their missionaries paddled to its sources and portaged the divide—and many of them never came back. It was the favourite route for the commerce and exploits of the coureurs-des-bois, who are to the world the most attractive figures in Canadian history. Nor is the country north of the Ottawa and the Great Lakes new territory to the French-Canadians. Pierre La Vérendrye and his associates travelled it many a time, and its lakes and rivers still retain French names.

The Hinterland of Ontario is wooded, and the French-Canadian is America's best axeman. The

Americans of the United States by many thousands, have taken up the land of Canada's treeless Western plains, but Ontario's arable lands, covered by woods, they have left severely alone. The French-Canadian is at home in the woods and can protect himself there; the Swedes and Norwegians are alone his competitors. The Hinterland's acres of clay-loam have a capacity for mixed farming; and the French-Canadians are no mean adepts at that sort of agriculture; having well occupied the Province of Quebec, they are making their way up the Ottawa River to the land which the English-Canadians have allowed to remain a wilderness.

Even now the stranger, unacquainted with conditions, may see no signs of trouble. He may even reason that, since English-Canadians generally prefer to live in cities, they ought to be pleased to have a people, capable of clearing the land and willing to brave the perils of forest fires, move into this vast unsettled hinterland; such settlement is for the good of Ontario, the good of Canada, the Empire, and the hungry world generally.

But if the French settle Northern Ontario, obstinately refusing to learn English, the trade of Northern Ontario will go to Montreal and the industrial cities of Quebec, complained the English-Canadian merchants of Ontario who refuse to learn French. Here was an economic motive for attack which, swaying important business interests, attracted the politicians who were already sounding the keys of religious and race prejudice.

Here was an ideal pool (to change the metaphor) for the politicians, a mixture of nationality and economics, which, properly whipped, might return eleven English-Canadian votes to one French-Canadian vote—a clear majority of ten, multiplied by thousands. But there was this difficulty: the pool was no party's preserve. The majority fish—and in that alone the politicians were interested—would go to the party which whipped the pool with the greatest goodwill and skill. Both Liberals and Conservatives were scrupulously willing; and each, led by its press, proceeded to outdo the other. Scarcely a day passed without a leader in the English press of the Province seeking to persuade English readers that the land of Northern Ontario must not be settled by a French-speaking population. Significantly enough, the press did not devote as much space to urging that it ought to be settled by English-Canadians.

It is W. E. H. Lecky who tells us, in "The Map of Life," that no one "can study the anonymous press without perceiving how large a part of it is employed systematically, persistently and deliberately in fostering class, or race, or international hatreds, and often in circulating falsehoods to attain this end. Many newspapers notoriously depend for their existence on such appeals, and more than any other instruments, they inflame and perpetuate those permanent animosities which most

endanger the peace of mankind." "Systematically," "persistently" and "deliberately" have Ontario's newspapers inflamed men of the English
tongue and the Protestant religion against French
Catholic settlement in New Ontario.

Since the days of Guy Fawkes, Englishmen have
been a bit nervous of plots, and especially those
with a clerical tinge. If a politician can once appeal to an English-speaking Protestant constituency, with an apparently full-fledged clerical plot
in his possession, he may safely order his wife's
gown for the opening ceremony of Parliament.
No one better than Sir John Willison—at the time
editor of the "News" of Toronto—knew the political value of a clerical plot in Ontario, and in 1916
he proceeded to devlop one for his readers. Writing editorially of the priests of French Canada, he
said : "The dream of reconquest and of ascendancy
they have never abandoned. They have made race
serve religion, and religion serve race. All that
could be done they have done to preserve the
French language and to discourage the spread of
English, no matter what handicaps they may have
imposed upon their people. They are directing migration into Ontario and the Western Provinces."

Bacon reminded us that "There is nothing makes
a man suspect much, more than to know little."
Sir John had said little but had said enough. The
French-Catholic clergy were directing French-
Catholics to New Ontario and the West. What

visions of intrigue for ascendancy were suggested to imaginative minds?

Now let us have the facts of the part taken by the French-Canadian priests in the "colonisation of Ontario and the Western Provinces." The subject deserves more than passing attention, since whole nations are frequently impelled to action through suspicion.   It is true there are priests organised for the express purpose of directing French-Canadians "into Ontario and into the Western Provinces." I have on my desk a document which supplies this information. "Voici les noms et adresses des missionaires colonizateurs s'occupant du rapatriement des Canadiens-Français: Rév. Bouillon, Manitoba; Rév. Bourassa, Nouvel Ontario; Rév. Normandeau, Alberta Centre, 172 St. Antoine, Montréal; Rév. Giroux, Rivière La Paix, Alta.; Rév. Caron, Abbitibi, Qué., 82 St. Antoine St., Montréal." But that is not all.   There are men stationed in the United States whose duty it is to supply expatriated French-Canadians with first-hand information of the country, and point out the easiest routes by which it may be reached. As might have been suspected, the names indicate that they are, with one exception, of the French nationality. I give the names and, to satisfy the incredulous, the addresses: Max. A. Bowlby, 73 Tremont St., Boston, Mass.; J. A. Laferrière, 1139 Elm St., Manchester, N.H.; J. B. Carbonneau, Jr., Biddeford, Me.; J. E. Laforce, 29 Weybosset St., Providence, R.I.

Even that is not all. I have in my possession a number of booklets printed in the French language, with beautifully coloured maps describing the resources of Canada: of "Ontario and the Western Provinces," "the Lands of Promise;" and am assured that these books have been circulated by the thousands in the Province of Quebec, and in the Eastern States that have French-speaking populations. These men of the French-Canadian nationality are told of New Ontario:

"La nouvelle ligne du Grand Tronc-Pacifique, ou plûtot du Transcontinental National, qui en sera la section orientale, traversera la partie nord de cette région, livrant à la culture une vaste zone de terre argileuse arable d'une étendue de 16,000,000 d'acres.

"Ce district septentrional couvre une superficie de plus de 140,000 milles carrés soit plus de la moitié de la superficie totale de la province. Une grande partie de cette étendue se compose d'excellents terrains agricoles. La colonisation y a déjà pris des proportions très respectables, surtout dans les districts de la Rivière-à-la-Pluie, et de la Baie du Tonnerre.

"Cette zone argileuse, offrira un grand attrait pour les colons lorsque toutes ses parties seront plus facilement accessibles. Son climat, tempéré et fortifiant en été, n'est pas rigoureux en hiver, ce qui le rend favorable à l'agriculture. D'autres parties de cette section septentrionale sont arables, et le réseau de lacs et de rivières qui la couvrent constituent des voies accessible faciles. C'est une des parties les plus richment boisées du monde."

The French-Canadian is informed, in the language of France, as to the location of the railway facilities, the extent and character of the arable land, the nature of the climate and the value of the woods and waterways of Northern Ontario; he is reminded elsewhere in these French written books of the deeds of his ancestors, the exploits of the coureurs-des-bois, and the sacrifices of the Catholic missionaries in the land called Ontario. Seductive appeals are made to the pride of race as a stimulant to colonisation.

Now, if these things constitute a plot, "born of the dream of reconquest and ascendancy," it is significant that the blame was not put where it belonged, on the Ottawa Government—not on the poor curés—since it was the Department of the Interior which hired the priests, directed their activities and printed the French literature from which I have quoted. The book that I hold in my hand was "publié sous la direction de l'hon. W. J. Roche, Ministre de l'Intérieur." But will anyone, for a moment, believe that a Conservative Government financed—nay, more, counseled and directed —the curés in a campaign of "reconquest and of ascendancy."

The Government, in encouraging French-Canadians to settle the lands of Ontario and Western Canada, was but following a policy laid down many years ago for the settlement of Canada's idle, arable land; a policy designed to make these lands productive. Production, not religion, not nationality, was the incentive. There was no plot; there was simply a well thought out plan for colonisation.

I would not be misunderstood on this point. The

country's need is settlement as a means toward agricultural production; French-Canadian settlement is an issue simply because the French-Canadians apparently have alike the willingness and ability to make these idle lands productive. The French-Canadians are "unprogressive" in the sense that they have held on to the old community life longer than most peoples. They are the natural colonists for this land of woods. When they move they take their Church and their school with them. They commence life in the new land with the anchors of civilisation. Not so the English-Canadians, who, each for himself, treads a lonely way. There are English-Canadian frontiersmen in Ontario, several thousand of them that, destitute of Church and school, by violation of eugenic laws have sunk into indescribable conditions of mental and physical degeneracy. Some years ago the "Toronto News" lifted the lid that prevents these things being discussed in public, and after giving the public a glimpse of the deplorable situation, suddenly clapped it on again and returned to the attack of French-Canadian settlement, which, with separate schools, under clerical direction, was apparently considered an even greater menace. Why? I cannot say.

The French-Canadian willingness to settle Ontario lands has been interpreted—and misinterpreted—as a plotting of French-Canadian Catholic Clergy; it would be equally good reasoning to suggest that the English-Canadians are being herded in towns and cities by the plotting of Protestant Clergy, an evident absurdity. If there be any religion at work in the issue, it is only to the extent that the Roman Catholic Church has, through its schools and its sermons, preached the gospel of contentment. No, there is something more; for the priests of Quebec are teaching their parishioners the doctrine that a thing well done on the farm is a thing worth while for its own sake. When unknowing men talk of priest-ridden Quebec, I think of an order of missionaries in the province, who periodically make a retreat for meditation and study. And the objects of their thought? The care of bees, the best fruits to grow on the farm, melon-culture, manuring, the breeding of horses, co-operation, dairying in all its branches, aviculture, apiculture, horticulture, and, in general, all that has to do with agriculture. They are "Agricultural Missionaries, organised by the Catholic Bishops of the Ecclesiastical Province of Quebec in the year 1894." In one year they carried the gospel of God's land to 145,250 listening farmers. They had audiences, and that is, unfortunately, more than can be said of many of our Ontario Farmers' Institute meetings; and they preached with the fervour of men who carry glad tidings. The priests of Quebec have organised the rest days, which lighten the labour of the farm, and are an active force in holding up the sanity of country life. But these things are open to all. Neither the French-Canadian nationality nor the

Roman Catholic Church has a patent upon these common sense doctrines. Others may preach and practise them

Not many years ago, I visited a farm monastery in Quebec. In the fields I found a young monk, with bared, sunburnt arms, engaged in the back-wearing exercise of thinning and weeding turnips. He paused in his work as I came near, wiped the dripping sweat from his forehead, straightened himself out to a full six feet of manhood, squared a pair of broad shoulders and breathed the deep breath of a worker in the fields. I recognised in him a priest whom I had met at Ottawa some months before, and we discussed the usual topics of the farm and the season. "I thought you were a religious priest," I said in parting. "I hope I am," he replied, "and what a beautiful religion it is," said he, looking over the well-tilled field. "So strenuous," he added, taking the hoe and bending once more to his work.

Yes, agriculture is a beautiful and strenuous religion. And only as a religion, only when loved for its own sake, does the land yield its fullest benefits to mankind. And English-Canadians have been looking upon farming as a mere trade, measuring its values by dollars and cents. They have priced the farm for what it yielded in money; and, contrasted with the results of city occupations, it has fallen short. That is why English-Canadians have deserted Old Ontario and refuse to settle New Ontario. That is why farms within driving distance of Toronto—even at present prices of farm products—are to be bought for less than the original cost of clearing, fencing, and draining the land, and erecting the buildings. That is why the farms of the Eastern Townships are passing out of English-Canadian control. After all, it is a matter of religion; but it is the religion of God's land. If it is true that Canada's expansion can be no greater than the development of Canada's land, it may be, that having deserted the farms, we cannot permanently maintain ourselves in the city.

With the restoration of "contentment" to the English-Canadian vocabulary, Canada may become the home of many millions of people who regard production simply as a means to a sane, healthy development in life. Contentment is not necessarily a bar to progress; slavery to production ultimately is. We must learn, in town and country, the secret of doing things, simply because doing them well is worth while. It may be that the French-Canadian ideal, which tempers production by social enjoyment, is indigenous to the country; and that the English-Canadian objective of getting rich by "following the leader," is not permanently realisable in this country, its seeming success this last twenty years having been only a flash in the pan.

If there is to be national rivalry in this Province, that was carved out of Quebec and made safe for civilisation by French valour, let it be a force, under new ideals—or rather, returning to our father's ideals—for the country's good. Which will be first to occupy the Clay Belt, the Old or the New Inhabitants? Which will do more to clear these lands and convert them into contented farm homes, the English-Canadians or the French-Canadians? There is no need for conflict; the wilderness is big enough to absorb the surplus energies of the two nationalities, wide enough for both English and French settlements, each developing, under its own culture, in mutual toleration.

No people is entirely master of its own conduct; there are obligations to civilisation which all must perform. No people may hold vast areas of land capable of feeding millions, within striking distance of the high seas; refusing to cultivate them and refusing to have them cultivated by others (their fellow countrymen) who are unwilling to pay the supreme penalty of denationalisation; no people may do that and shamelessly face the scrutiny of civilisation.

BOOKS OF REFERENCE

Madison Grant, *The Passing of the Great Race.* Scribner.
The Canada Year Book. King's Printer.
W. E. H. Lecky, *The Map of Life.* Longmans.
Atlas du Canada (1913), King's Printer, Ottawa.
Dominions Royal Commission Reports. Wyman & Sons.

CHAPTER X

BENEATH THE SURFACE OF THINGS

Too often we overlook the fact that Canada's problem in nationality is essentially a world-problem, and too seldom do we attempt to analyse and determine our real national conditions and seek guidance in the world's experience.

Through a political disagreement of our respective forefathers, we, the descendants of English and French, have been placed side by side on the North American Continent. Having got into our present apparent difficulties through European politics, it may be that we can find a way out of them by a study of European politics. It would seem reasonable that, in a matter of this grave importance, we should not rely solely upon our own sporadic wisdom. We have established a code of morals for the individual upon the teachings that were given to the people of Judaea many years ago, and we regulate our individual rights and wrongs by a system of jurisprudence which, as the name implies, was borrowed from Rome. What is then more natural than that equally useful help may be obtained by searching abroad for information as to the relations which nationalities ought to bear to each other, and to the State, when they have to live together under a common political organisation?

169

But before we go abroad, we ought to make certain that we have clear ideas of the several concepts we have to take with us.

Have we a clear common answer to that historical question: Who is the State? Who is this body that would dispose of nationalities as if they were clay and it a potter? A few years ago— as years run in the lives of nations—Louis XIV of France asked the question, and then promptly replied "I am the State." But before the age of Louis and the kings, there was the head of the family, then the chief of the tribe and the lord of the manor, but always the idea of the *pater familias*. Kingship but continued the original idea. The king was father, the subjects his children, more or less his obedient children; like a father, he protected the weak from the strong, and like a wilful father, he now and then chastised both.

Then came a revolution. There had been revolutions before. Often a throne had been upset, but it had always been set up again and sat in by a new man, crying in one breath, "Who is the State?" and replying in the next, "I am the State." If there was not too much of a pause between breaths, and if the answer was backed up by enough trusty arquebuses, the chances are that the answer was accepted. In the new revolution, which spread over the greater part of the world, reaching even to China a few years ago, and to Russia a few months back, there was no resetting

of the throne.   Democracy said, "I am the State";
and said it so sternly that there was no room for
argument.   Incidentally, democracy held the
arquebuses.

What is democracy?   Every schoolboy knows
that "democracy is the government of the people,
by the people, for the people."   At least he has
been told so by those who generalise on political
conditions.   But our open eyes tell us that democracy can be no more than the government of all
the people by a majority of the people; and further tell us that, in the Province of Ontario, it has
been a government—for the majority of the people.
Now, obviously, where there is a majority, there
must be a minority; in creating one, it is necessary
to create the other.   And within the means of
creation is concealed a condition which is pregnant
with importance to the business of our investigation.

In all democratic countries there are invariably
two or more groups of men that devote themselves
to politics.   These men we habitually call politicians, relieving monotony occasionally by referring to them as statesmen.   They are the real ten-
ants of the throne which fell away from kings.
Their tenancy is obtained from the majority, and
on certain set moving days they go hunting for
majorities.   The politicians have no use for minorities, because it is not within their power to lease
the all important throne.   There are various ways
by which a majority may be secured.   Sometimes

the politicians promise the men engaged in one industry a rich living upon the fruits of another industry; and thus by the promise of protection, factory is not infrequently turned against field. In countries which are fortunate—and unfortunate—enough to have diverse nationalities, the politicians often seek to turn one nationality against the other, or others, always aiming to pick up the nationality with the most noses; for it is noses that make up what we call the Sovereign People.

In the old days the politicians, as we have seen, hunted for power with arquebuses. That was a poor way of determining right and wrong; and yet it must be remembered that back of the arquebus was a reasoning, average man. In getting away from this awkward manner of settling disputes, have we more closely approximated an equal opportunity for all men to assert their opinions? Those who defend democracy, retreating from pillar to post, assert that it is a spirit in which every man has an equal opportunity of arriving at power. But is even that true? Powder and shot were within reach of the average man, but their modern successor, under normal political conditions, is the newspaper; and not by the wildest stretch of imagination can we say that the influence of the newspaper is within reach of the average man.

The great metropolitan dailies which make and unmake majorities, which enthrone and dethrone politicians, are worth at least a million each, and are thus only within reach of millionaires—and of only a particular group of millionaires. For news-gathering is a monopoly shared only by consent of the men within the combination. Those who attempt to establish a newspaper without access to the news-gathering service, are likely to succeed no better than imbeciles who, conceivably, might try to build brick houses without bricks.

The Canadian people are dependent upon ten or twenty newspapers for their information as to conditions. If the newspaper's function were to report conditions as they are, or if the owners of the newspapers were superhuman in being all wise and free from the prejudices that affect ordinary mortals, then the danger of evil would not be so great. But neither of these "ifs" are realisable in actual practice. It is a well-known fact that the reports of events in newspapers and the editorials are coloured to suit the aims and opinions of the editors, and, in the final analysis, of the proprietors. Let me illustrate with a personal experience. I once had occasion to make several statements before an Ontario public service commission, and in reporting what I had said, a newspaper, whose owner was unfriendly to my position, made me say three out of four things in exactly the contrary way to which I actually said them. There was no chance for disagreement as to what was actually said, for I obtained the official stenographic report of the proceedings and forwarding it to the editor, explained what had been done. I received a sympathetic letter in reply. But no correction was made of the mis-statements. If the subject, as mis-reported, was of importance to the public, surely the subject accurately reported was not less important. That is only one instance of the many which I might give where newspapers within my own experience have mis-reported public proceedings. It is by this means that public opinion has been formed on several issues in which newspaper proprietors hold identical opinions. The public is never given a chance to determine the issues upon the facts.

At a recent meeting in Toronto, Ontario farmers bitterly complained that the economic conditions of the country are being constantly misrepresented by the millionaire proprietors of the city-published papers. It may be that the men who own the newspapers are protecting a just cause; but, in the opinion of the farmers, they are protecting it by misrepresentation. Not long ago, there was a general election in Canada, and in the Province of Ontario all the city dailies, except one—and that of comparatively small circulation—devoted themselves to representing only one side of the issue and, some think, to misrepresenting the other. Again, it may have been that the newspapers were protecting the better cause; but the decision as to which was better was left to the small group of men who own the papers upon which we are dependent for our knowledge of events and opinions. Heaven help the men who cannot *by* the press defend themselves and their interests *from* the press! They are as helpless as the men who, in the olden days, now and then vainly tried to protect themselves with pitchforks and scythes against the attacks of the arquebus-armed troops of the feudal barons. The French-Canadians have had the solid opposition of the English-speaking press of Ontario. The newspaper owners may urge that they have presented opinion, on this subject and others, which is contrary to their own; and the "Catholic Register" might, with equal fairness, maintain that it now and then presents Protestant opinion; but few there are who will ever by that means become aware of the merits of Protestantism.

There are some who think that the occasional agreement of the ten or twenty men that control the press of the country is due to the influence of money, senatorial appointments, and titles. But an explanation may be found without imputing any of these things, and, personally, I prefer to accept it. Newspaper owners are, after all, as they say in fairy tales, "only flesh and blood mortals" composed of the ordinarily varying parts of wisdom and unwisdom, prejudice and unprejudice. It is not strange that, like many another group of even greater size, they sometimes all support the wrong cause; it would indeed be strange if they did not.

We often indulge in panegyrics of democracy and elaborate upon its superiorities over autocracy. But the progress towards equality in opportunity of asserting opinion is more imaginary than real.

The mortal men that own the newspapers, that colour and disseminate the information, that creates the majority, that places the politicians on the throne, are our real rulers. Let us recognise the fact. That is a substantial something in our effort to see things as they are. And let us also not forget that since newspapers, like farms and stores, usually pass from father to son by inheritance, professing democracy we have completed the circle and once more are subject to the control of an hereditary autocracy.

When an election has been fought out on the issue of nationality, the dominant nationality becomes the Sovereign People. Under kingship, the weaker children had, at least, a figment of protection from the stronger; under majority rule, they have none. They are, in fact, His Majesty's Loyal Opposition. Opposition, it is true, but the use of His Majesty's name, is a subterfuge. His Majesty, in a democratic country, is a figure-head. We may even call him such without danger of losing our own heads. We admire and respect him, and regard his services as essential to the best interest of the State; but we do not rely upon him to protect the weak from the strong, the minority from the majority. He may have a moral influence on other matters; but what have morals, under our accepted philosophy, to do with this question? and, as a result of the stirring of the pools, he is powerless. Often the politicians, having reached the throne, are themselves powerless to undo their own work.

Democracy means freedom—for the majority. It means more: it means license—for the majority —under the Treitschke doctrine identifying right with might; it has times again shamefully oppressed minorities. The minority must swallow its medicine, and a bitter nostrum it is. For fear some may think I have over-stated the case, let me quote Dr. Bussel, an Anglican clergyman, who, in "The New Government for the British Empire," says: "The worst offenders against local freedom, the worst oppressors of minorities, have never been monarchs—rather those plebeian governments which, holding up the idea of royalty to scorn and hatred, have in truth modelled on it their powers, their policy, and their demeanour." The difference between oppression by an autocracy, and oppression by a democracy, is thus not that of principle, but rather that of a division of spoils. There is no more virtue in the injustice of a democracy than in the injustice of an autocracy. This we must remember, as we seek to trace the relations of nationalities to each other and to the State, and usually they amount to the same thing. When we say the State seeks to establish homogeneity, we invariably mean that the men who control the State machinery would have all men within the State learn their language, accept their ideals, and conform to their way of living. High sounding phrases may conceal the intent, but cannot destroy the spirit.

"What is meant by homogeneity?" That is another concept about which we should be clear minded. The question might not have remained in my mind if it had not been asked by a learned college professor. Absolute homogeneity, in the sense of all men being of the "same composition or structure throughout" (my dictionary's definition) is plainly unattainable. Possibly one of the first serious thoughts that comes to maturing youth is the unlikeness of men; the innumerable varieties of men. When we stand on the streets of a crowded city and watch the thousands and thousands move slowly by, no two alike in features, and, reasoning from experience, know that no two are alike in character, when we realise that we can travel America and Europe—Asia and Africa as well —and never find anyone just like ourselves, we are impressed with the truth of the old proverb that it takes all kinds of men to make a world. There is a design behind these unlikenesses, for they mean strength to the world. Each of us brings a contribution, some thought, some act, which is peculiarly our own in the sense that it emanated from our own distinctive personality; small though it may be, it goes to swell the sum total of the world's thought assets.

As we have seen already, men are further divided into national groupings, and these again have distinctive characteristics, and it is in the sense of having all men within the one State of the same nationality, of the same group character, that the word homogeneity is used in the subject under discussion. To that end, it is contended, all ought to speak a common language.

"Conscious perception," concludes Max Müller, "is impossible without language." This distinguished Anglo-German savant was the dean of philologists. "Language is necessary to thought, and there can be no thinking without language." That may be true, but the converse must not be carried too far: for many men use much language with little thought. Whether or not thought is possible without language, language is certainly a guiding factor in thought, for it is the key to culture. As the philosophers point out, this would be the sorry world of many centurites ago, when men killed their food with stone hammers and knew not of fire with which to cook it, if we were to be deprived of the accumulated wisdom of our forefathers; if we had no access to the thought of the great men of our age, and all ages, and were each compelled to rely upon the products of his own thinking. No provision would have been made for the strong to help the weak. The old paths, with their blind ends, would have to be travelled over and over again every time a human being came into the world.

Men have done their thinking in groups, and have expressed their thoughts and experiences in one of nearly three thousand languages, a round dozen of which have attained the eminence of culture. These languages are so many storehouses upon which man may draw if he has the key; and the key that unlocks the storehouse is education. Thought makes man, and if all have the same key, if all draw upon the same storehouse, then all men will think alike: will, in fact, be homogeneous. That is the reasoning of those who strive for a common language. Since the State is the arbiter of the language to be chosen—and, under democracy, the State usually means the major nationality—the result is an effort of the majority to impose its language upon the minority.

There are some who do not fall in with this reasoning, and contend that just as the world is better for its infinite diversity of character, so the State is better for diversity to the extent of the capacity of its machinery to provide preservation for several national cultures. But the bulk of the reasoning has been the other way; it is only within recent years, for causes which will soon become apparent, that men have come to the conclusion that not only on the old moral grounds, but for reasons of self-interest, the State should protect and preserve as valuable assets its national cultures.

The theory of those who would have all within the same state of the same national character, has been called that of "the Nation-State." And here again we must be clear-minded. The idea of the Nation-State is of comparatively recent origin. Ernest Barker, a Fellow of Oxford, in contributing an interesting essay to the "Unity of Western Civilisation," says that in the Middle Ages "there was a contracted world, which men could regard as a unity, with a single centre of coherence. There was a low stage of economic development, which on the one hand meant a general uniformity of life, in fief and manor and town, and on the other hand meant a local isolation, that needed, and in the unity of the Church found, some method of unification. With many varieties of dialect, there was yet a general identity of language, which made possible the development, and fostered the dissemination, of a single and identical culture. Nationalism, whether as an economic development, or as a way of life and a mode of the human spirit was as yet practically unknown. Races might disagree; classes might quarrel; kings might fight; there was hardly ever a national conflict in the proper sense of the word. The mediaeval lines of division, it is often said, were horizontal rather than vertical. There were different estates rather than different states. The feudal class was homogeneous throughout Western Europe; the clerical class was a single corporation through all the extent of Latin Christianity; and the peasantry and the townsfolk of England were very little different from the peasantry and the townsfolk of France."

The last of the Crusades ended in 1272. Then began the disintegration of Western civilisation. All Europe was compelled to face a returned soldier problem. Men who had felt the pulsation of the wide world found it difficult to contain them-

selves in obscure villages and the humdrum life of
the farm. The transport had been followed by the
ship of trade. New wants were created and new
commodities had to be acquired for their satisfac-
tion. There was town work for the returned soldiers and their great-great-grandchildren. The
villains and copyholders of the land became villains and copyholders of the town. Commerce
supplanted agriculture, and gradually assumed
regional identity because of regional capacity.
Then came competition, one region with the other,
and the protection of the regions' trade interests by
powder. The Mohammedans could continue their
journeys to Mecca undisturbed; no longer was
there need to kill Christians; war with Christians
became a Mohammedan pastime, not a Mohammedan necessity, for the Christians were killing
themselves. Martin Luther converted the Pope's
bull into ashes on December 10, 1520. Henceforth the Christian religion ceased to be a centrip-
etal force. For no sooner had Protestantism been
accomplished, than religion—as in heathen days
—became regional. And religion served as a text,
or pretext, for inter-regional combats. An innumerable number of totem-designed standards supplanted the common banner of the Cross. The
Christian religion then became a centrifugal force.
Latin no longer served to satisfy the classes; becoming conscious of an identity with the masses of
their regions, they turned to the local dialects and
sought to weld them with their Latin (classic and

vulgar) into national tongues.   Languages also
became regional.   So ran the course towards
regionality and nationality.   In a few minutes we
may turn the pages of history in which it is written, and the very ease with which we read it serves
to prevent us from realising the length of ages
involved in its completion.

In spite of these mighty forces, the idea of nationality, as identical with a region and a state
organisation, did not come to fruition until the first
half of the nineteenth century.   People with different cultures continued to live (and not always happily) under common political organisations.   There
were wars then, as now; and a casting about for a
political panacea resulted in the idea of the Nation-
State.   It was at first accepted as an inspiration
from Heaven.

Boundary lines were no longer to follow economic lines, to be determined by navigable rivers,
ports, coal mines, and the balance between agriculture and industry.   National characters were
to guide statesmen in the laying out of self-governing countries.   That was the policy which would
make for harmony.   Although this doctrine was
no man's special preaching, one name stands out
prominently in its preaching, that of Joseph Mazzini.   Born at Genoa in 1805, twenty-five years
later he was lining up a Young Italy Republican
Organisation.   There are several of them in New
York, but this one aimed at Italian, not American
politics.   Mazzini was not content to wield the

pen alone; he yearned for the sword. But his efforts in the military field were a failure, and in 1849 he and Garibaldi were compelled to flee for their lives, their revolution crushed. However, substantial ruins were left; and upon these King Victor Immanuel, aided by the great ability of his minister, Cavour, succeeded in making the Italy of to-day.

With the military campaigns that made Italy a nation, we are not here concerned; but with Mazzini's doctrine we are very much concerned. "The map of Europe will be remade," wrote Mazzini, the enthusiast. "The countries of the peoples will arise, defined by the voice of the free, upon the ruins of the countries of kings and privileged castes. Between these countries there will be harmony and brotherhood . . . Then each of you, strong in the affections and aid of many millions of men speaking the same language and educated in the same historic tradition, may hope by your personal effort to benefit the whole of Humanity."

As will be seen, Mazzini confused democracy with freedom, and ignored the fact that seldom is there a geographical distribution of nationalities which provides the way for boundaries to cover a national body politic as a garment covers the human body. The doctrine designed for good, through this fatal error, worked incalculable suffering in application. In the nineteenth century nationalities struggled for the possession of statehood, and eloquent were the pleas made for the sacredness of race and national self-expression. "But that very growth of national consciousness which inspired the struggle for freedom," says L. T. Hobhouse, "turned to exclusiveness and imperiousness as soon as it had achieved its end, and nationality as an exclusive principle—as a kind of collective egoism justifying itself, as ordinary egoism is never allowed to justify itself, in contempt for law and justice and the corresponding rights of others—has become the dominating force in twentieth century politics." The sacredness and inviolability of nationality were apparently only for majorities, only for those who were strong enough to protect themselves. As the old proverb has it, "The strong is always right."

Canada attempted to solve its differences of nationality by a practical application of the Nation-State when it created the divisions of Upper and Lower Canada. It was clearly the intention that Upper Canada should be mainly English, and Lower Canada mainly French. The change of names to Ontario and Quebec in later days did not alter the situation. These provinces were to be nation-provinces in the sense that English-Canadians would control one and French-Canadians the other. And only in that sense, for there were French in both provinces and English in both. Success was thus assured only in the event of the controlling nationality avoiding "a contempt for law and justice and the corresponding rights of others"; avoid-

14 c.

ing the "collective egoism" which, leading to a belief in its own superiority would urge it to force its own mentality upon the other.

Let it not be forgotten that that tendency and its consequences, which have led up to the present situation in Ontario, were foreseen by some of the fathers of Confederation. M. Dorion, who was one of the fathers, said in the debates: "There is at this moment a movement on the part of the British Protestants"—note the combination of nationality and religion—"in Lower Canada to have some protection and guarantee for their educational establishments in this province put into the scheme of Confederation, should it be adopted; and far from finding fault with them, I respect them the more for their energy in seeking the protection for their separate interest. I know that majorities are naturally aggressive, and how the possession of power engenders despotism, and I can understand how a majority, animated this moment by the best feelings, might in six or nine months be willing to abuse its power and trample on the rights of the minority, while acting in good faith, and on what it considered to be its right." The situation then in Ontario was in some respects that of Ireland to-day; where a minority, holding to separate religious ideals and traditions, fears the aggression of the majority. The fact that the Irish minority is Protestant and the Ontario minority is Catholic, does not alter the principle involved; although I fear it alters the line-up of supporters.

But M. Cartier thought there was no need for words precisely protecting the minorities in Quebec and Ontario, to be written into the Constitution; and he was also a father of Confederation. "What would be the consequence, even supposing any such thing were attempted by any one of the local governments?" he asked. "It would be censured everywhere. Whether it came from Upper Canada or from Lower Canada, any attempt to deprive the minority of their rights, would be at once thwarted." In other words, while "British Protestants"—using M. Dorion's words—were to control one Province and French Catholics the other, in both, the rights of the minority were to be protected by a sense of fair play. The "British Protestants" in Quebec were to be continued in the freedom of self-expression, by the spirit of toleration which M. Cartier believed would characterise the major nationalities in both provinces. That was the spirit of the fathers of Confederation. Through the Debates, we find the words "British" and "Protestant" used in the same sense. As evidence of the understanding, I submit that for some years in that spirit the affairs of Ontario were administered. No attempt was made to deprive the French-Canadians of freedom in cultural self-expression. It may be good law, but it is a gross violation of the spirit of Confederation, to now contend that the British North America Act was designed to protect merely Catholic rights in Ontario and Manitoba, and Protestant rights in Quebec, and not French-Canadian rights and "British-"Canadian rights as well.

Astute M. Dorion! Confiding M. Cartier! From where was the censure to come? How far would the feeble voices of the French-Canadians carry? There are more French-speaking men, women, and children, in the Province of Ontario, than in the whole of Alsace-Lorraine; but the French of Alsace-Lorraine have a bigger brother in France than the French of Ontario have in Quebec. Of course, this question must finally go before the bar of the world's opinion; but, in the meantime the minority must suffer, and the majority, the State itself, must suffer, for nothing eats farther into the vitals of a body politic than the existence of a body of people whose cries for justice fall upon ears that will not hear.

In neither Province has the majority a free hand to exact its pound of flesh, under the wording of the British North America Act, any more than kings in the days of Rule by Divine Right were justified in pursuing their own selfish ends. Conclusions as to acts involving religion and nationality are so often drawn as a result of prejudice, that I must cite the opinion of an authority in this connection whose devotion to Protestantism and Anglo-Saxonism is beyond suspicion. In the issue of May 23, 1916, the "Witness" (published in Montreal) stated: "As to the argument that the English language alone should have unquestioned rights in Ontario because it is an English Province, would not the corollary be that the French language alone should have unquestioned rights in Quebec as it is a French province? When was it ever settled that Ontario should be entirely English and Quebec entirely French? It is only necessary to put these questions fairly before the mind to realise that the educational policy in any of the provinces cannot be divorced from the larger political considerations which were in mind when Confederation was formed. To ignore these conclusions is, we believe, dangerous, and destined to introduce serious elements of disruption in the country." But I fail to find in the English press of Ontario—and upon Ontario rests the decision —an equally Christian view.

Let us now submit our Canadian situation to the light of the world's experience.

BOOKS OF REFERENCE

Ernest Baker and Others, *The Unity of Western Civilisation.* Medford.

L. T. Hobhouse, *Questions of War and Peace.*   T. Fisher Unwin.

M. Moncalm, *The Origin of Thought and Speech.* Kegan Paul Trench Trübner & Co.

CHAPTER XI

THE FUTILITY OF FORCE

THE night before Alexander of Macedon went East on his celebrated journey of conquest, Aristotle, with the privilege of an old master—he had been Alexander's tutor for eight years, and was then conducting a private school in the Capital —took his former pupil aside for a few words of advice; the kind of talk one would expect under the same circumstances, from an old dominie.

"You are about to start upon an enterprise which will bring you into many lands," said Aristotle, "and amongst many nations, some already celebrated in arts and arms, some savage and unknown. But this last counsel I give you: whithersoever your victories lead you, never forget that you are a Greek, and everywhere draw hard and fast the line that separates the Greek from the barbarian."

"No," answered the headstrong, youthful Alexander. "I will pursue another policy. I will make all men Hellenes. That shall be the purpose of my victories."

Alexander was successful in mighty feats of arms; he overran Persia, subdued Phoenicia, conquered Syria, was made King of Egypt, and received the allegiance of all Afghanistan and part

of India. He took from the men of many lands
their liberties, destroyed their cities and made
slaves. But he didn't make Greeks.

There was then no recognised code of morality
directing the conqueror to respect the group
culture of the conquered; no "squeamish senti-
mentality" about the rights of minor nationalities.
"You know as well as we do," said the Athenians,
in 416 B.C., to the representatives of a small people of that day, "that right, as the world goes, is
only in question between equals in power; while
the strong do what they can and the weak suffer
what they must." And yet then as now, the strong
were impotent to spread culture by the sword. The
men who lost their cities and their liberties refused
to become Greeks; those who were left free, to refuse or to accept as they pleased, whose eyes were
not filled with tears of sorrow, or blinded with prejudice, found in the culture of Aristotle a pearl of
great price, and willingly placed it in the family
storeroom, but remained nationally what they were
—barbarians to the Greeks.

The spirit of nationality becomes intensified by
restraint, for it is only under threatened deprivation that its value is fully appreciated. Air is indispensable, and yet only those who have gasped
for want of it, really appreciate its supreme value.
Nationality has been as free as air to English-
speaking Canadians, and that is why they have
seldom stopped to consider what it means to them
and what its deprivation means to others. National

culture is as sacred as the memory of a mother's prayers. It is the "home fire" which every man, woman, and child, has the instinctive impulse to keep burning. Just as the Parsis—again a story of compulsion—carried from Persia centuries ago the sacred fire of their fathers to India and to this day keep it burning, so do men jealously guard their national culture as an inheritance of the past and keenly realise the responsibility of handing it down intact, brighter and better, to future generations. That is why men will not yield their nationality before physical force. It is more precious than the individual lives which have been given often in its preservation.

The explorations of La Salle and La Vérendrye; the adventures of the coureurs-des-bois; the sacrifices and martyrdoms of the Jesuits; the struggles of Hébert, who first of white men tilled the soil of Canada; these things are the heirlooms of the French-Canadian nationality, the common possession of poor and rich alike, and they may not be taught in the French language in Ontario, except in the first two years of the pupil's school life, when the pupil is too young to understand. They are educational assets, more valuable in character-building than arithmetic, geometry, and algebra. The assets of mankind; preserved in the French language, they are the special assets of the French-Canadian; for the father's example has ever had a special meaning for the father's son. The lesson is gone, the unselfish incentive to strive is lost, when these things are taught in an alien tongue. In English these exploits and sacrifices are interesting incidents; in French, to the French-Canadians, they are patterns of character. Let us bring the thing home to ourselves—if we can—as English-speaking men. The story of Nelson's famous battle, and his still more famous legend, "England expects every man to do his duty," are related in every schoolhouse in the United Kingdom, in Canada, everywhere the English language is spoken, as an incentive to greatness. If Englishmen were forbidden by law to have that story and others so freely written over the glorious pages of English history, told to English children in the English tongue, it would illustrate only the decline of greatness—not its glory.

There is no conflict in the United States, simply because men and women of alien tongue went to that country only after having decided that they preferred to draw from the English-American cultural storehouse; many were tempted by American dollars to abandon the old and draw from the new. The few who were of a conquered alien nationality had not the will to continue. But where a nationality has become established in a country and has built around its rivers, lakes, mountains and plains, a culture of its own, it will not give up at the demand of an alien nationality made dominant by conquest or immigration. That is the point to remember. I must be pardoned for repeating it, since it is the gist of the lesson. The old language will not be given up—if it is a suitable tool, or can be made such for the necessities of the spiritual and economic life of the people. "As a native of the Highlands," writes Dr. Alexander Duff, the Indian educationist, "I vividly realised the fact that the Gaelic language, though powerful for lyric and other poetry and for popular address, contained no words that could possibly meet the objects of a higher comprehensive education." Thus the language of the Northern Scot, slowly but without compulsion, yielded to that of the Englishman. If there had been compulsion? The story of the Covenanters is a sufficient answer. Economic advantage, science, and literature, all would have been submerged in the will to preserve.

Let me try to make this point plain to those who have no will to understand, for it is fundamental. I do not seek to maintain that nationality is imperishable. Indeed the world is in a constant state of flux; families are constantly changing from one nationality to another—but only when left free to choose, when unhampered in the use of the old. Nationality may be steered, but it cannot be towed; it will not yield to force. That is the teaching of history. Mr. Toynbee says in "The New Europe": "Where a minority has abandoned its mother tongue, it has done so without pressure, as the Irish have exchanged Erse for English in their national literature. Where a minority has clung to its native speech it has been allowed to retain it, as

Welsh has been retained in parts of Wales as an instrument for poetry and primary education. Only the more lately emancipated languages of Central and Eastern Europe, have become committed to a disastrous struggle for existence." Mr. Toynbee's study was confined to Europe, because it was designed to diagnose conditions affecting the war. If he had included the New World in his range, he would have found another people who, in British North America, are "committed to a disastrous struggle for existence."

The Jews, perhaps, furnish the best object lesson of the futility of restriction. For many years, different States of Europe tried to destroy this race, religion, nationality—call it what you will—shut it up in a ghetto; prohibited it from owning lands; limited it in the choice of occupations; and often compelled it to wear a "badge," as if the Jew were a leper barred from contact with the rest of society. In spite of all, the Jew held on, the more a Jew because of the repression. That was repression at its best—or at its worst—certainly at its strongest.

Turkey is Germany's most legitimate partner in the present war. For years the Turks tried to hammer the peoples, who composed their vast, conglomerate empire, into homogeneity. For many generations, the distinctive nationalities within the Balkans were subjected to Turkish rule and subjected to the Turkish crucible and yet "the Diplomatist," author of "Nationalism and the War in

the Near East," tells us "on the reflux of the Turkish inundation the Bulgar reappeared a Bulgar and
all the more a Bulgarian for having so long been
a Greek rayah and an Ottoman subject, the Serb
reappeared as the most Slav of Slavs, and all the
more Slavonic for having been a Turk, an Austrian
or a Hungarian according to the vicissitudes of the
time. It would seem as though the deeper the sub-
mergence and the more sweeping the inundation,
the more does anything atrophied or alien get
purged out of the national character." The
Armenians, wilfully persisting in living up to the
traditions of their fathers, were scourged by Turk
with torch and sword—and still there are Armenians. Turkey passed school regulations to destroy
the nationality of the Albanians, submitted them
to property and civil disqualifications—and still
there are Albanians.

About the time of the British North America
Act, Holstein and Schleswig became parts of Germany. Previously they had been under the direct
rule of the King of Denmark, although Holstein
was even then a part of the loosely-joined German
Confederacy. The population of Schleswig-Holstein was mainly of the German tongue, but was
apparently satisfied with its political condition
until an attempt was made to force linguistic conversion upon it. The situation was complicated,
as will be seen from this paragraph by Dr. Rose
in "The Development of European Nations":
"The fervent nationalists in Denmark, while leav

ing Holstein to its German connections, had re-
solved thoroughly to 'Danify' Schleswig, the northern half of which was wholly Danish, and they
pressed on this policy by harsh and intolerant measures, making it difficult or well-nigh impossible
for the Germans to have public worship in their
own tongue and to secure German teachers for
their children in the schools. Matters were already in a very strained state, when shortly before
the death of King Frederick VII of Denmark
(November, 1863), the Rigsraad at Copenhagen
sanctioned a constitution for Schleswig, which
would practically have made it a part of the Danish
monarchy." Then came the crisis.

But Germany was not ready for immediate
action. In those days Germany did not want a
world-war. A little state like Denmark it did not
mind violating, especially since Denmark had
violated the principles of nationality by attempting
to cast the Germans of Schleswig in a Danish
mould. Casting about for public support, Germany found in Napoleon III, who sat upon the
throne of France, a ready tool. The Third
Napoleon, in the historian's opinion, was more
than a bit of a fool. As M. Falloux said of him:
"He does not know the difference between dream-
ing and thinking." He had accepted the Mazzini
doctrine, but had failed to see its legitimate outcome. "I shall always be consistent in my conduct," he said. "If I have fought for the independence of Italy, if I have lifted up my voice for

Polish nationality, 1 cannot have other sentiments in Germany, or obey other principles." Napoleon saw only the Germans in Schleswig-Holstein—and indeed they were the more numerous—but there were Danes. And no sooner had they been brought under German jurisdiction than Germany sought to Germanise them. The Germans of Holstein were out of the frying-pan, but the Danes of Schleswig were in the fire.

Let us briefly follow the results. With map of Europe in hand, the reader will at once see that Schleswig is geographically a part of Germany; the economic interests of its inhabitants naturally swing south towards the 60 million and more Germans, rather than north towards the 2½ million Danes of Denmark. The highly developed social and intellectual life of the German people might ordinarily have been counted on to absorb the Schleswigers. There was no bar of religion between the two nationalities as in Canada, for the Danish Church is a modified form of Lutheranism. The ground had seemingly been prepared by Nature for homogeneity. And in the opinion of competent Danish students, homogeneity would have been secured in time, had not the Germans— "political asses" that they are, to use Herr Althoff's expressive words—failed to recognise that the road to homogeneity lies in freedom of culture, not in its repression. The Germans perversely chose to ignore the teachings of history, and set about securing unification by the discredited means of force. The work was conducted with that commendable thoroughness which the German applies to every job, from pig-sticking to ship-building.

The school regulations required a thorough teaching of German, as the Ontario regulations since 1912 require a thorough teaching of English in the French districts. Ontario has vacillated in the work of restriction; Germany, for as many years as there are years in the Canadian Confederation calendar, has sternly and systematically and persistently attempted to force the Schleswigers to learn the German language. Yet all that while the Danes have been passing through the German schools only to disdain the use of the German language in after life; only to cling to the Icelandic tongue of their Viking forbears; in short, only to remain German subjects of Danish nationality.

Little Belgium also furnishes a lesson in the futility of attempting to secure homogeneity by the school crucible. She gained her independence; was separated from Holland in 1831; was, in fact, born of a protest against the attempt to submerge national sentiment, and has in the course of her career, passed through many experiences illustrative of the relations which nationalities should, and should not, bear to each other within a common State. Of the birth of Belgium, and as it exists to-day, Joseph McCabe tells us: "William of Holland made the world-old and world-discredited mistake of aiming at uniformity. The threat to their religion and their language stirred at length the slow-moving Flemings, and they supported the revolt of the more fiery and more aggressive Walloons."

The people of the new kingdom were of two nationalities, the Flemings and the Walloons. Protesting against being forcibly converted into Dutchmen, the two partners hardly had got started in the business of running a State themselves, before each nationality set about making over the other, and as usual by way of the schoolhouse, repeating the "world-old and world-discredited mistake." The Walloons, for the most part, spoke French, and the Flemings spoke Flemish. Each nationality thought its language should be that of the schools, the courts and the State. The two nationalities are divided in Belgium almost as are English-Canadians and French-Canadians in Ontario and Quebec, the one inhabiting the North-Western portion of Belgium, north of a line drawn through Courtrai and Louvain, and the other being south of that line. But dispersed through the two parts are settlements of the minority, as in Quebec and in Ontario. It was in those dispersed settlements, that the conflict arose and ran its most turbulent course.

The Flemish tongue is of comparatively little value in international trade, argued the Walloon; and besides, we want unity in the development of our nation. Let us take the language of France; it is valuable in commerce and rich in literature.

The argument seemed good to all the Walloons
and to none of the Flemings. Our tongue is distinctive, replied the Flemings; and a very good
tongue it is. Most of the inhabitants of Belgium
speak it now. If it be given up for French, it
is only a matter of a short time when Belgium will
be given up to France. That seemed a good
argument to all the Flemings, and to none of the
Walloons. Incidentally, the latter half of the
Flemings' argument has been made before, and
made by Englishmen, on behalf of the French
language in Canada; for in the early days it was
considered that individuality in language was the
best guarantee that this country would not be
eventually absorbed by the virile young United
States just across the way.

From argument, the rival nationalities in Belgium proceeded to invective. "Patois!" they
shouted at each other. The cry of inferiority is an
ever-ready stone in the clashing of nationalities.
The Walloon nicknamed the Fleming a "Flamingant," and the Fleming replied by derisively
calling the Walloon a "Fransquillon." Each
sought to belittle the other's accomplishments; not
in commerce, because that affected the common
purse, but in literature and in social life. Each
nationality considered it a matter of loyalty to
refrain from learning the other's speech. "A country committed to bi-lingualism for all eternity!"
"It is unthinkable!" They argued in words that
are frequently heard in Ontario. There was Hades

15 c.

in Belgium; of course, not as much as since 1914, but enough to make things uncomfortably hot. "When the question of language comes up in Parliament, everyone speaks at once, and we hear nothing," mournfully complained the Speaker of the Chamber of Deputies.

At first, the Flemings had the worst of it. French was the language of Court life, of polite society, and of big business. Flemish was limited in the schools, and practically excluded from the courts of justice. There was much in the contention of the Walloons that Flemish had failed to rank among the cultural languages of the day. The Flemings are, broadly speaking, descended from Frankish tribes, who, tired of moving about Northern Europe, squatted in what is now Belgium, in the fourth and succeeding centuries, but subsequently came the Belge, who was Gallic, and the Saxon who was Low German, and out of the mixture of Frank, Belge, and Saxon, was created a new subdivision in races—the Flemish. Their language is described by the philologist as southern Dutch in vocabulary, structure, and grammar, bearing a very close resemblance to middle Dutch; but in details, choice of idioms, and turns of expression, it exhibits a certain measure of independence. The philologist adds that "Flemish gives the impression of being an uncultivated, unliterary tongue" —an altogether unlovely material out of which to make literature.

But charges of inferiority pressed the Flemings

together, made them resolve that their language should become impeccable. A national society was formed, which strove with all the intensity of a movement writhing under the sting of the charge of inferiority, to place Flemish freely in the schools and courts. Men strove for fame in literature, in the consciousness that they were benefitting not merely themselves, but also and mainly the national circle to which they belonged. Then came Maeterlinck and Conscience, to whom the literary world paid homage. The Flemish were no longer "Flamingants"; they had won a place in national culture. They were Belgians. The court appointed Henri Conscience, the great novelist, as tutor to the Royal Princes—and society, as ever, followed its lead. Conscience did more than teach the Royal Princes; he went into the schoolhouses and taught the language he loved to the children from the homes of rich and poor alike. On the pedestal of his statue in Antwerp—if it has not been destroyed by the Germans—are these words: "To him who taught our people to read."

Not to know Flemish was no longer a badge of superiority: it was just plain ignorance. The Walloons who had turned up their French noses at the dialect of the "Flamingant," found a strange and previously unseen beauty in the Flemish language —after it had been admitted to the Civil Service, and the best positions went to the men who could speak the two languages of the country. Possibly a beauty now hidden in the French and English languages would be uncovered to some if a knowledge of both were made obligatory in Canada's Civil Service.

Belgium came gradually to the consciousness that it was irretrievably bi-lingual, and reformed its schools accordingly. "Since the knowledge of Flemish has become absolutely indispensable in many professions, and above all in the legal profession, the schools have devoted themselves, all over Belgium, to giving the pupils a thorough practical knowledge of the two languages," reported T. R. Dawes, a Welshman and the head master of the Pembroke Dock County School, in 1902, after an investigation of the school system of Belgium.

Of course, there were "die-hard" Flemings and "die-hard" Walloons; but the better sense of the country was for harmony through mutual respect, and besides, years of struggle had revealed the futility of relying upon schoolroom restrictions as a means of securing homogeneity.

The results of freedom and restriction are contrasted in the experiences of Alsace and Lorraine under French and German dominations. It must be remembered that the people of these provinces were originally of Baltic blood, and further, of its Teutonic subdivision. Their commonly used tongue was originally, and is to-day, akin to German. In 1871, Lorraine had been a part of France for only 100 and Alsace for only 200 years; and yet both Alsatians and Lorrainers, if not of French nationality in 1871, certainly preferred to remain a part of France. They had become tied to France by the silken cords of affection.

Contrast their treatment by France with their treatment by Germany, and contrast their feelings for France with their feelings for Germany. Surely here is an apt lesson for us! What are the means by which the affection and the loyalty of a nationality are secured? the means by which its disaffection and disloyalty are avoided? That is the lesson we seek.

Professor Hazen of Columbia tells us that, on the one hand, by France "the traditions of the land were respected. No attempt was made to force the Alsatians to use the French language. No military service was required of them. The result of this wise policy was to create the felicitous impression among the people concerned that nothing or almost nothing was changed. Friction was thus avoided. Life moved along normally and in the same old grooves. The new régime could strike roots, slowly it is true, but all the more solidly. No racial opposition was aroused. Changes were effected, but so gradually and so beneficently that only the advantages of the new connection were apparent." In the course of time the Alsatians and Lorrainers saw with the clear eyes of free men the advantage of learning French.

"The House of Bourbon, from the Treaty of Westphalia to the French Revolution, never thought of preventing or hampering the use of German in Alsace, never considered its suppression necessary as a means of hastening the assimilation of the province."

That the many in Alsace and Lorraine did learn French, was due to the attractiveness of French literature, French culture and, above all, to the winsomeness of French character. The Alsatians and Lorrainers became French simply because in course of time they learned to like the French and what the French stood for.

Professor Hazen tells us that, on the other hand, Germany's "first act was to eliminate almost completely the study of French from the curriculum of the schools, at the same time ordaining universal and obligatory attendance and increasing the salaries of the teachers. When the study of French was not entirely suppressed, it was relegated to a peculiar place. The curriculum of the school in Mulhouse, as described by a speaker in the Reichstag in 1872, prescribed the teaching 'of history in German, of geography in German, of penmanship in French (laughter), of drawing in French (laughter.' " It is a question whether Ontario is now more generous than Germany was then, for under Regulation 17, penmanship and drawing may not be taught in French, since English becomes the language of general instruction as soon as the pupil is old enough to draw and write. "The Germans have had forty-five years in which to reconcile these people of German descent to their re-union with the parent stock," writes Ramsay Muir. "They have utterly failed. They have only succeeded in arousing against themselves an intense and enduring distaste."

Could there be a plainer and more insistent lesson in history than that loyalty is the consequence of liberty? disloyalty, the consequence of restriction? The Alsatians were left free to speak German under French rule, were assisted in educating their children by means of the German tongue— and remained French; the Alsatians were forced to speak German, to have their children educated in German, under German rule—and refused to become German. The French successfully steered nationality; the Germans failed to tow it. And humanity is much the same the world over.

Those who are astounded at the stupidity or the blindness of the Germans in failing to discover the path towards homogeneity, have only to survey conditions in Canada. Here the French-Canadian nationality is immeasurably farther away from assimilation than it was before Regulation 17 was devised for its immersion in the English language. For years, France had not held sway over the hearts of the French-Canadians. The younger generation was convinced of British justice, British stability, and British integrity, and had become sincerely attached to British traditions. Instruction in the two languages was regarded as a necessary means to education. The educated of the French nationality spoke the English language as

well as their own. But the progress towards assimilation has been stayed by the conviction that
Regulation 17 was intended to be a means of denationalisation; nor are the French-Canadians to
be blamed, for as such it has been staged before
the public in the Province of Ontario.

Those who speak French in Canada have had
several hundred years of life in a country in which
men of sound physique and strong will are bred.
They have the strong man's will to continue. They
refuse to allow their nationality to perish in a land
which was once their fathers'. Would we,
their compatriots, have it otherwise? A generous
foe will always admire a stubborn enemy. Even
the Germans—and in these days we have little
respect for their fairness—admit that "the energy
with which the Poles organised their resistance to
the German attack on their soil deserves admiration." We English-Canadians call Ontario "our
soil," but always must we remember that, like
Schleswig, it once belonged to the men of the
minor nationality.

It is a curious law of retribution that the nation
that attempts to destroy another's culture, invariably fails to hold its own; and yet not curious,
when we remember that to attempt the suppression
of a national culture is "fighting against God."
The Germans, who have led the way in forcing
their language upon others, as immigrants are the
first to merge themselves in the individuality of
the State of their adoption. In Brazil there are

thousands of Germans of the second and third generation who have willingly accepted Latin culture
and allowed their knowledge of German to depre-
ciate into a doggerel tongue. Even in Westphalia,
to which many thousand Poles were removed, the
Germans became largely incorporated into the nationality of the Slavs, practising their religion,
speaking their language, and partaking of their
national aspirations. W. H. Dawson relates an
amusing incident arising out of a visit paid by Herr
von Bethmann-Hollweg who, at the time, as Minister of the Interior, was visiting one of the villages in which Germans had been planted in the
effort to Germanise the Poles. Meeting a German
colonist the Minister asked: "Well, and how do
you like your new home?" "All right" was the
cheery reply; "except that we cannot yet sufficiently
understand the Poles. But" (reassuringly) "never
mind, we shall learn Polish yet." It is Prince von
Bülow who regretfully admits that, "in the struggle between different nationalities, the German has
so often succumbed to the Czech and the Slovene,
the Magyar, and the Pole, the French, and the
Italian." And with such an admission, the Germans fruitlessly, hopelessly, struggle on to make
all within the German Empire, Teutons.

Alexander of Macedon would have made all
men Hellenes. This morning my shoes were pol-
ished by an heir of this noble Hellenism, and I
could not but think of Alexander's bold words.
The Greeks, proud of their attainments, had sought

to substitute their culture for the culture of other men, and in the inevitable struggle had lost their own. Assuming it to be their special mission to polish other men's heads, they wound up by polishing other men's boots.

<small>BOOKS OF REFERENCE</small>

A Diplomatist (edited by Lord Courtney of Penwich), *Nationalism and War in the Near East*. Carnegie Endowment for International Peace. Clarendon.

Arnold Toynbee, *The New Europe*. Dent.

J. Holland Rose, *The Development of the European Nations*. Constable.

Arnold Toynbee, *Nationality and the War*. Dent.

Joseph McCabe, *The Soul of Europe*. Dodd, Mead & Co.

Alfred E. Zimmern and Others, *The War and Democracy*. Macmillan.

Ramsay Muir, *Nationalism and Internationalism*. Houghton, Mifflin & Co.

Prince Bernhard Von Bülow, *Imperial Germany*. Cassel.

Charles Downer Hazen, *Alsace-Lorraine Under German Rule*. Holt.

A. H. Buxton, *Indian Moral Instruction and Caste Problems*. Longmans, Green & Co.

T. R. Dawes, *Bi-lingual Teaching In Belgian Schools*. Cambridge. Dent.

M. Fishberg, *The Jews*. Scribners.

CHAPTER XII

THE conflicts between nationalities, their motives, means, and results, are everywhere much the same. The full course of the clash has been laid bare by historians and philosophers, who have recorded and analysed the relations of Teuton and Pole. A comparison of their findings with conditions as they have been, and are, in Canada, reveals an almost uncanny identity, illustrating the obvious truth that when men start from the same place towards a common object, they necessarily travel in parallel paths.

Towards the end of the eighteenth century, Germany obtained a slice of Poland—her bit of the land which was regarded as essential to the protection of the people who call themselves German; and with it, several million human beings possessing a distinct nationality. No sooner had the conquest been effected than Germany, having the coveted land, began to wonder what she should do with the people. The Russians, confronted with the same problem, had attempted to crush their share of the Poles, by force of arms; resistance had followed force, and massacre had followed resistance. Of course, this procedure succeeded only in making dead Poles; it wholly failed to make

211

living Russians; and, worse than failure, the world was shocked.

Germany did not intend to repeat Russia's mistake. The Slavonic Poles would be made over into Teutonic Germans by process of law. Germany would do everything according to the code, and therefore the world should not be shocked! For Germany believed that the Treitschke doctrine of State omnipotence had obtained acceptance everywhere. But let me set down the course through which the conflict moved, and with it the parallel in this country under the English-Canadian régime.

Teutonic sentiment is primarily religious and Protestant—militantly Protestant. The German philosophy that denies the existence of God, or limits His attributes to a point where personality vanishes, has not taken hold of the average Teutonic mind; the great mass of the people are essentially religious and sincerely—and, as we think, mistakenly—see God's personal hand directing their collective undertakings. To use the words of Gustave le Bon, in the "Pyschology of the Great War": "A vast number of books, most of which have been published during the last thirty years, demonstrate that the Germans have a greater conception of their own superiority, than was ever before entertained by any nation, except perhaps by the Jews of Bible times and the Arabs of Mohammed's day. This idea is based chiefly upon the illusion that the German race, which is actually

composed of the most heterogeneous elements, is a
chosen race, specially selected by God for the conquest and subsequent exploitation of the world."
It naturally follows that God's "peculiar way"
for the Germans is through the State Church, the
Lutheran Church, which the Prussians fondly
regard as the bulwark of Protestantism. To again
use le Bon's words: "In Treitschke's eyes history
is simply a divinely regulated development whose
object is to secure the triumph of the Protestant
faith, and he considers that the conquest of the
world has been set apart for the German race,
which owes its greatness to Luther. With this
reformer, indeed, the progress of humanity begins."

It surely cannot be considered too much to say
that English-Canadians, that have assumed the
heavy part in the attempt to make over the French-
Canadian nationality by means of the school crucible, have much the same feeling. Later on we
shall have proof of the contention. In both countries, there is a sentiment for homogeneity for other
reasons; but in both the most turbulent side of the
stream, the current that never lags in its intensity,
is religious; and in both countries, it is directed
against Catholicism. For the Slavonic Poles of
Germany and the French-Canadians are alike in
being nearly solid in their adherence to the tenets
of the Roman Catholic faith.

In Germany and Canada alike the major nationality fears the destruction of its religion and cul-

ture at the hands of an aggressive minor nationality. To Canada, there came few of the French tongue to implement the strength of the minor nationality; and from Germany, mainly to the United States, there was a constant stream of Polish migration; but, in both countries, it was pointed out that the birth-rate within the minor nationality was higher than in the major nationality, and figures, ever ready in knowing hands to prove anything, were made to prove the certainty and the imminence of the minor becoming major.

The Roman Catholic Church sternly forbids race suicide, and while the Protestant Churches do not encourage and presumably discountenance it, the fact remains that the birth-rate is generally higher in Catholic communities than in Protestant communities. In Canada, using the latest figures available (1914) the birth-rate per thousand living is 38 for the Province of Quebec—mainly Roman Catholic—and 24 for the Province of Ontario—mainly Protestant. The other Provinces show wide variations, Manitoba having a birth-rate of 33 per thousand, and Nova Scotia 25 per thousand. The methods of gathering the statistics in the several Provinces are by no means the same, and the results are inconclusive. But Quebec is undoubtedly the Province of largest families, having 273 children of nine years or under to every thousand of population. Ontario has only 200 to the thousand, but Ontario is a notorious laggard, evidently given over to race suicide, and with

British Columbia stands at the bottom of the Provincial list. Manitoba has 248 children to the thousand, and in 1901 had 270 to the thousand; so that the disproportion between the races is not as great as is generally understood. And yet the cry is insistent that some day Anglo-Saxonism and Protestantism will be swept away by the higher birth-rate of the French-Catholic population.

Dr. Sarolea is my authority for stating that the Germans believe the same of the Poles who "increase much more rapidly than the Prussians, as indeed, to use the expression of Prince von Bülow, 'they breed like rabbits.' Some means must be used to check the Polish advance. It is essential to the integrity and preservation of the Empire that the Eastern and South-Eastern frontiers shall not fall into the hands of a disaffected race." Here we have at the outset parallel dangers which the majorities in both countries are unwilling to meet by the obvious antidote of competition.

Then there was also the question of mixed marriages. While the Roman Catholic Church does not actually forbid the marriage of its communicants with those of other faiths, the restrictions placed in the way of such marriages make substantial assimilation by the marrying route impossible. In Germany, intermarrying was once regarded as the solution of the vexed problem. "The surest means of giving this oppressed nation" (Poland) "better ideas and morals will always be gradually to get them to intermarry with Germans, even if at first it is only two or three of them in every village," was the opinion of Frederick the Great before 1772, the year of Poland's partition. But neither in Germany nor in Canada was assimilation possible by what the Great Frederick regarded as "the surest way"; although in both countries there was an assimilation between the nationalities by the intermarriage of Roman Catholics of Slavonic and Teutonic origin, and Roman Catholics who spoke English and French. But their Roman Catholic populations were insufficient to turn the tide of population increasing by natural means towards the major nationalities.

What was Germany to do? "Prussia must be ruled and administered from the national German standpoint," writes Prince von Bülow. "If we had allowed the Slavonic element in the East of the Prussian Kingdom to extend and flood the German element, as has happened in part of Cisleithania, instead of having a hard fight for German nationality in the Eastern Marches to-day, we should have had a fight to maintain the unity of the Prussian State; we should not have had a Polish problem, we should have had a Polish danger." In Canada, it has been similarly maintained that this country must be ruled and administered from the national Anglo-Saxon standpoint, and not infrequently reference has been made to the Divine destiny of the Anglo-Saxon race to rule. The dangerous old idea of a tribal God, ever ready to smite the unchosen races—megalomania—dies slowly.

In Ontario it is pointed out that if we were to allow the French-Canadians to extend and flood over Northern Ontario, we should some day have to fight for the predominance of Anglo-Saxonism. Within the past few months hundreds of thousands of chauvinists' dollars were devoted to publicly advertising the imminence of the peril which threatens Anglo-Saxonism—and I am not referring to official political party literature. In Germany there are only 55 Slavonic Poles, as against 925 Teutons, to the thousand of population; in Canada, 28 French-Canadians to the hundred—slight evidence of danger in either country—but chauvinism is essentially a matter of sentiment and prejudice, not of reason; and chauvinism, in spite of its brave words, is easily frightened by shadows.

In neither country was the aim to drive away the minor nationality. "Nobody dreams of wishing to thrust our Poles outside the borders of the present Kingdom," says Prince von Bülow. Canada must have felt likewise, for she has been spending substantial sums of money to bring back the French-Canadians who have gone to the United States.

If the Poles and the French-Canadians were constantly increasing by birth-rate, were not assimilable by marriage, were not to be sent out of the country, and would not voluntarily give up their national culture, what then was to be done to secure the homogeneity which, in the thought of the dominant parties in both countries, was essen-

tial to their own best social and economic lives?
In both countries, the eyes of statesmen turned to
the schoolhouse; it was there that men were made.
It was in the schoolhouse that mentality was formed, likes and dislikes imbibed. Hitherto the school
had made for heterogeneity; hereafter it should
make for homogeneity.

In both countries the school situation was
much the same. When Poland—or rather a part
of it—became a part of the German Empire, its
inhabitants had been given assurances of the preservation of their religion, and with it the maintenance of the Polish language. The assurances, direct
and implied, were much the same as those given
to the French-Canadians in the days of the Quebec
Act, when it will be remembered the French-Canadians were told by Thurlow that they were to retain all their "customs and institutions" which
did not directly affect their relations to the new
sovereign. But in both countries conditions had
changed with time.

"On behalf of the Prussian Government, it is
contended," says W. H. Dawson, "that there is constitutional justification for the invasion and ulti-
mate cancelling of Polish 'particular' lingual
rights. Granting that at the time of the partition
special franchises were promised to the inhabitants
of the appropriated territories—franchises which
were to include even 'national representation and
institutions' long before they were thought of as
suited to the rest of the Prussian Monarchy—it is

pointed out that half a century ago the rights of
King and people underwent a complete change, in
that they ceased to be regulated by tacit and unwritten agreement, and were put down in black and
white in the form of a political constitution. It is,
therefore, argued that the Prussian constitution of
1851 must be regarded as superseding all pre-existing political arrangements, hence that by accepting
that document the Poles forfeited all right of appeal to earlier promises and guarantees. While,
however, such an argument may be capable of
satisfying the official conscience, it fails to remove
the objection of the Poles that the suppression of
their language is a blow aimed at the race and at
the sanctities of hearth and home."

On behalf of the Ontario Government, it is contended that there is constitutional justification for
cancelling any privileges which may have been
previously allowed; which may have been implied
in the Quebec Act. Granting that at the time of
the Conquest the French-Canadians were guaran-
teed the preservation of their religious faith, and
that then schools were universally considered as a
matter of religion (exclusively so in Canada)
granting that the French-Canadians, were for
many years, continued in the free use of their language, even after Confederation (after the Ottawa
River had become a boundary line) it is pointed
out that their special lingual rights had ceased to
be revealed by tacit and unwritten agreement after
they had been put down in black and white in the

British North America Act. It is therefore argued that the Canadian Constitution of 1867 must be regarded as superseding all pre-existing political arrangements; hence, by accepting the document, the French-Canadians have forfeited all right of appeal to earlier promises and guarantees. May I repeat a sentence from Dawson, which I have just quoted, simply changing the word "Poles" into "French-Canadians": "While, however, such an argument may be capable of satisfying the official conscience, it fails to remove the objection of 'the French-Canadians' that the suppression of their language is a blow aimed at the race and at the sanctities of hearth and home." In both countries the code, the written law, has been appealed to; and in both judicial decisions sustain the legality of State action, but did not attempt to pass upon the morality of the business.

Until 1873 all Polish children were instructed in the language of their parents; it was provided that after that year all instruction was to be given in German. Since that time the regulations have varied from nothing to a substantial something in the extent to which teachers have been permitted to instruct their pupils in the use of the parents' language. It is necessary that the reader who has not closely followed the controversy, should here bear in mind the distinction between the teaching of a language and teaching in a language. The German Government, in its work of denationalisation, has proceeded upon the theory that the one thing needful was to have instruction in general subjects, such as mathematics and history, imparted solely by means of the German tongue. Germany, after all, desired that the son of the conquered race should have a Teutonic mind. He might speak Polish, or Danish, or French, but what of that? Many Prussians of the old stock spoke them all. But if the pupil were forced to suck his education through the Teutonic straw, he would acquire the all important thing—a Teutonic mentality. That was the end towards which all German regulations were applied to Polish schools after 1873.

It is all very well for the press of Ontario to talk of the generous provision (an hour a day) made for the teaching of the French language (a few minutes for each class) ; but the central idea of Regulation 17—and the bone of contention—is that instruction in the subjects of the curriculum shall be exclusively in English. A precise setting forth of the ways and means by which it is to be accomplished is impossible. Regulation 17 would puzzle not only a Philadelphia lawyer : it almost defied the greatest body of legal wisdom in the realm, the Judicial Committee of the Privy Council, which it will be remembered, found the rule obscure and difficult to understand, but concluded that the complaint of the applicants "was mainly directed" to the paragraph "which regulates the use of French as the language of instruction and communication" and decided that:

"In the case of French-speaking pupils, French, 'where necessary,' may be used as the language of instruction and communication, but not beyond Form I, except on the approval of the Chief Inspector in the case of pupils beyond Form I, who are unable to speak and understand the English language."

Thus clearly the real object of the Ontario regulation is that French-Canadians shall have all their mathematics, history, geography, drawing, and the whole course which is supposed to constitute education, imparted to them in English. Since the French-Canadian child enters the first form when five or six years of age, the effect of Regulation 17 is the practical proscription of French for purposes of all general education.

"Just as the twig is bent, the tree's inclined."

The controversy in Ontario is not primarily pedagogical; it is, as in Poland, a clash between two nationalities in which one believes that the other is seeking its destruction—and the evidence compels us to admit not without reason. Mr. C. B. Sissons of Victoria University, in his recently published book "Bi-Lingual Schools in Canada," reports this statement from a former Attorney General of the Province (the late Hon. J. J. Foy) that "no other language (than English) should be taught in the schools," and that "there cannot lawfully be any bi-lingual schools in the Province of Ontario." One is at a loss to know upon what Mr. Foy based his opinion that there cannot lawfully be any bi-lingual schools in Ontario, but that is not

the serious feature of the statement. The importance lay not in what was said, but rather in who
said it. Mr. Foy was then a Minister of the Crown
in Ontario, the Minister responsible for Ontario's
law, and his statement must have been accepted by
English-Canadians as the government's opinion
that the French-Canadians had already too many
rights; and by French-Canadians as equally
authoritative that the government was in reality
preparing for the complete destruction of the
French language in Ontario. Some may say that
Mr. Foy was "only speaking politically," but that
is just the kind of speaking that is most widely
reported; the kind that, in the heat of elections,
stirs up trouble which cannot be allayed in calmer
moments. Nor were the appeals for restriction
limited to Ontario. Mr. Sissons also gives another
specimen of the language used by a candidate on
the Provincial hustings: "It has been stated that I
am in favour of bi-lingual schools. I will say this,
that I am entirely opposed to the teaching of
French in the public or separate school of the
Province of Ontario. I never at any stage felt any
doubt as to where I stood. I want to tell you, good
people, that English is good enough for me. It is
good enough for the Dominion of Canada. As
long as I have anything to say in the Legislature I
will fight for English and English alone."

There is in this phrase, "It is good enough for
the Dominion of Canada," more than a veiled hint
that the French language ought to be abolished

from Canada. Nor is that by any means isolated opinion. It is the sort of thing that has been said from the pulpits and hustings of the Province, and repeatedly in public print, and all the while vehement protests were being made by pulpit, hustings and press against the interference of the French-Canadians of Quebec in "the affairs of Ontario."

The French-Canadians of Quebec have been accused of using intolerant language; of stirring their Ontario compatriots into resistance. And in truth, M. Bourassa and other champions of the French-Canadian nationality have had many bitter things to say of the English-Canadians of Ontario. But we must not forget our inevitable parallel from Poland, and this time we may have it in few words. Mr. Dawson says: "That the Poles have only answered intolerance with intolerance, bitterness with bitterness, must be frankly admitted, and Polish human nature would be very different from any other were it otherwise." In Canada it is not a case of "the pot calling the kettle black." The French-Canadians are being deprived of "natural" rights or privileges—call them what you will—that they have been enjoying in the schools of Ontario with only fitful interruptions since before Confederation. They are—view the matter as you will—the injured party, and would be more than human to suffer without resentment. But this must be said for them: the French-Canadians have not, in their resentment, re-

taliated in the one place where retaliation could
have been made effective—in the Quebec Legislature. The English-speaking minority or the "British Protestants," as they are called in the Debates
on the proposals for Confederation, are legally
entitled to no greater educational rights in Quebec
than the "French Catholics" in Ontario—and yet
their interests, in spite of the bitterness of the conflict, have been splendidly conserved.

Mr. J. C. Sutherland, who looks after education interests of the minority in Quebec, tells us
"In the Regulations of the Catholic Committee—
a large book of 222 pages—there is a heading in
bold black type to the pages dealing with the course
of study which reads: English for English schools,
French for French schools. It is the emphatic
symbol of the liberty which is honored in the Province of Quebec." I wonder if any other nationality
in the world, the Poles for example, could have
resisted such a temptation to retaliate.

In both Ontario and Poland the children were
first to lead a revolt that was not of words. At
Ottawa, the largest city affected by Regulation 17,
the school children threw down their books and,
parading the streets, cried out for justice. Left
to their own free will, they might have chosen
the language of commerce; but, with boisterous
childish voices, refused to accept it by force.
In Germany, as Dawson tells us: "The famous
'school strikes' of 1906—a fitting counterpart to the
equally memorable Wreschen school-scandals of

1901—came as a reminder of the depth of aggrava-
tion caused by the language prohibition. These
strikes began in the autumn of 1906 and lasted into
the following spring. They originated in the
diocese of Posen, but spread to other parts of the
Polish enclave and even to Breslau. In the diocese
of Posen alone, 40,000 children 'struck.' The rebellion began with a refusal to answer questions in
German, and it ended in abstention from school
altogether." The Ottawa strike came in the first
days of the war, when men's minds were naturally
turned towards oppression within the German Empire, and Mr. Asquith, Britain's Premier, analysing the causes of the war, named the strike
of the school children in Polish Prussia, and its
accompanying circumstances "a black chapter even
in the annals of Prussian culture."

And to clinch the parallel, there is a "land grievance" in both countries. If the Poles have had
slightly worse treatment than the French-Canadians in the matter of the schools, they have had
kinder treatment on the land, in the sense that the
Germans have not violated the security of property.
The land situations are different, in that in Poland
the dispute has been over occupied lands, and in
Ontario over unoccupied lands. In Germany the
State has attempted to take lands from Polish
proprietors and turn them over to Germans.
At first sight that appears to be a drastic measure.
But the lands were taken only by recourse to the
market. So far as I can find, no attempt has

been made—even in the white heat of the clash
—to make violation of school regulations a means
for confiscation. To give the Teutons their due,
they have, in this matter, played the game according to the laws of civilisation; and if they have
played into the hands of the Poles, well, it was impossible to play otherwise, and preserve the fundamental consideration of government, the security of
title to property. As a matter of fact, the Poles
have been paid exceedingly high prices for their
holdings, amounting in some instances to fifty per
cent. above market values, and the consideration
received has been often used to purchase more
lands, with the net result of more Poles on the
land. But what was to be done? Confiscation as
a penalty for violation of school regulations apparently did not occur to the German mind.

Plainly the Teutonic practice of purchasing
lands from the minority was commercially unfeas-
ible for Ontario. The Germans replaced Slavonic
farmers by Teutonic farmers; while in Ontario, as
we have seen, English-speaking farmers, so far from
being willing to replace French-Canadian farmers, are by thousands giving up their land—sometimes not waiting for a purchaser—and moving
to city and town. But there were the King's
lands in New Ontario. Over these English-speaking Canadians, possessing a majority in the Provincial Legislature, were trustees. The Provincial
machinery could be used to prevent French-speaking subjects of the King from preserving their

lingual interests in this part of Canada. What did
it matter that Canada's crying need was food, and
more food? What did it matter that the Mother
Country had cabled: Speed up farm production?
What did it matter that Ontario had for many
years vainly endeavoured to find colonists for these
fertile, unplowed lands? All these considerations
were submerged in the resolve that the King's
subjects who spoke French and attended mass,
should not secure a further footing on the King's
lands in Ontario. Plainly the situation was extraordinary and could be met only by extraordinary
measures. But the government was not abashed;
it went the full distance and required applicants
for the King's lands to sign papers that they would
obey unreservedly "all Provincial laws, statutes,
rules, and regulations, of every character whatsoever," on the understanding that failure to comply
with any of these rules and regulations should
"entail forfeiture without compensation" of "all
rights and of any moneys paid on account of purchase of the land."

A moment's reflection will serve to show the far-
reaching importance of such action.   Will the
reader think for a moment of the vast amount of
"Provincial laws, statutes, rules and regulations of
every character whatsoever that may be in force
from time to time," and say that there is not somewhere in his hidden past—particularly if he own
an automobile—a blemish which stands for a violation of law or regulation that would under this

regulation have put his home in jeopardy? That the government is aiming at violation of the school laws, and not its veterinary or automobile regulations, affects the principle only to make it worse. There is nothing that more readily saps respect for law than the existence of government regulations which it is not intended to enforce. That it may be intended to enforce the regulation only against French-Canadian violation of school regulations and not against that of English-Canadians—and statements to this effect are being freely made from the hustings—affects the principle only to make it more vicious. The foundation of loyalty is justice. The State expecting equal loyality from all, and now demanding equal military service from all, ought to give justice equally to all. Equality is a "postulate of democracy." It will shock many to find subjects of the King of all Britain, seeking to settle in the King's wilderness, forced to contract themselves out of that right of justice which, since the early days of history, has been supposed to be inalienable to the white, red, yellow, brown, and black men who constitute the humanity of the British Empire.

Men are being forced to swear away their rights to a common participation in the protection accorded property in the land of Ontario—and yet the press to which we might naturally have looked for a defence of justice, raises no outcry at its destruction. It is not the properties of its owners, nor the properties of its readers and advertisers that are being deprived of the protection of the Courts. So far from condemning Ontario's action, the English press of the Province has defended it as a fitting punishment upon men and women who resolutely struggle for the preservation of their fathers' tongue in a land discovered and explored and made safe for civilisation by their fathers. The defence, as was to be expected, is halting and lame, attempting to conceal and smother the intent with verbiage, rather than justify it, as will be seen by the following words of the (March 15, 1918) "Toronto Star": "The order does not mention" (Regulation 17) "this celebrated document. It binds the intending settler to obey the military service laws and also all Provincial laws, statutes, rules, and regulations of every character whatsoever that may be in force from time to time. Of course this included Regulation 17," continues "The Star" ingenuously, "so long as it remains in force; but," adds "The Star" with a fine show of generosity, "it does not stand in the way of any attempt to modify it by the usual constitutional methods. It may be taken for granted, however, that the effective teaching of English in all schools is the permanent policy of Ontario."

Surely no further evidence is required for condemnation of the land regulation than these words written in its defence. The express object of the order authorising the government to confiscate the homes of pioneers is to strengthen the hands of the

English-Canadians in the national clash over the language of the schools. No one had suggested that the "order" had converted or could convert Regulation 17 into an unchangeable Median law. Surely, having abandoned justice, we should not surrender the courage of manhood by attempting to conceal our course in evasiveness. Turn and twist as we may, we cannot escape the plain truth that, as Lord Acton has said, "the great political idea sanctifying freedom and consecrating it to God, teaching men to treasure the liberties of others as their own, and to defend them for the love of justice and charity, more than as a claim of right, has been the soul of what is great and good in the progress of the last two hundred years."

Those who are guilty of destroying justice in Northern Ontario have habitually ascribed injustice to others. With perfect reason they have defended the cause of struggling minorities in Germany, Austria, and Turkey; and have condemned the harsh measures of majorities. Yet inconsistently enough the conflicts of nationality and race, disfiguring the Old World, have uncovered nowhere a majority more willing than that of Ontario to strike at a minority's sanctity of home. We have habitually boasted that no matter what others may do, British men fight fairly. We have talked of British "fair play" as a thing inherent in the souls of British men. The English-Canadians of Ontario may still talk of it, but they cannot boast of having incorporated it into their Provincial conduct. It was Lord Chatham who said: "The poorest man may in his cottage bid defiance to all the forces of the Crown. It may be frail; its roof may shake, the winds may blow through it, the storm may enter, the rain may enter, but the King of England cannot enter." But the days of that boast are gone—at least on the King's lands in Northern Ontario. There, if British men—and British men may be born to speak French—violate even the least of the regulations laid down by the King's stewards, then the stewards (the representatives of English-Canadians) may, at their own ungoverned will, enter the home; the log houses and barns; the gardens and fields; and seize all that has been built thereon, throwing the pioneer and his family, homeless and despoiled into the wilderness. And the authority—as the "Globe" reminds us, "the English-speaking majority" are "twelve times as numerous as the French-speaking minority." To put the doctrine in Shakespeare's words:

> "Force should be right; or rather, right and wrong
> (Between whose endless jar justice resides)
> Should lose their names, and so should justice too.
> Then everything includes itself in power,
> Power into will, will into appetite;
> And appetite, a universal wolf,
> So doubly seconded with will and power."

The lifetime savings of the one may, at the will of the twelve, become the unearned property of the thirteen; such is the logical outcome of the Treitschke doctrine of State omnipotence. It seems almost incredible that such things may be in a British country.

Prince von Bülow admits that after twenty years of coercive effort there are no appreciable results in the shape of more Teutonic Poles; but seeks to cheer up his Chauvinist following with the idea that eternity is a long while. In Canada the two nationalities, as a result of oppression in Ontario and Manitoba, are farther away than ever before from assimilation. To speak the French language is now regarded as a patriotic duty of those belonging to the French nationality. The French-Canadians have become embittered against the dominant nationality, and their bitterness is that of men who feel that they are the victims of oppression. Their attitude may be again best described in Dawson's words, written of the Poles: "The language grievance which lies at the root of all these charges, is one which falls upon the Poles" (and French-Canadians) "with peculiar severity, because it is the grievance which is most universal, and which touches them in the most susceptible part of their being, wounding alike national, domestic and religious sentiment."

BOOKS OF REFERENCE

Gustave Le Bon, *The Psychology of the Great War*. Macmillan.

W. H. Dawson, *The Evolution of Modern Germany*.

C. B. Sissons, *Bi-Lingual Schools in Canada*. Dent.

Prince Bernhard von Bülow, *Imperial Germany*. Cassel.

Charles Sarolea, *The Anglo-German Problem*. Nelson.

17 c.

CHAPTER XIII

HOMOGENEITY AND SOMETHING BETTER

NATIONALITY is a mental condition, essentially a mystic force, none the less real for being intangible, but all the more difficult to understand and regulate. While there is a well-recognised difference between collective psychology and individual psychology, much can be learned of the group by drawing upon our experience with individuals. If the reader has a neighbour whose outlook upon life differs from his own, he may understand, by personal application, the wrong way and the right way of securing homogeneity. The reader, if he be physically stronger, might, under given circumstances, compel his neighbour to work for him. In that way slavery was instituted, but the reader cannot, by the same means, compel his neighbour to think with him. It must be remembered that Alexander made slaves but could not make Hellenes. The reader may even compel his neighbour to say out loud that black is white, green or another colour, but the chances are that the neighbour will go on thinking that black is something else. We know that from the Turk's experience with the Armenians. Many a man has said "Great is Allah and Mohammed is His prophet"; but down in his heart he has retained the conviction that Mohammed was an imposter. Physical force is more likely to strengthen than weaken a mental condition. School regulations that are unacceptable to a national minority, have historically failed to destroy that which was forbidden; have succeeded only in deepening the attachment to it. Nor is argument an infallible remedy for heterogeneity. We have seen that both Walloons and Flemings had very good arguments and yet failed to convince each other. What, then, is the secret remedy for heterogeneity? what the hope of those who, in a State with diverse nationalities, regard homogeneity as the means of salvation?

Modern philosophers in attempting to analyse nationality, appear to have forgotten Thomas Buckle—he has been dead for more than fifty years—or, remembering, have omitted to credit him with a valuable contribution to the subject, a work produced many years ago, but still standing the criticism of the times. Mr. Buckle was the Conan Doyle of his day. Given the conditions under which men lived, he could tell you, without personal inspection, what sort of men they were; and more than that, what sort of men they would be in the course of ages. Sherlock Holmes, the masterful creation of Sir Conan Doyle, was only a child in inductive power beside Buckle. "Battles, kings, law-makers, writers, and founders of religion," were the natural products of conditions which are to be found in the influence of Nature on man, and man on Nature. Here is the lay of his philosophy, the key with which he solves the riddles of nationality. "If we inquire what those physical agents are by which the human race is most powerfully influenced, we shall find that they may be classed under four heads: namely, Climate, Food, Soil, and the General Aspects of Nature; by which last I mean those appearances which, though presented chiefly to the sight, have, through the medium of that or other sense, directed the association of ideas, and hence in different countries have given rise to different habits of national thought."

Although the inhabitants of North France and England are first cousins, yet, separated by a narrow channel of water, within sight of each other, one people living on an island and the other on a continent, differences in "climate, food, soil, and the general aspects of Nature," left marks on the two peoples; lead them into different courses of art, politics and industry—into different habits of national thought. For us these facts have this importance: the descendants of the two peoples have been set down side by side on the North American Continent, both subject to the same physical conditions of Nature, and both will eventually have the same habit of national thought—if Buckle is right. There will develop a new nationality, and it will be neither French nor English; it will be Canadian. The Englishman fondly imagines that he can remain an Englishman in Canada, he and his children. But they cannot, according to Buckle, for they are no longer subject to the influence of the "climate" (its rains and its fogs, for instance), "the food, soil, and the general aspects of Nature" of the British Isles; by the inexorable law of Nature they must become eventually different human beings. The French-Canadian for years imagined himself nationally French. Many of his neighbours thought the same, and saw in the display of the tri-colour an evidence of the nationality of France. Perhaps neither nationality fully realised that the French-Canadian had ceased to be French until the Great War. It is true that he retains many of the characteristics of French nationality, but three hundred years have left the foundation of a new nationality which he himself has called Canadian.

All Canada is north of the 42nd parallel of latitude and subject to extreme heat in summer and extreme cold in winter. Quebec houses most of the French-Canadians, although every seventh family in Quebec is of English, Irish, Scotch, Welsh, or Jewish descent; Ontario houses most of the English-speaking Canadians, although every twelfth family in Ontario is of French descent. Taking these two provinces for investigation, it will be found that their average climatic conditions are not appreciably different, except in the severest winter months. Too often do we forget that Port Arthur and North Bay are in Ontario, when we compare Ontario's climate with that of Quebec. The comparison is usually between Toronto and Montreal.

While settlement in Canada is practically on latitudinal lines, settlement in the United States is longitudinal as well. One half of the United States is in the wheat-belt and the other half is in the cotton-belt; and at one time, if not now, the men south of the Mason and Dixon line believed that slavery was an economic necessity, socially desirable, and morally defensible. Yet the men north of the line were as fully convinced that slavery was an economic mistake and horrible immorality. Both sides doggedly maintained their points of view, and finally fell to fighting. The wide difference in their views can only be accounted for by the effects of climate on character. There is to-day a difference between the man from Alabama and the man from Maine. In fact, as we are reminded by Edwin S. Corwin, there were men, who, at the time of the Confederation of the United States, would willingly have abandoned to Spain the territory now included within several of the Southern States on the ground that "the virtues required by a republic were to be had only in a hardy climate." Gouverneur Morris of New York was of the opinion "that to hand over the navigation of the Mississippi to Spain from the mouth of the Ohio would be accordant with the best interests of the United States, inasmuch as it was the only measure calculated to keep the growing population between the Ohio, the St. Lawrence, and the Mississippi dependent on the republic." To-day the men of the South, as a result of war—that direct or indirect effect of climate—are associated together in common political action. There is still in the Federal politics of the United States a "solid south."

The man on the street in Canada says that there is a solid Quebec in the politics of Canada. So there is to-day, but the conditions of to-day are not normal. Let us find out how far he has been wrong in saying it for years, for he is seldom right. The Conservatives have had an average of 29 supporters from Quebec in the twelve general elections following 1867; and, inasmuch as there are 65 members elected, the Province came within 3½ members—if a member be divisible—of distributing its political opinions equally between the two parties. At the 1911 election, it will be remembered, the Conservatives and Nationalists, working together, elected 27 supporters, and the Liberals 38 supporters in the Province of Quebec. The evidence in the electoral or legislative records of the country shows that the French- and English-Canadians have fully coalesced in the political thought and organisation of Canada.

Sir George Ross included in his interesting book, "Getting into Parliament and After," a page on the relations of English- and French-Canadians. With the exception of a vote upon a motion of Sir Mackenzie Bowell, in the House of Commons in 1874 to expel Riel from Parliament, Sir George found that: "The severest critic cannot show that on any question on which Parliament has given a decision since Confederation, he has acted under less generous motives or with a narrower view of the interests of Canada than have his English-speaking fellow-subjects. Even where religious questions were involved, as in the Jesuit Estates Bill, the Remedial Bill of 1896 and the granting of a Constitution to Alberta in 1905, his vote was divided, as was the vote of the English-speaking representatives."

From spring until autumn, the industrial activities of Canada are in full blast; there is work for everyone, and employment for all the country's capital—save in the occasional years of depression. The farmers, manufacturers, bankers, financiers, artisans, railwaymen, everyone who has a place in the country's life, are fully employed; but when the winter comes there is a falling-off of activities: the great building trade comes to an end; the lakes and waterways are closed to navigation; the agrarian activities are confined indoors. Lumbering is shifted from the mills to the woods. There are few activities that do not feel the change; the many are influenced by it and the work and trade of the country is sharply directed into seasonal movements. We have seen that, generally speaking, the French-Canadian is fonder of staying on the land than the English-Canadian, but after all that is only a tendency; in course of time the inexorable levelling process will run its course and the two, English and French, will be alike disposed to field and factory—if Buckle is right.

The winter tie-up vitally affects the intellectual

life of Canadians—English and French—directing
it as well as material things into common seasonal
movements. The lessening of the work on the farm
enables the children to continue their school training longer than is usual in rural countries, and the
farm holds or controls the movements of more than
one-half of Canada's population. As a result,
although there may be few of great learning, there
are few of great ignorance in Canada. The win-
ter-bound months afford a well recognised opportunity for reading, meditation, and discussion. The
politician looks upon the early spring as the birth
season of political and social opinion; Nature,
while apparently inactive under ice and snow, is
in reality renewing her fertility; and mankind, in
comparative physical rest, takes a new hold upon
things intellectual, or relaxes in pleasure. The
winter is the season of stock-taking. The merchant
counts his goods; the farmer sums up last season's
results and lays out his plans for the coming year;
the artisan formulates his demands for the May-
day scale of wages and terms of employment.

Thus climate is a great levelling influence upon
Canadian character!

The social life of a people is vitally influenced by
the comparative density of population and the
means for intercourse. Quebec has only 5.69 people to the square mile; Ontario has 9.67 people to
the square mile. In both Provinces there are
frontier men living apart, in communities practically unorganised; even in the old settled districts,

by reason of the bad highways, communication is limited, as compared with better settled countries. Road improvement is on the way in both Quebec and Ontario, but it will be many years before it is possible to have the intimate social life of Old England. Quebec has a greater percentage of rural population than Ontario, 51.56 per cent. of its people being classed as rural, as against 47.35 per cent. in Ontario. The significance of these figures towards homogeneity becomes plain when we remember that there are 370 people to the square mile in the United Kingdom and only 22 per cent. of its population is rural.

We have found difference in the aptitude of each nationality for trade, and yet both are engaged in trade. The French-Canadians are by no means exclusively farmers; nor are the English-Canadians exclusively townsmen. In agriculture both nationalities conform pretty much to the same practices; they are not separated by the wide gulf that often divides men in intensive and extensive agriculture. And both are mainly freeholders, owning land in equal amounts and of practically equal values. Contrast this position with that of Cousin Hodge in England, who is almost invariably a tenant. Fortunately for those who abhor heterogeneity, the economic interests of the two nationalities are practically identical.

We seldom pause to think how near the two stock nationalities are to each other; we emphasise too often only the differences. It is between Western Canada (Manitoba, Saskatchewan and Alberta) and Eastern Canada (Ontario, Quebec and the Maritime Provinces) that lie the real differences in Climate, Food, Soil, and the General Aspect of Nature which "gave rise to different habits of national thought." It is here, in course of time, that Canadians must face the real problem in heterogeneity—if Mr. Buckle is right. Let those laugh who will at this prediction; they are thinking of to-day, not of to-morrow.

The men who speak French have been in this country, subject to Buckle's influence of "its climate, its soil, its food, and its aspects of Nature" for several hundred years. "The French-Canadian loves this land because he has taken root in it," writes C. W. Colby, of McGill. "He feels that his ancestors fought the savage and tamed the wilderness, without much help from outside. His face is not set toward France, nor, so far as I can make out, is it set toward Europe at all—save in matters of religion. Mme. Hébert, the wife of the first genuine colonist, declined to take her children back to France when Quebec fell before the English in 1629. She had fixed her fortunes in the New World and meant to remain. There is something symbolical in this."

Some day men who speak English in Canada will feel much the same way—if Buckle is right. We often forget that Canadians who speak English are such comparatively recent comers. From the statistics of population it is fair to assume that the average English-speaking Canadian family has been in Canada for not more than two generations; and yet, within this short time, the change from English to Canadian is apparent. The Canadian may be taken for an American on the streets of London, but rarely for an Englishman. Nor is it the tone of voice, the inflexion of words, and the cut of clothes, although these things count in making the distinction; there is already an apparent organic difference between the men of British North America and the men of the United Kingdom.

If I import sheep from Shropshire for my Ontario farm, I must not expect to clip real Shropshire wool for more than a limited number of years. I may call it "Shrop," to distinguish it from other wools of the country, but it will, in course of time, become unlike that which clothes the sheep that mow the grass on England's Welsh border county. The story of the influence of climate, of soil, and of food, is told in the changing texture of the wool. The General Aspect of Nature may not affect the sheep; but we know that birds and animals are vitally affected by what they see in their surroundings; and so are men. Even on a little island like Corsica, my friend M. L. Santini, tells me there is a race difference between hillsmen and plainsmen. The two nationalities in this country have been spared Nature's obstacle to homogeneity, which works with the others, for change in mankind.

Some years ago, when a meeting of the British Association for the Advancement of Science had brought literary and scientific "lions" from the United Kingdom to this country, one of them was my guest. He had spent some previous weeks in investigating Canadian conditions, and, naturally, I was interested in his conclusions. "Are we producing a distinctive race type in Canada?" I asked. "Certainly," he replied. "It is quite evident; and will be more apparent as the years go by." "It is true of the French-Canadian, but is it true of the Canadian who speaks English?" I asked. "Just as true of the English-Canadian as of the French-Canadian," was his reply. "You must remember that the French-Canadian was here several centuries before the English-Canadian. The very hills and streams make a people what they are. English are no more immune than French from the influence of environment upon character. Homogeneity is inevitable—in time." He had been reading Buckle.

Canadians of both nationalities have affection for the land of Canada, and that love is patriotism. It is the same soil, the same hills, lakes, and rivers, which the one loves in French and the other in English—the same patriotism. A common love, has ever led men into common paths. As time goes on, there will be a clearer distinction between love for the country of origin, and love for the home country—both equally admirable in their way. Ages will remove the memory of the hedgerows of Old England—regret the inevitable if you will—and change the affection for English soil into an admiration for the sterling qualities of the English people, and a deeply set respect for their administration of Empire.

The length of the course towards homogeneity will depend entirely upon the man-made obstacles placed in Nature's way. If the reader be sincerely desirous of speeding Nature on her course; if he be anxious to have his neighbour work with him, think with him, he will surely realise that the surest way, and perhaps the only way, is to have his neighbour like him. If he wants men to accept his way of thinking about things, then that way must be made attractive. Experience has taught us that as individuals, and experience has taught us that as a nationality. Shakespeare did more than any other man to bring Scot and Englishman into approximate homogeneity; and Burns did his part, for while he intensified the national spirit of the Scot he made the Scot less "unspeakable" to the Englishman. Out of such influences came the will of both Scot and Englishman to work and think together.

And yet homogeneity in the United Kingdom is only approximate. There are still Scots and Englishmen and Welshmen, and Irishmen; and, personally, I hope there always will be. For homogeneity is a false god, an unlovely idol that is none the stronger or more durable for having a congruity of parts. And, personally, I hope there will always be English-Canadians and French-Canadians. Each has a service to perform which the other cannot do; and the State machinery is capable of being directed in preserving and developing that individual capacity for service, that culture to which the "old inhabitants" cling, as well as the culture of the "new inhabitants," and still leave a reserve power sufficient to care for the more limited culture and lesser capacity of the easily forgotten "aborigines." Personally, I am not any more anxious to force my mind upon my neighbour than to have him force his mind upon me. It has been my good fortune to know both John R. Robinson of the "Telegram" and M. Henri Bourassa of "Le Devoir"—outstanding figures in the Canadian clash. Much alike in several respects, by reason of differences, they are each capable, under a truce to the national feud, of carrying separate offerings to their common country. I would not for anything have Robinson made over into a Catholic-French-Canadian, nor have Bourassa made over into a Presbyterian-Scotch-Canadian. That would mean loss to the State, not gain; and an inestimable loss, if it were followed by conversion of their compatriots and co-religionists. The United Kingdom is the stronger for its measure of heterogeneity; and likewise Canada is stronger. We must not forget that granite is not homogeneous, and yet, according to the man who makes the dictionary, it has strength, durability, and "takes a high polish," three very desirable elements in a State, particularly the "polish." I cordially subscribe to the statement of Dr. Sarolea that "We believe in nationality, not because any one nation has monopolised all the virtues, but because no nationality can possibly monopolise or has monopolised all the virtues; because each nation has only received certain specific gifts; and because other nations and other conditions are required to develop other gifts which may be equally important." Canada is not unfortunate in possessing men and women determined to hold fast in the New World to the two cultures of the Old that have done most for civilisation.

Some day Dame Nature will have ironed out our kinks, and we shall be regarded as men indigenous to the climate, soil, food, and general aspects of Nature of the country in which we live—if Buckle is right. Some day we shall have the same habit of national thought—if Buckle is right. Let us then draw the fires of the man-made crucible, and let Nature do her work in the "natural" way. But until that some day—and I do not look forward to it with the pleasure of anticipation—let us have an English-Canadian nationality, and a French-Canadian nationality, and a Canadian nationality. Three nationalities and still one nationality; although apart, we shall still be together. We shall not be homogeneous, but, better still, we may be harmonious in diversity.

BOOKS OF REFERENCE

Henry Thomas Buckle, *History of Civilisation in England*. Hearst.

Edward S. Corwin, *The French Policy and the American Alliance*. Princeton University Press.

Sir George W. Ross, *Getting into Parliament and After*. Briggs.

C. W. Colby, *Canadian Types of the Old Régime*. Holt.

Charles Sarolea, *The Anglo-German Problem*. Nelson.

CHAPTER XIV

TOLERANCE

MOHAMMEDANS had an easy way of deciding the vexed questions of religion and nationality; with them the two were identical. "All true believers are brothers," said they; and being anxious to increase the family relations, gave non-Mohammedans so many minutes to come into the family circle or get out of the world. Mohammedanism grew. Its growth, however, was largely due to its propagation in lands where men changed their religions as did the Vicar of Bray—with the government. But there is this to be said for Mohammedanism: when you are in, you are in; and it cannot be said for Christianity: for when you are in, you are usually out unless the neighbours are of your particular cult.

Less than one-third of the world, according to Dr. Jordan, an authority on comparative religions, is Christian; and that third is a seething mass of suspicion and conflict—and of the two, open conflict is in some ways preferable. Five-sixths of King George's subjects—again according to Jordan —deny the inspiration of the Christian teachings, and live in greater harmony than do the one-sixth that profess to regulate their lives by those teachings. Just why men believing in the birth,

life, and death of Jesus and the precepts of the
"Sermon on the Mount," should be so intolerant,
has never been satisfactorily explained; and with
an explanation we are not now concerned.

It is the effect of those differences on Canadian
nationality with which we are alone concerned—a
subject upon which a layman writes only after he
has surrendered all hope of living at peace with his
neighbours.   According to the last census returns,
40 out of every 100 Canadians are Roman Catholics; the 60 are mainly members of the various
Protestant Churches.   There are pagans in Canada,
white and red; there are Mormons half-openly
avowing a belief in polygamy; Jews denying the
Divinity of Jesus; Doukhobors denying all authority of the State; Confucianists, Buddhists, and
Hindus; but the main conflict is within the
Christian Church, between Protestants and Roman
Catholics, who, in the last analysis, believe in the
same fundamentals of religion, and whose social
life is practically identical.

The French-Canadians, practically all Roman
Catholics, constitute twenty-eight per cent. of the
country's population; leaving twelve per cent. as
non-French Roman Catholics.   National lines in
Canada do not entirely follow religious lines, for
many of the English-speaking Catholics are bitterly opposed to French nationality.   In fact, upon
Bishop Fallon, an Irish Catholic cleric, rests much
of the responsibility for the present crusade against
French-Canadian pretensions.   Notwithstanding

this, most of the arguments advanced against the French-Canadian claims have a religious bias. It is contended in the press of Ontario that Cardinal Begin and the hierarchy are keeping the French-Canadians ignorant of the English language to keep them Catholic. Is the converse then true? are the French-Canadians being forced to learn English in order that they may be converted to Protestantism? The one supposition is no more absurd than the other; but the truth is that a French priest is French, and an Irish priest, Irish! Buttoning a clerical collar every morning does not affect a man's nationality.

Yet language has an effect upon religion. There is but one God: whatever their differences, English- and French-Canadians, Protestants and Catholics, agree upon that. But there is "God" and "le bon Dieu"—both the same, unless your children are forced to think of "le bon Dieu" as God, to make their prayers to God, instead of to "le bon Dieu"; and that is the inevitable result of conversion in language. Then there comes a real living difference. All the adjectives which are applied to the Divine Being—loving, guiding, protecting, with the mental pictures and associations which they imply—all are changed; and when the change is made by force, even to the wisest and most scholarly it seems vital. To the less wise and less scholarly, to the average man and woman, it is a loss of the best friend; to the race, it is a calamity.

The feeling against the French in Canada, in certain sections of the country, is based upon the belief that they belong to an intolerant Church. But intolerance is not the exclusive property of any Church. There are few Churches which in the past have not been guilty of intolerance. There are men who are antagonistic to the French-Canadians because they belong to a Church which they suppose to be disloyal to the British Crown. But disloyalty is not the property of any Church; it is an attribute of a people repressed, and may become that of a Church only if it believes itself to be the victim of persecution.

I write feelingly upon this phase of the subject, for my family came to the New World in search of brotherly love. In the colonial days they landed on the shores of New England, and finding it a Protestant community, proceeded to make themselves at home. Much to their surprise, Cotton Mather and his sect would have none of them, tied them with ropes to wagon-wheels, and then prodded the oxen. The Protestants of New England mutilated what was left of my ancestors and drove them from the country.

There were men of their faith, according to a memorial transmitted by Edward Burroughs to King Charles II, who received 370 stripes from a whip with knotted cords; "two unhappy wretches were cut to bits by 139 blows from pitched ropes; others were put neck and heels in irons or burnt deeply in hand"; some had their ears cut off by the hangman, while other free-born subjects of the King were "sold for bondmen and bondwomen to the Barbadoes, Virginia, or any of the English plantations." And these things were done in the name—not the professed spirit—of Puritanism in the New World only a few generations ago.

Not that my forefathers were lacking in Protestantism! They protested against the Pope and all his priests—but they protested against the Protestant priests as well. Sorrowfully I must confess, they protested too much. Travelling their weary way to what is now New Jersey, they lived there until the days of the American Revolution; when, having protested most of all against war, they surrendered their principle of non-resistance and, with the unerring instinct of the family for unpopular causes, accepted militant loyalty to the British Crown. Immediately after the war they were imprisoned on Staten Island, and finally found a refuge in the land now called Ontario—which had remained British by the loyalty of the French-Canadians and the influence of the Roman Catholic Church.

I have related so much of the history of my unfortunate family, because a man's religious views are influenced largely by tradition, and for another reason: it will be seen from this story, insignificant as it is, that I have good reason for saying that the Roman Catholic Church did not, in the days of religious persecution, possess a monopoly of intolerance; and so far from being disloyal to the British Crown in Canada, has been the reverse. Of the fourteen colonies which Great Britain had in America at the beginning of the last quarter of the eighteenth century, thirteen were English-speaking and Protestant; only one was French-speaking and Catholic, and only that one was loyal. It is set down in every history of the period that when the French-Canadians hesitated between Britain and America—they had been British only a short time—the Church threw its great weight on the side of Great Britain. It is true that this was done, not through a mere unreasoning sentiment, but because the Church relied upon the promise of its freedom that had been made at the Conquest. Reasoned loyalty is invariably based upon a feeling of security in the things most prized.

It is impossible to say what the attitude of the English-Canadian majority would be towards French nationality if the French were Protestant—for they are not Protestant. Certainly some of their opponents would withdraw from active opposition, and have publicly said so. "The Hamilton Times" thinks (September, 1912) that "If the French-Canadians were Protestants there would be no French question"; while the "St. Thomas Times" was (November 28, 1912) of the opinion that "The reason why Canada is opposed to the French language is merely a matter of religion. The majority in Canada has decided that they live in a Protestant country." It is ever a question of

majority : might is right. Certain it is that the conflict of nationalities has been intensified and embittered by the added conflict of religions. Religious
intolerance is by some—and I confess myself of the
number—regarded as the hot-bed from which
spring forth our unfragrant national dissensions.

The average Ontario Protestant firmly believes
that the French of Canada are priest-ridden, and
with fraternal zeal would be his brothers' keeper.
Not long ago I was travelling through the Province
of Quebec with a friend who, pointing through the
car window to a little French village that clustered
around a massive grey-stone church, said :

"There is a picture which illustrates the burdens
imposed upon the people of Quebec by the Church
of Rome."

"Do you know Richmond Hill, just north of
Toronto?" I asked; and he did. "About the same
population," I suggested; and he agreed. "There
are five churches at Richmond Hill," I continued,
"with five separate costs for heating, lighting, and
preaching. Which do you think pays the more
for religion—the people of the village we have
just passed, or the people of Richmond Hill?"
Then we talked of other things.

The average English-Canadian believes that the
French priest takes a hand in politics, and perhaps
he does. In 1896 there was more than a rumour
that the Quebec hierarchy had declared in favour
of the Tupper Government. In 1917 there were
Protestant clergy who, from the pulpit, preached

the doctrine of eternal damnation for those who
voted against the Union Government. The only
difference that I can find between the incidents,
is that in 1917, the Ontario laity accepted the
dictation of their clergy, while in 1896 the Quebec
laity refused the dictation of theirs. On both
occasions the clergy believed that vital issues
were at stake and directed their people accordingly. I am not protesting against clerical interference in politics; I am only asking the reader
to remember that interference in politics is not a
practice peculiar to the Province of Quebec and
the Roman Catholic Church.

I refuse to believe that Sir Wilfred Laurier, Sir
Lomer Gouin, Judge Maréchal, Senator Belcourt,
Senator Beaubien, the Hon. Thos. Chapais, Aimé
Geoffrion, Charles Wilson, and many other strong,
able, French-Canadians that anybody can think of,
are priest-ridden. They are admittedly competent to think for themselves in material matters;
it is absurd presumption to pretend that they are
not equally competent to select for themselves a
course in matters spiritual. After all, is not religion "a phase of the whole struggle for existence."

It is difficult—oh, so difficult—for one man to
understand another man's alien religion. He looks
through his own stained windows into the stained
windows of the other man, and believes that what
he sees is the other man's religion; but in reality he
has only a distorted concept of colouring. If he be
a Catholic and wants to know what the Protes-

tants believe he calls upon Archbishop McNeil, and if he be a Protestant and wants information of the Roman Catholic faith he raps at the door of Archdeacon Cody. But scholars in comparative religions as they are, neither of them has the sympathetic understanding of the other's belief. As a result of this method of obtaining second-hand religious information, neither religious party ever really understands the other; and, misunderstanding, each proceeds to critise the other. The harmony of the world would be immeasurably improved if men were to accept the spirit expressed by the Catholic historian, Lord Acton, when he wrote to Mary Gladstone: "I scarcely venture to make points against the religion of other people, from a curious experience that they have more to say than I know, and from a sense that it is safer to reserve censure for one's own, which one understands more intimately."

We cannot all think alike in religion, for the simple reason that we are not all alike. That which helps one most may not help another as well as something else. If religion means harmony with the Infinite, then the Churches, after all, are but vehicles to carry men to a realisation of God, and an understanding of His will. Likewise, nationalities are a means of carrying men to a fuller development of life. Once we accept that position, it naturally follows that we must have an intense conviction of the duty of toleration. Am I tolerant? becomes the question which each man must put to himself—and answer. "Every man should let alone others' prejudices and examine his own," said John Locke. "Nobody is convinced of his by the accusation of another; he recriminates by the same rule and is clear." Bishop Creighton, in his little book on "Persecution and Tolerance," expresses the same thought—and it is the vital one —with the statement that while men realised the evil of intolerance, "there was the practical question, Who was to begin? If you were to tolerate your neighbour and allow him to win a majority of one, would he tolerate you? Cromwell would 'meddle with no man's conscience,' but he would not allow him 'to exercise the mass,' or to use the Anglican Liturgy. Tolerance was not the doctrine of any sect or party. It was not the product of superior enlightenments, still less of growing indifference to religious questions. It was the result of social development; and it rests solely on the basis of empiricism. Practically we are tolerant because no harm comes of our being so."

No harm from being tolerant! Think of these words, written by the celebrated Anglican bishop who delved most deeply into the history of intolerance; and then of the suffering, the awful pain that, since the dawn of history, has been following in the wake of intolerance. We have got beyond the cruelties of Tyburn trees, and the fires of Smithfields, and the tortures of the thumb-screw, but we have not got beyond inflicting pain by intolerance. There is suffering in the loss

THE CLASH

in one's native land of a mother's cultural tongue, and there is suffering in the intolerant spoken word, often the unconsciously intolerant word, which belittles and sneers at that which others hold dear. There is "no harm" in tolerance and yet there are men who have twisted their minds into a belief that they are serving God, and King, and mankind, by opposing nationalities and religions other than their own.

Surely the standard of conduct which regulates our relations to Church and national groups should not be less high than that by which we regulate our relations to individuals. And yet there are men who, shrinking from the thought of self-excellence, become downright braggarts in speaking of the nationality or Church to which they belong; who, scorning to deride their fellowmen as individuals, spend themselves in ferreting out the faults of an alien nationality and, colouring and magnifying them, publish them within range of their influence. Motive is, after all, a fundamental test of conduct. Do we honestly seek to benefit mankind when we criticise nationalities and religions other than our own, or do we rather find in it a delicious and seemingly respectable vent for our prejudices?

I am told of a school in Quebec, where instructors dilate upon the shortcomings of English-Canadians as revealed in history, and teach their pupils to regard the English-Canadians of to-day with distrust. I *know* a school in Ontario where under the guise of solving Canada's national problem, boys who someday will be called upon to shoulder a part of the country's administration, are being sedulously innoculated with what the masters believe to be a knowledge of the shortcomings of French-Canadians. No matter the defence as to intention; the boys are coming out of that school having learned to distrust and despise their compatriots of the French tongue and the Catholic religion.

How far have we progressed from perpetrating "the miserable and impudent falsehoods which a large class of English writers formerly directed against the morals and private character of the French." It was Henry Thomas Buckle, who wrote the words which I have quoted, and "these things," continued Buckle, "tended not a little to embitter the feelings then existing between the two first countries of Europe; irritating the English against French vices, irritating the French against English calumnies." Buckle died in 1862, and yet lived late enough to think that "the progress of improvement by bringing the two countries into close and intimate contact, has dissipated these foolish prejudices and taught each people to admire, and what is still more important, to respect each other, and the greater the contact the greater the respect."

We in Canada are lingering behind in the progress of toleration, we are *now* where the English of England, and the French of France *were* in the era of chauvinism; we are each continuing to put the emphasis upon the other's failings rather than upon the other's virtues. And through our whole course of criticism runs the element of religious antagonism.

There are five or six railways that carry between Buffalo and New York. In my opinion, one of them is best, and by it I always travel; and yet each railway has its patrons and its partisans. Sometimes there is a wreck; but, as a rule, all the travelers on all the roads reach New York—and now and then people get there by walking. It would be presumptious egoism for me to challenge the judgment of the sensible men and women who prefer a different way to the one I think "best." Perhaps, after all, my way may be only "best" for me. Of course, if I am an official of "the best railway," I may pardonably point out its advantages, may shout them from the housetops, paint them by brush and pen; but a sense of decency and the ethics of commerce will forbid my running down the other lines. Surely Church ethics should not be less generous. Churchmen may feel that the other ways lead to Helena, instead of to Gotham; but they ought to stop and consider that there are men and women, whose judgment is ordinarily as good as their own, travelling by the other ways.

I know no Church that has not men of deep spiritual character within its membership. I could not believe in a God, if men, surrendering themselves to Him with the soul's cry "Lead Thou Me On," following where they were led, are in a presence which is not God's. No, we cannot all attain a realisation of spiritual truths by the same way, any more than we can all by the same way attain equal knowledge of things that are not spiritual. Nor can we all render the same service. May it not be that each Church, and each nationality, is complementing the services of the other; doing a something which the other cannot do.

What is, and what ought to be in religion and nationality, was illustrated to me the other day by the conversation of two little girls whom I know. They had been discussing religion rather vigorously when the aggressor—a Protestant, by the way —said, "I hate your Church and you hate mine; and that's all there is to it." Grown-ups rarely say the thing so bluntly, but after all the Hymn of Hate is none the less unlovely for being concealed in the heart or expressed in redundant verbiage. "No," answered the Roman Catholic child, "I love my Church and you love yours; that's what there should be to it." Does not candour compel us to admit if Roman Catholics and Protestants, English-Canadians and French-Canadians, were to accept that spirit each would be living in closer conformity to what is best in life.

Religion is inextricably tied up in our national problem, and has been since "the late Definitive Treaty of Peace concluded at Paris 1763, to grant the liberty of the Catholick Religion to the inhabitants of Canada." This definite engagement, written into Britain's deed of possession, should not be lightly passed over in a study of the national problems of the country. At that time the United Kingdom itself had not full religious liberty, and it was the intention, as expressed in the debates over Canada's first constitution, that there should be "in some part of His Majesty's Dominion an asylum where Roman Catholics might go if persecuted." In the days of the Quebec Act Great Britain was only imbibing the spirit of toleration. The standard of religious toleration within the Empire was thus first planted by British men in Canada, and it must not be lowered by those who, under autonomy, have inherited their authority.

It is true there are timid souls who honestly fail to realise that Roman Catholics, as well as others, have emerged from the Middle Ages; who have forgotten that Copernicus was opposed by Protestants as well as Roman Catholics; that Kepler had to give up the idea of being a Calvinist minister because his views on the planetary movements were not orthodox; who have no confidence that freedom can exist in a state controlled by Roman Catholics. To them I commend these words of Charles Fox, taken from the Debates on the Quebec Bill: "No one has urged the circumstance of the people of Canada being Roman Catholics as an objection to an assembly, and I trust I shall never hear such an objection stated; for no one who has ever conversed with Roman Catholics can, I think, believe that there is anything repugnant, in their views, to the principles of political freedom. The principles of political freedom, though not practised in Roman Catholic countries, are as much cherished and revered by the people, as in Protestant countries."

To-day there is, in the Province of Quebec, a State governed by the representatives of a people essentially Roman Catholic in spirit and numbers; and, as Fox prophesied, the Protestant minority does not have to plead in Quebec for freedom. The English-speaking Protestant press of the Province is practically a unit in declaring the impartiality of the French-Canadian Catholic administration. The English-speaking Protestant minority in Quebec has been given practical autonomy in the administration of its educational affairs, and yet its numbers are only slightly greater than those of the French-Catholic minority in Ontario and less than half the total Roman Catholic population of Ontario. Is it too much to expect as much impartiality, as much national and religious toleration from the English-speaking and Protestant Provinces of Confederation, which have, under the British North America Act, an authority no greater than that of Roman Catholic Quebec?

Tolerance in religion and nationality does not imply the surrender of a man's love for his own. The English-Canadian and Protestant may stoutly cherish his own and at the same time encourage the culture and religion of the French-Canadian. As

19 c.

Dr. Hobhouse well says, "We have to work toward peace through nationality and not against it." And he might have said the same of religion. For the principle is the same. "God has divided man into men that they might help each other," said that old heathen, Seneca. And he told a wholesome truth. Let each nationality respect the other; each help the other in preserving and improving that which each thinks is best in its own culture; and out of respect and sympathy must come, not homogeneity, but that better something else in our national life, in our religious life, in life generally— harmony in diversity.

> "It is the secret sympathy,
> The silver link, the silken tie,
> Which heart to heart and mind to mind,
> In body and in soul can bind."

Books of Reference

Canada Year Book.

Lord Acton, *Letters to Mary Gladstone.*

M. Creighton, D.D., *Persecution & Tolerance.* Longmans.

H. & E. Egerton and W. E. Grant, *Canadian Constitutional Development.* Musson.

Max Nordau, *The Interpretation of History.* Heinneman.

CHAPTER XV

SOMETIMES it is well to commence an investigation with a few figures in mind, and before attempting to dissect French Canada's part in the Great War, we ought to know in what proportion the several elements within the country voluntarily contributed to the overseas forces of Canada. We will take our figures from an opponent of the French-Canadians, Dr. Edwards, a member representing an Ontario constituency in the Dominion House of Commons. From the floor of Parliament, he said: "Out of a population 3,564,702 English-speaking Canadians born in Canada, 125,245 have proceeded overseas, or over three and one-half per cent. Out of a population of 813,714 English-speaking people born outside of Canada, 155,-095 or 19 per cent., have answered the call of King and country."

Clearly, as English-Canadians we ought not to go further without an explanation. We cannot very well throw stones at the French-Canadians while we are living in glass houses. If numbers contributed to overseas forces are to be the measure of loyalty, we English-Canadians are at the outset under a suspicion of comparative disloyalty, and are the last men who should prefer a similar charge against our neighbors. And yet is not that what we have done? Are we not in the unenviable position of those who, having been caught red-handed in wrong, protest that someone is even more guilty? Since good and bad are determined by comparison, and English-Canadian enlistment was bad when placed beside that of the British-born, did we not seek to make it good by comparison with that of French Canada? There are men—myself among the number—who believe that English-Canadians are as loyal to Great Britain as are Englishmen; and yet the numbers of English-Canadians enlisting are in comparison with the Englishmen of Canada—the Scots and Irish as well—woefully deficient. There are English-Canadians who explain away their own shortcomings in forty different ways, without impugning English-Canadian loyalty, and then naively confess that French-Canadian failure to enlist is explainable only by clerical dictation. We ought not to refuse to have others tried by the evidence with which we discharge ourselves. But let us deal with our own case first, and allow the French-Canadian case a few minutes' respite.

A realisation of the necessity of fighting for freedom in Europe came none too readily to any of us who were not of Europe. England was only thirty or forty miles away—within sounding distance of the guns—and it was months before Englishmen realised that the last pound of English energy and the last pound of English sterling had to be thrown into the cause. All that time—if we are to believe the London papers—the French people were asking "When are the English coming?" The brave little army of English regulars fighting with incredible valour, was swallowed up in the hordes of Frenchmen and Germans who swayed back and forth in indescribable slaughter—and was finally practically lost by extermination. There was a reason why England did not, at the outset, put her young men by the millions into the field. What we can do to-day largely depends upon what we have done yesterday. England had trained her people for peace and could not over-night fit the nation mentally and physically for war. Her hands were tied by the past.

We Canadians, three thousand miles away, for weeks after the declaration of war, turned in our half-sleep and murmured, "It must have been a bad dream; we shall surely awake in the morning to find there is no war." The Great War did not at first seem real; it did not seem possible; at least to those of us whose fathers' and fathers' fathers had been born and reared in the centre of the North American Continent. The thought-world is the real world, and few of us had thought of war in connection with ourselves. The stirring days of the seventeen seventies, were far away and indistinct; the invasion of 1812 was remembered best by the old-fashioned, picturesque uniforms of its participants; while, 77 years later, the rebellion of 1837 appeared little more than a good-sized election row. War did not seem to us a business with which we ourselves were connected. I am now expressing the sentiments of the native-born of English Canada, and I speak with a conviction born not merely of my own mind, but of the extent of the response of my compatriots.

The call for overseas service in English Canada was first answered by the militia men. They, of all classes within the community, came nearest to understanding. They had, at least, thought of war and had pictured themselves in many a sham-battle as actually fighting, killing foes—and sometimes Germans—and defending homes and principles. The militia men, and men who in their youth had been militia men, shouldered the burden of raising the first contingents. It was they who pleaded with the men of substance for the funds with which to carry on recruiting. Just why it was necessary to secure by private subscription from ten to twenty thousand dollars for each battalion raised in Toronto and Montreal, just why field-kitchens and battalion-trucks had to be purchased out of private funds, I do not know. Nor is knowing material; that these things were, is material. None can tell how few English Canada would have contributed to overseas forces if it had not been for the arduous labours of the men who were, at the time or had once been, officers and privates in the militia. They were the foundation upon which our overseas contributions were built,—and it is hard to build without a foundation.

Militia men paraded the streets with bugles and drums, raising the martial ardour of the people; they coaxed and scolded from street corners for recruits; and canvassed for them from house to house, and factory to factory. And when it was all over—one half of Ontario's voluntary army was secured from one-eighth of Ontario's population— the British-born.

Dr. Edwards estimated that only seven-tenths of one per cent. of the French-Canadian population had enlisted. Comparing this figure with his previously quoted figures, it will be seen that the British-born did six times as well as the English-Canadians, and the English-Canadians five times as well as the French-Canadians. That is Dr. Edward's computation of patriotism, based on voluntary enlistment in Canada. But are we as sure of Dr. Edward's figures comparing English-Canadian and French-Canadian enlistment, as we are of those comparing native-born and foreign-born? Volunteers gave their places of birth, but did not submit their genealogies. Then by what method was the nationality of the native-born determined? Presumably by counting the French names on the enrollment lists—a procedure obviously open to criticism. If the reader had been asked to classify Private Wilson, would he have put him in the French list? I confess I should not have known what to do with him; for my Wilson acquaintances are about equally divided between the two nationalities. What about Corporal Pratte?

Again I should have been in a quandary. I
have a very good friend, born in England,
now living in Canada, who answers to that
name; and I know a full half-dozen more of
the name who, born in Ontario, are exceedingly
proud of being Catholic French-Canadians. There
are at least two well known men in Canada by
the name of Martin: one of them is a Presbyterian
Scotch-Canadian and Premier of Saskatchewan;
the other is a Catholic French-Canadian and
Mayor of Montreal. It may be thought that the
Christian names would keep the conscientious in-
vestigator straight in his count—and we must assume that those who counted the list wanted to be
impartial—but not so. Mayor Martin is the son
of Solomon Martin, and only a man prejudiced in
favour of the French-Canadians would have credited a man by that name to their list. Surely we
commonly think of George, Arthur, Paul, Ernest,
Joseph, Charles, Edmond, Albert, Henry, Archie,
Ferdinand, Simeon, David, Alfred, Oliver, and
Frederic, as English Christian names, and yet I
find that all were used years ago by French
priests in christening boys who are Senators and
Members of Commons to-day. I assume that the
reader would not hesitate to place a Canadian-born
Peter Brown on the English-Canadian side of the
house. And yet the Captain Peter Brown who won
the military cross was educated by French priests at
Mount St. Louis College, and believes himself to
be a French-Canadian. There are scores of names

such as Brown, Nelson, Wilson, Baker, Harwood, Fraser, Lindsay, Harvey, Scott, Otis, Barry, Martin, Daniel, Brien, Campbell, David, Miller, Richard, Raymond, Nichol and Thomas, borne by men whose nationality may be either English or French.

I am not seeking to maintain that French-Canadians enlisted in proportion to English-Canadians. Whilst their enlistments were not as small as described, they were smaller than they would have been under normal conditions—and conditions were not normal. The French-Canadians, like the Englishmen and English-Canadians were influenced by the past. Max Nordau has said that "the multitude have no historical sense"; they have "an incapacity to detect underlying connections or to trace back the causes and effects of phenomena," but I assume that the reader is not of the multitude and sincerely wants a correlation of the facts which account for French-Canadian failure to respond generously to the call of freedom in Europe.

There are some who maintain that the French-Canadians and the Roman Catholic church in Canada have been historically unwilling to support Great Britain. Even at the cost of digression we must, of necessity, dispose of that chronic charge by a survey of conditions when, on another occasion, British power was threatened in America.

When the English-speaking British of America threw off their allegiance to the King of Great Britain, back in the seventeen-seventies, "no stone was left unturned, no means were left untried to induce the French to revolt," says the historian. "Inflammatory proclamations inciting to rebellion were issued from the printing presses of Boston and Philadelphia, and posted at dead of night by mysterious, unknown hands, on the doors of the Canadian churches. The agents of the republic infested every village along the St. Lawrence, alternately cajoling and threatening the inhabitants. Freedom and assistance were promised to those who threw off the yoke of slavery; and the sword of the avenger was denounced on the cowards who meekly submitted to the British tyrants at the critical time when the rights of man were endangered and the friends of liberty in peril."

At the outbreak of the revolution there were only about a thousand British regulars in Canada, and not a single armed vessel. Of the civilian population, only a few hundred were English-speaking and many of these we are told, were "recalcitrant," by no means enthusiastic in the cause of Great Britain; many of them having come from the disaffected colonies were more inclined to throw off than to hold on to British sovereignty. Except for the handful of British regulars and the few hundred half-loyal English, the inhabitants were French-Canadian; clearly, by numbers and training the French-Canadians were masters of the situation.

With the Quebec Act in operation only a few weeks, the people were not wholly convinced of the genuineness of its guarantees. So the response to the Governor's call for volunteers was not immediate. There was no bi-lingual question in those days, no one to dispute the right of self-expression of the French-Canadian nationality in the land east or west of the Ottawa River, but the "new subjects" wanted assurances for the future.

There was also dissatisfaction because the inhabitants were not allowed to choose their own officers. Many of the seigneurs had returned to France after the country had been turned over to the British, and leadership fell largely upon the Church. Fortunately, the principal laymen and clergy of the colony believed that the assurances of the Quebec Act were something more than an expedient of the hour, and accepted them as an enduring pledge of the maintenance of French civil laws, of French customs, and of French culture in Canada. The young men were rallied to the British standard in sufficient numbers to resist the invaders and preserve the colony for the British.

An attempt has been made to picture the Canadians of that day as unintelligent yokels, whose assistance was not of material service. But we know better. Francis Parkman has given us a graphic description of the country and its inhabitants at the close of the French Régime, only a few years before. It may be true that many French-Canadians of that period were unschooled, although New France was probably as far ahead in education as New England. Whatever the faults of French colonial government, its system had, at least, one advantage needful for the day. As Parkman tells us, "It favoured military efficiency. The Canadian population sprang in great part from soldiers, and was to the last sympathetically reinforced by disbanded soldiers. Its chief occupation was a continual training for forest war; it had little or nothing to lose, and little to do but fight and range the woods."

For many years the Canadians had successfully defended their country from the inroads of American colonists, who, it must be remembered, had the backing of the British Government; and had they been so minded at this critical period, without the shadow of doubt could have established their independence, or at least have thrown off British sovereignty.

The outstanding fact of the period is the French-Canadians elected, of their own free will, to remain British.

Although France, in the Treaty of Alliance, concluded at Paris and ratified by Congress in 1779, expressly "forever renounced any part of the Continent of North America which, before the Treaty of Paris in 1763, or in virtue of that treaty," belonged to Britain, there was another course open by which her ancient colony might have been wrested from Great Britain and at the same time have been prevented from falling into the open arms of the United States. That plan lay in in-

dependence under French protection. That was
the plan of Vergennes, then the masterful direc-
tor of French foreign policy. He hoped to expel
the English and establish a free "agricultural and
commercial state which should govern itself under
the protection of France. In that way, he argued,
the country would be peopled by the French
themselves, and 'by any who choose to go there,'
and a national spirit, grounded on similarity of
language, customs and national character, and
kept alive by constant intercourse, would be
created substantially identical with that of France
herself."

The plans of Vergennes were defeated by the
stubborn loyalty of the French-Canadians to Britain.

There was also more than a suggestion of independence in the proclamation of Baron D'Estaing,
Commander of the French fleet in American
waters, calling upon the French-Canadians in the
names of Lévis and Montcalm, to assert themselves
against the loosely-held British power. Further
still, we are told that the three commissioners, Benjamin Franklin, Samuel Chase, and Charles Car-
rol, appointed by Congress to win over the French-
Canadians, finding that impossible, "tentatively
suggested that Canada might retain an independent
position in its relation to the rest of the states."
Whether Canada would have become independent,
or a State of the Union, if the French had listened
favorably to these suggestions, will never be

known; for, *relying on the inviolability of a British pledge of the right to self-expression, they remained true to Great Britain in the years when the Empire appeared to be crumbling to pieces.*

We, then, approach a consideration of the attitude of the French-Canadians of the year 1914, towards the Great European War and Britain's position in it, remembering that Canada is to-day British because French-Canadians refused to have it something else.

It will be remembered that a few years before, a bill had been submitted to the Canadian Parliament providing for the creation of a Canadian navy. The proposal met with violent opposition from two sources: those who thought the measure went too far and those who thought it did not go far enough. There were English-Canadians in Ontario who ridiculed the idea of a Canadian navy; its ships were "tin pot"; they would be useless in war and absurd in peace. The argument against the bill was the other way in Quebec. There a small group, calling themselves Nationalists, accused the Government of designing to sell the country to further Great Britain's greed for Imperialism. The Quebec opposition was not at first formidable. It lacked the one thing needful in politics. In these days political organisation is a considerable undertaking; it requires finance, and although M. Bourassa, its driving force, controlled a daily newspaper, his movement must have been confined within narrow limits without support of a practical and substantial nature. Curiously enough, that support was provided by a group of English-Canadians who, preaching Imperialism in Ontario, either found political consistency in supporting anti-Imperialism in Quebec, or did not mind inconsistency. Thus the propaganda of non-participation, through the coalition of Ontario genius for finance and Quebec genius for oratory, was spread throughout French Canada. Eloquent appeals were made on behalf of pacifism; harsh words were said of Great Britain; pathetic pictures were painted of hardships which participation in Britain's wars would bring to Canada.

When the war came, in 1914, none of the affected countries had been prepared except Germany. There was neither armament preparedness nor mental preparedness—and both were desirable; but if there had been no adequate campaigns for mental preparedness in the allied countries, there had been no deliberate campaign against it. There had been no systematic preaching of the gospel of pacifism—nowhere except in French Canada and Russia. But in the latter country the campaign was conducted in subterranean channels, and in the former in open air, supported by an alliance with one of the country's two great political parties.

When party politics are involved, men lose their critical faculties. Wrongs become rights, and rights wrongs; while means are measured by their prospects of success. We have habitually damned a certain clerical organisation with the odium of believing that "the end justifies the means"; but in truth the maxim properly belongs to the realm of party politics. "The Veteran," the official organ of the Great War Veterans' Association, says that they were "Conservative Imperialists who subsidised M. Bourassa and his friends to confer upon the population of Quebec the benefit of a prolonged education against participation in the wars of Great Britain." But—with partisan merits and partisan demerits, we are not concerned; and, remembering them, emphasising them, we shall serve no good purpose and may destroy our essential perspective of the true business in hand—the clash of nationalities in Canada, and its underlying forces. They were English-Canadians that, in 1911, backing a non-participation campaign in French Canada, a few years later, bitterly blamed French Canada for its success. That is the point to remember.

It is unjust to blame the French-Canadians for having accepted, in such numbers, the teachings of non-participation; for it must be remembered that after the campaign of 1911, men who derided the idea of Canada assisting Great Britain were chosen His Majesty's advisers. They became M. le Ministre This and M. le Ministre That. How can the men on the side-lines of Quebec be blamed for thinking that the people of Canada generally believed what, as political leaders, these ministers had preached so recently from the hustings in Quebec: that pacifism was righteousness, and

Canada ought not to take part in overseas warfare in Britain's behalf.   Under our system of government, men are supposed to be selected as Cabinet Ministers because their political views are agreeable to the majority.

Let me repeat: the outbreak of the war found no section of the world deliberately educated against war—except French Canada and Russia.

The French-Canadian Ministers, in the course of time, retracted what they had said as politicians seeking the confidence of the people.   But the retraction was not preached as energetically, as forcefully, as eloquently, as extensively, as the original doctrine.   Indeed, a number of years had passed before many of the converts knew there had been a change of heart in their former teachers. Even had the recantation been spread broadcast, it is still doubtful what the result would have been, for men cannot be pushed that way to-day and pulled back to-morrow.   But we must pass on to another phase of the complicated situation.

At first the Canadian armies were recruited solely by voluntary enlistment.   In English Canada appeals for recruits were made in the name of freedom.   It is true, as we have seen, no clear explanation was given of the nature of the freedom involved in the war; little or no attempt was made to define freedom; English Canada was not particularly interested in definitions and details.   Britain was at war; that was enough for many.   Even those who refused to enlist were ready to ad-

20 c.

mit the virtue of the cause.   But French Canada
was critical.   The word freedom had a particular
meaning for French-Canadians, for were they not
even then struggling to protect a freedom of self-
expression they had once exercised in Ontario
and Manitoba, in a land that had belonged to
their forefathers.   Whether the exercise had been
by privilege or right, does not, for our present purpose, matter; there had been exercise and there had
been deprivation; that is what we must remember
if we would understand the mental attitude of the
French-Canadians.   It was then being commonly
asserted that French-Canadian nationality had
freedom for self-expression only in that part of the
land acquired at the Conquest, marked off by the
boundaries of Quebec.   Under that doctrine there
were   "English-Canadian   Provinces"   and   a
"French-Canadian   Province."   Hence   French-
Canadianism was forced to become provincialism.

The recruiting agent could not very well declaim
in French Canada of Britain's indelible adherence
to freedom; could not point out that nowhere within the British Empire had culture been denied
freedom in a country acquired under conquest;
nowhere within the British Empire had a minority
insisting upon maintaining its national self-expression, been forced into an alien mould, nowhere—
except in Ontario and Manitoba.   It was the exceptions in which French Canada was concerned.
Admirable is the British spirit of freedom, would
have been the reply, but is it not in that spirit that

the "national" affairs of Canada should be administered?

> "If she be not fair to me,
> What care I how fair she be?"

It was almost equally hopeless to attempt distinction between what Britain had done and what
Ontario and Manitoba were then doing. The
French-Canadians would probably have admitted
that so long as Britain exercised direct control over
Canada, their national interests had been respected
and preserved in all the land acquired under the
Treaty of Paris, and that only with the coming of
responsible government under English-Canadian
domination, had they been curtailed. But that argument and that admission would not have helped
matters, for the French-Canadians would have answered: this is a British country which ought to be
administered in accordance with British principles.
And the answer seems to be unanswerable.

The war emphasised the necessity of unity. That
was its first outstanding lesson. But neither Ontario nor Manitoba held out an olive branch to the
French-Canadians; neither Province abated one
whit its demand for the limited use of the French
language in the schools. The press of Toronto, so
far from seeking a *via media* out of the difficulties,
continued to launch attacks against the French-
Canadians, with vitriolic appeals to race and religious passion. The gravity of war failed to temper
its course. For fear the reader may think I am using stronger words than necessary to describe the

all-important action of the Ontario press during
those trying, difficult, first months of the war, let
me give an illustration. On June 20, 1916, the
"Toronto News," then edited by Sir John Willison,
stated that "some of the clergy boasted that they
would compel Ontario by force of arms to submit
to Quebec's demand for enthronement of French in
this Province."   At the time, men's nerves were
painfully raw, yet the "News," edited by a direc-
tor of public thought in the community, cried
"Civil War."

Let us pause for a moment, even at the cost of
another partial digression, to analyse the form and
results of this call to arms. The Dominion of
Canada was armed as never before; great machine
shops were turning out ammunition, mainly under
English-Canadian direction; huge armies, consisting mainly of men born in the British Isles,
were in concentration camps.   Invasion of Ontario would have been mad suicide. It would
have been an untrained, unarmed mob, courting
annihilation at the hands of an efficient, powerful
army. And strangely enough, such a war, or rather
massacre, was apparently not abhorrent to some
English-Canadians. To raise the cry of Civil War
could serve no good purpose in English-Canadian
preparedness. If "The News" had reliable information that the clergy were planning to force
Ontario to submit by arms, the information became
legitimate news that should have been withheld
only for State reasons; but if the information was

unreliable, the printing of it became—well, I shall
let the reader fill in an appropriate adjective. "The
News" has saved us the trouble of investigating the
reliability of its information. It came not from the
paper's regular correspondents, who, surely, were
informed of conditions, but from "a visitor from
the United States." "The News" frankly said so.
Yet the announcement upon this scandalously
scanty foundation, was printed in scare-head type
in the editorial columns of a government organ. If
twenty visitors from the United States, or, for that
matter, twenty visitors from Jamaica, or any other
part of the world, had told "The News" that
twenty French priests had boasted that they would
compel Ontario to submit "to Quebec's demand for
enthronement of French," repetition of their irresponsible chatter would still have been condem-
nable.   Had the words been ever so true, their
repetition in "The News" could have had no other
effect than to sow dissension in a field where harmony was needed as the water of life. And that is
but one illustration of the many that might be given
of what Ontario's press—Conservative and Liberal
—was saying while recruiting agents sought to
stimulate enthusiasm for Britain's cause in Quebec.

Almost from the first days of the war the Ontario
press vented its sarcasm and caustic epithets not
merely upon the slackers of Quebec; no, upon Quebec as a Province, upon the French-Canadians as a
nationality. Ontario assumed that Quebec was going to be disloyal, and proceeded to prod it into

the trenches. If we remember the feeling that existed between the two Provinces, we can at once realise the results. It seems incredible that the press of Ontario should not have known that it could not raise soldiers in Quebec; should not have known that its activities in Quebec could not produce men; should not have known that it was daily harming, rather than helping, the cause for which it so volubly professed a love. If England had said to Ontario, to Canada, to Australia, and to South Africa, what Ontario said to Quebec—and she might have said more, with better reason—the Empire could not have held together. The Empire must have foundered in a turbulent sea of reproach. Nothing but England's generosity, England's sympathy, England's bigness, held, in the perilous first days of war, the roughly joined organism which men named Great Britain. If England followed the path towards unity and success, then Ontario trod the way that leads to disunity and failure.

We have seen that Ontario built its overseas battalions upon the foundation of its militia. But there was "only one French-Canadian infantry unit, with headquarters in the great City of Montreal, against three English-speaking infantry units; as against cavalry, artillery, army service and army medical corps, all practically English-speaking," in Montreal, according to an English-speaking officer high in the service. French-Canadian paucity of militia men before the war cannot

FRENCH CANADA AND THE WAR 287

very well be accounted disloyalty; for if French
Canada before the war had been strong in militia,
it might have been taken as evidence of preparation for overt disloyalty. Few thought then that
Canada would ever be engaged in a life and death
struggle with a foreign power, and there were
many who talked lightly, as did the "News," of a
conflict between French and English in Canada.
But let us hold tightly to the thread of the argument. Quebec in August, 1914, was exactly where
Ontario would have been without its thousands of
militia men trained to think of themselves as a part
of war. Quebec was without a foundation upon
which to build battalions for active service—and it
is hard to build without a foundation.

No! Quebec or rather French Canada, was not
where Ontario and English Canada would have
been without its militia. Her hands were tied by
the past—that was not all of her own making—and,
with the coming of the war, unfriendly hands were
to draw the knots still tighter. A body cannot be
pummelled without being bruised—not even a
body politic. And French Canada, when the war
opened in August, 1914, was black and blue and
bleeding; but still struggling to be all free. No one
loves and respects freedom for its own sake more
than our French-Canadian countrymen. No one
is more willing to give his all in its defence than
the French-Canadian. But many eyes were blinded
by tears of rage and sorrow at the loss of national
freedom in a part of the lands that were once their

fathers. Many did not at first clearly see the issue of freedom in Europe.

When the war broke out, voluntaryism was a principle of the British people. The principle may have been wrong; but it was ours; and we were proud of the fact that British men might serve or abstain from serving in the King's army, as they pleased. Like many another treasured ideal, voluntaryism went down in the cataclysm of the Great War. Voluntaryism failed to fill the ranks in the United Kingdom; failed in Australia; and failed in Canada. Then—there was nothing left but conscription. And after all, it is a postulate of democracy that all should bear equally the burdens of war. The argument seems plain; and yet it must be remembered it did not at first appeal to English men and women who for months after the war clung to the old system of voluntaryism Not until English coasts had been ravaged and destruction had fallen from the clouds upon English homes, did the government introduce conscription; there were murmurs of dissent, but they were downed by an aroused public who knew then that neither business nor politics could be carried on "as usual."

In Australia the people were consulted and refused to reverse the traditional British policy. There is no disloyalty to be implied in its rejection. Crawford Vaughan, a former Prime Minister of South Australia, recently told a Canadian Club audience that while "he himself had been an advocate of the democratic principle of conscription, the majority believed that the voluntary system would be adequate, and the result could not more be attributed to the Labour party than to any other party; even the men at the front so firmly believed in the higher morale of volunteers that they had voted against conscription on the ground that they did not wish 'to be mixed up with slackers.' "

Conscription was no more necessary for Canada than for Australia; and necessary for both, simply because the all-absorbing war had exhausted the resources of voluntaryism. That was the one fact that had to be squarely brought home to the people. Unhappily that one essential fact was smothered in Canada by an appeal to the passions of race and religion. From the first, before the government had announced its decision on the subject, before there had been an alignment of public opinion, the necessity of conscription was represented by men whose voices carried from one end of Canada to the other, as the result of French-Canadian failure to enlist for overseas service. Sir Robert and other English-Canadians manfully tried to stay the hand of those who made of conscription a race and religious issue, but their voices were drowned in the avalanche. Was it humanly reasonable to expect from French Canada substantial support for even a just measure urged upon these grounds?

Nor did Ontario conscriptionists rest here; as if to make doubly sure of French Canada's opposi-

tion, assaults were made upon the independence of
her laity and the loyalty of her clergy. At the back
of French-Canadian lethargy lay the directing
hand of the priest, it was urged. It may be true that
there were French-Canadian clergy as well as laymen affected by the campaign of non-participation
spread over Quebec in 1911 by English-Canadian
finance; but the advocates of conscription, omitting
that stage of our political development from consideration, carried the responsibility for non-participation direct to the doors of the Church. Especially upon the priests who had fled from France
in the days of her Church persecution, was heaped
the burden of abuse. "They seek revenge," it was
whispered from door to door, and gaining strength
by repetition, the charge was repeated openly from
the hustings. It may be that there were clerical
exiles who saw an intimate connection between
their own sorrows and the sorrows of France, but
nowhere is there a finer record of devotion and
sacrifice for native land than that which has been
left by the French priests who were in Canada at
the outbreak of the war. All but the aged and un-
fit answered in a body the call of the mother land.
While these charges of disloyal intrigue were being
made, Franciscans, Jesuits, Sulpicians, Christian
Brothers, Capuchins, Oblates, Trappists, Marists,
Eudists, Dominicans, all were represented *in the
ranks* of those who, with rifle and bayonet, fought
off the invading foe. While their detractors were
standing on the safe flooring of hustings several

thousand miles from danger, nearly a round score
of these priests had made the supreme sacrifice, and
lay buried beneath the Christian cross that marks
a soldier's grave; while others, more than a score
in number, bore upon living breasts, the military
crosses with which France decorates her brave.
There are among these French priests, wantonly
accused of disloyalty, more than a score who will
return to Canada as cripples, some armless and
others legless, and one who, returning, will never
more see Canada, for he is blind. When the history of the war is written, one of its inspiring pages
will be the deeds of these French Roman Catholic
priests who left Canada to defend as private soldiers their mother country, and not its least humil-
iating page will be the story of those who, exalt-
ing prejudice above patriotism, succeeded in setting race against race, and Church against Church
by defaming the names of those of French nationality and the Roman Catholic religion who gave
their all to the common cause.

It was bitterly unfortunate. We are told we
should forgive; and we should. But—

"Forgiveness to the injured does belong
But they never pardon who have done the wrong."

Nor will forgiving the past solve the problem of
the present; provide for unity in the future. The
wrong must be righted. The past is unsever-
ably tied into the present and let us not
forget that to-day will be the past of to-

morrow.   These things are not merely off-
shoots of a domestic situation; we can now see
them as the inevitable results of "a world-old and
world-discredited mistake."   Let us return to the
experience of the outside world, not for consolation, but for the purpose of looking at ourselves in
the clear light that comes from viewing a situation,
in the making of which we had no part. It will be
remembered that in an early chapter we had this
applicable quotation from "War and Democracy":
"There are governments in Europe so foolish as to
think that men and women deprived of their national institutions, humiliated in their deepest feelings, and forced into an alien mould, can make
good citizens, trustworthy soldiers, or even obedient subjects."

CHAPTER XVI

IN REVIEW

WE have found nationality standing for those thoughts and habits of life which are dearer than others because they are "our own." Because they are the dearest possessions of mankind, Great Britain has respected national things; in Canada, in South Africa, in India, the people who became British were left free as Canadians, Boers, and Hindus, to continue their group development in the land around which their traditions had grown; were left free to cherish the achievements of the past, and free to work along their own lines for the greater achievements of the future. That is what is meant by national freedom. Do we believe in it? Of course we believe in our own freedom, and so does every other people; but such belief is not enough. Do we believe in national freedom as a principle? Time and time again we have said so; how then can we reconcile our words with our action in curtailing the freedom of a nationality that, by the force of war, has become subject to our domination in its native land.

"Modern Europe cannot allow a people to be seized like a herd of cattle; she cannot continue deaf to the repeated protests of threatened nationalities, she owes it to her instinct of self-preserva-

tion to forbid such abuses of power." So cried
Alsace and Lorraine in 1871 when on the verge of
losing the free exercise of those thoughts and
habits of life which were dearer to them than any
other because they were their own. So cries
French Canada in Ontario and Manitoba to-day.
Do we believe in national freedom? We began
our enquiries with this question, and after surveying the field we are compelled to ask it again. It
is the issue that will not down; no amount of legislation, no decisions of the Privy Council, will
change the fact that a people once free to pursue
its development after its own fashion is being
forced in this, its native land, into an alien mould;
is being compelled against its will to have its
children prepared, in an alien language, for life's
work. Germany answered the disturbing cry of
Alsace and Lorraine with the statement: It is the
law. And it was the law, as sound a law in Alsace
and Lorraine as in Ontario and Manitoba. But
neither in Alsace and Lorraine, nor in Ontario and
Manitoba, is it national morality or national justice.

In Ontario and Manitoba it is something more
than immorality and injustice: it is ingratitude.
To give the Teutons their due, they were under
no obligations to the Alsatians and Lorrainers
for national services. But we English-Canadians should never forget that French Canada
refused to become part of the American Revolution. The past cannot be blotted out. Whether

we will or will not, we live in the past. When I think of this country's national past, I remember having heard that only three generations ago, one of my ancestors crossed the Niagara River and, reaching Canada, thanked God that he was again under the Union Jack. No! My ancestor was not playing a part in melodrama; he was simply a hard-headed man from the Jersey side of the Hudson River, believing that, in spite of the impost on tea, liberty could not flourish in America without British protection. It will be remembered that his belief in the unsafety of religious liberty in America was grounded on family experience. Convinced of the value of English national traditions, he sought a home where his children and children's children could build upon those traditions. *He came not to destroy the convictions of others, but to build upon his own.* He left the shores of the dividing Niagara River cursed—in English—as a Britisher, and landed on British soil to receive a "bienvenu." I cannot forget that the first kindness my ancestor received in his new home was from a French-Canadian. He and his benefactor did not understand each other's language, but what were mere words to men who understand each other's spirit. Those pioneers of the New World who stuck by King George in the upsetting days of the seventeen-seventies had much in common: both were Loyalists and both were Royalists; both looked upon the Union Jack as a symbol of national and religious freedom. The French-

Canadian had retained his freedom through Britain's sense of freedom, and Canada had remained British because of French-Canadian appreciation.

When we were the minority and they the majority in those early days, the hospitality of the Canadian wilderness was proverbial. There were few inns. The stranger—English or French—was made welcome in the home; and the guest of to-day was the host of to-morrow. The fires were kept burning under the kettle; pea-soup and soupe-aux-pois were one and the same thing when served in the rough-hewn log houses. There was a difference between English and French it is true; but it was that between p-e-a-s and p-o-i-s. Throughout the land there was a spirit of the brotherhood of man which, with the herding of men in cities, has become only a thing of meaningless words.

As recorded in the history of that period, the Recollet Fathers loaned a church to the Presbyterians whilst their own place of worship was being built. The Presbyterians were grateful—as was to be expected—and recorded their acknowledgement in one of the first minutes of their church meeting, presenting the Fathers with "one box of candles, 56 lbs. at 8d., and one hogshead of Spanish wine at £6, 5s." The preservation of the details is not merely an illustration of Scotch thrift: it is primarily an illustration of the relations between French, English and Scotch, Catholic and Protestant, in the days before politicians and editors became directors of public sentiment.

But in time's course we became the majority and
they the minority. In the reconstruction days after
the war men came from English-speaking parts in
tidal waves, from England, from Scotland, from
Ireland and from the United States. Then we de-
manded and received self-government. Surely no
specific restrictions were necessary to preserve the
interests of the French-Canadians from despoila-
tion at our hands! Surely belief in national freedom and gratitude for past national favours ought
to have ensured the continued existence of French-
Canadians as French-Canadians within the self-
governing Province! Surely self-government is not
identical with selfish government! Did French-
Canadians preserve this country for Britain only
to lose their national freedom when they became
a minority of one, or even as one is to twelve? To-
day the Boers are as confident of the protecting
power of the Union Jack in Africa as the French
once were in Canada. Last year (May 15, 1917)
General Smuts, the veteran Boer leader, was given
a banquet by members of both Houses of the Imperial Parliament; and on that occasion set forth
his understanding of Britain's principle of freedom. He said: "Even the nations which have
fought against it, like my own, must feel that their
cultural interests, their language, their religion, are
as safe and as secure under the British flag as those
of the children of your own household and your
own blood. It is only in proportion as this is realised that you will fulfil the true mission which is
yours."

21 c.

For many years after the Conquest the French-Canadians felt as do the Boers that their cultural interests, their language, their religion, were as safe and as secure under the British flag as those of the children of the English household and the English blood. And with good reason. We have seen Britain's intention in the days of the Quebec Act expressed by Thurlow, Fox, and Burke. And it was all for freedom. In 1857 Egerton Ryerson, who laid the cultural lines of the land that is now called Ontario, made the statement that "French is the recognised language of the country, as well as English." For many years after Confederation French-Canadians felt reasonably safe, although then the advocates of "the other way"—the way that is not Britain's—had begun to threaten their security. In 1889 Sir Oliver Mowat, who for many years presided over the affairs of Ontario, said: "Our opponents insist that the Government should insist on all instruction being given to the French children in the English language. No such regulation was suggested by the Commissioners, and none such has been made, because such a regulation would be absurd; and, instead of serving the cause of education, would often prevent education altogether. How can you teach in a language which the children do not understand?" But Mowat's day came to its end and "the opponents" now have their way. Now all instruction is to be given to French children in the English language.

Some day the Boers may be a minority in South Africa, as the French-Canadians are in Ontario to-day. When the spaces of African land are filled with English-speaking men and women, is Boer culture and the Dutch language to be restricted by an English-speaking majority? Will the plea that the Boers have not occupied all the land—have left room for others—be sufficient to justify the majority in insisting that Boer children be instructed solely in English? in relegating the Dutch language to a minor place on the school curriculum beside geography? Will an English-speaking majority seek to force an English-speaking man's mind upon the Boer, as one seeks to force it upon the French-Canadian in Ontario and Manitoba to-day?

Is there no such thing as national freedom? Is there only State freedom? It was not the State that developed the treasured culture: it was the nationalities. Is there freedom for the culture of only the majority? freedom only when it can be protected by ballots or bullets? If that be true, then where does the British sense of freedom differ from that of Germany, of Turkey, or of any other country? Where is there freedom at all? Unless a man has freedom for his national culture in his native land, he has no freedom; he has nothing worth while.

> "For what avail the plow, or sail,
> Or land, or life, if freedom fail?"

In the light of the country's past and in the light

of the world's present, the French-Canadians are morally entitled to cultural autonomy in the land which Britain holds under the title deeds of the Treaty of Paris. It is a moral obligation, but surely moral obligations are our sacred obligations!

While the State is a casing, we must not forget that as a casing it requires strength if the thoughts and habits of life which are dearer than others are to be protected.   Here lies the argument upon which Germany most relies to justify its harsh, unbending course towards Teutonic homogeneity. Germany protests that the casing will be weakened by sheltering a Polish nationality; a Danish nationality; and a French nationality; and that in consequence the Teutonic nationality may be exposed. Likewise Ontario argues that it cannot house twin nationalities. "One school and one language" has been the cry; and in vehement English we are told only with one of each can we continue to have "one flag." It is but a reiteration of the old prechristian Athenian precept, "one Blood, one Speech, one Cult, one congruous Way of Living," expressed after the manner of the Americans of the United States. Have those who argue that way forgotten the plain teaching of history that, if all the American Colonies had been homogeneous in the days when Britain's fortunes were at their lowest ebb, if all had spoken the same tongue and attended the same Church, all would have been to-day under one flag, and that flag would not have been British.

But let us lay aside a sense of gratitude to the French-Canadians for retaining this country for Britain, as apparently those who argue for one school and one language would have us do, and regard our relations as only of the present and future. We will remember the argument for the necessity of homogeneity, at first sight, appeared formidable; but proceeding further, we found that homogeneity had never been secured by the birch of the school-master. That ought to be enough to make us desist from continuing "the world-old and world-discredited mistake." But were we to succeed in forcing our culture upon an unwilling people, where others have failed—a highly improbable supposition—even then let us remember homogeneity is no assurance against disruption of the State. Let us again remember our English-speaking Protestant Loyalist ancestors who fought against their English-speaking Protestant Revolutionary neighbours; and who after the war were imprisoned, were deprived of their property, and subjected to gross indignities. "Why should persons who are preying upon the vitals of their country," said the Governor of Connecticut, "be suffered to remain at large, whilst we know they will do us every mischief in their power"; and the Governor of Connecticut spoke the language of those whom he drove from the country. Nor did homogeneity in language save the United States—the homogenist's pattern of polity—from civil war in the eighteen-sixties. Protestant fought Protestant,

and in both armies, English words were the words
of command.   The fact that the Englishman of
England and the American of the United States
spoke the same language in much the same way
in 1812, did not prevent them from fighting.   We
had a domestic clash of arms ourselves twenty-
five years later, and men did not divide upon their
manner of spelling freedom, but upon their manner of thinking freedom.   No!   There is something better than "one school" and "one language":
And that something is harmony in diversity.

The very struggle that the French-Canadians
are making to-day, its tenacity and its depth of resolve against great odds, is our best assurance that
they are a fit people beside whom free men may
dwell in a common State.   If French-Canadians
have not shown quite the same readiness as English-Canadians to arm in defence of freedom these
past few years, it must be remembered that they
have not had the same incentive.   Would we have
done what they have done? is a rough and ready
rule by which men may judge the conduct of others.
If the situation had been reversed, if it were English-speaking people who had been forced, in any
one of the nine Provinces, to have their children
educated in an alien tongue and limited in the use
of their own, would they have done better than the
French-Canadians in fighting for freedom on the
Continent of Europe?   It was not the existence of
twin nationalities that weakened the casing; it was
the attempt of one of the twins to destroy the other.

It was in fact a repetition "of the world-old and world-discredited mistake" that brought the disaffection natural to its train.

We have found that, ethnically, we Canadians who speak French and English are first cousins. There is no immutable blood difference between us. Nationally we are not the same. We cannot stay to review the evidence of the nature and extent of the difference, but we would indeed be blind if we did not recognise its value. It takes all sorts of men, says the old proverb, to make a world. "It takes all sorts of nations," writes Alfred Zimmern, "to make a modern State." Diversity, not homogeneity, is the strength, not the weakness, of the British Empire. Speaking at the South African dinner given in his honor on May 22, 1917, General Smuts explained Boer ideas on this feature of the case in these words: "The policy General Botha and his associates have stood for is that we must have national unity in South Africa as the one true basis for future stability and strength—and that national unity is entirely consistent with the preservation of our language, our traditions, our cultural interests, and all that is dear to us in our past. The view we have taken is this, that the different elements in our white populations ought really to be used to build up a stronger and more powerful nation than would have been possible if we had consisted purely of one particular strain."

In Canada, English talent is complemented by

French talent; we are not alike, and yet we are not sufficiently unlike to render political cohesion impossible. We English-Canadians have neither all the virtues nor all the vices; and the same may be said of the French-Canadians. If I have uncovered more of the English-Canadian shortcomings than of the French-Canadian, from whom does it come in better part than from an English-Canadian, sharing all the faults of his nationality.

Seldom do we English-Canadians lay ourselves open to the charge of self-depreciation. Too often do we exaggerate our own virtues and regard our own vices tolerantly—sometimes affectionately—and vent our indignation upon the other fellows'. A few years ago there were evidences of corruption in the Quebec Legislature, and English-Canadians wagged their heads and said, "I told you so: the French-Canadian is innately corrupt in public life." This is an English-Canadian's standing charge against the French-Canadian: he does not hold fast to a high standard of morality in public affairs. When we are faced with the clean records of Sir Wilfrid Laurier and Sir Lomer Gouin, we smugly assume that their virtues are in some way due to contact with English-Canadians. They are exceptions, we protest: and exceptions are necessary to prove the rule. Not many years before the Quebec incident there had been evidences of corruption in the Ontario Legislature surrounding the Gamey charges, and shortly afterwards there was a big scandal in the Manitoba Legislature involv-

ing men in high places, later on another scandal
involving members of the Saskatchewan Legislature—and yet no one thought of interpreting these
things as evidence of the innate corruption of English-Canadians, corruption at Toronto, Winnipeg,
and Regina, was just plain corruption, regrettable,
but certainly not indicative of innate badness in
English-Canadian character. Nor was it; nor
was the Quebec affair indicative of French-Canadian character.

We English-Canadians have habitually had our
good eye upon French-Canadian faults, and our
blind eye upon our own. We have judged the
French-Canadians by their poorest men, the English-Canadians by their best; and have not, unnaturally, concluded that, financially, commercially, artisically, morally, socially, and generally, we
are superior.

Shortly after Earl Grey had taken possession of
Government House at Ottawa, in conversation with
a rich English-Canadian merchant, he asked of the
health and fortunes of Philippe Hébert, the sculptor. "I don't know him," confessed the merchant.
"Don't know him?" gasped Earl Grey. "My dear
man, he is one of the most distinguished Canadians." "Oh, a French-Canadian!" commented
the merchant, and continued in what at least Earl
Grey apparently thought were tones of deprecia-
tion: "We English-Canadians meet so few French-
Canadians." "That is your misfortune," replied
the Governor-General, "and a double misfortune in

the case of Hébert.   I assure you that in England
he was quite a lion.   The cultured and distinguished were honoured by his acquaintance."

Did the reader ever have a heart-to-heart talk
with a Chinaman about other matters than shirts
or salads?   Did he ever fathom his opinion of the
relative values of nationalities?   If he be a frank
Chinaman and the reader a sympathetic listener,
the Chinaman will say that his people are superior
to all others.   They have, in his opinion, forgotten
more than others ever knew.   Has the reader
watched the supercilious smile that played over the
face of his Indian guide when he wearily and blun-
deringly stumbled through the bush?   The Indian
has a conviction of the inferiority of the tenderfoot.
The bearded Jew, only a few years from the
ghetto of Russia, who buys our old bones, bottles,
and cast-off clothing, for less than the price of a
song at the opera, sincerely believes himself and
his people the chosen of God, and the Talmud the
receptacle of all wisdom.   The conviction of race
and national superiority lies deeply in the breast of
all men who rub shoulders only with their own.   We
have analysed that feature of our belief at length,
and dwell upon it in conclusion because it is indeed
the well of our troubles.   So long as we continue
to drink its intoxicating waters we shall never dwell
in harmony with the French-Canadians, nor any
other nationality, not even with the men whom we
called "bronchos" and "sparrows" before the war.

We know the worth of few things save by com-

parison; and seldom know our own worth, because
when it is involved we seldom make an honest comparison. At times we have bitterly resented the
Englishman persistently confusing us with the
Americans of the United States. I remember having heard the late Honourable Mr. Tweedie relate
an illustrating incident in his career as a Cabinet
Minister of New Brunswick. He had had occasion to visit officially the British Consul-General
of New York, and followed his card into the Con-
sular office. "Ah," said the official looking at the
card in a reminiscent way, "Tweedie of New
Brunswick—Brunswick—yes—I remember now. I
was there a year ago." And yet further conversation revealed that the Consul-General had not
been out of the United States since crossing the
Atlantic. He had been in the City of New Brunswick in the State of New Jersey, and had confused
it with the Province of New Brunswick in the
Dominion of Canada. "Stupid Englishman" we,
who had heard Mr. Tweedie's story, exclaimed.

But is this constant confusion of Canada with
the United States the result of English stupidity?
Is none of it due to our unimpressing individuality? Some years ago I met a distinguished English author who, having spent several weeks in the
United States, was in New York preparing to sail
for home. "And you have not visited Canada!" I
protested. "No; I was in the United States two
years ago, and that will do as well; for you are
certainly doing and thinking now what the Amer-

icans did and thought then," he replied quizzically.
"On this trip I am visiting you as it were two years
hence," he continued, as if to give a stronger punch
at our belated imitativeness. The remark was made
with a smile, but I must confess it was received
with a twinge. Was it altogether without truth?
Distinguished Englishmen and Europeans are constantly passing through the United States and passing by Canada. Are we really in English Canada
culturally nothing more than an "up-state" part
of the American Republic? We found in our enquiries that we are dependent upon the Americans
of the United States for many things that go to
make up nationality. But are we really bankrupt
in cultural individuality? Have we English-Canadians no thoughts and habits of life which are
our own? If that be true or even partially true,
then surely we cannot justly blame the French-
Canadians for holding fast to their own and refusing to accept an English-Canadian culture, the
existence of which the world persists in ignoring.
Are the waters genuine in that well of superiority?
It may be that some features of our domestic clash
would be settled if the Lord were to answer a
prayer made after the manner of the poet Burns:

> "Oh, wad some power the giftie gie us
> To see oursel's as others see us!
> It wad frae monie a blunder free us
> And foolish notion."

I must confess that I do not look upon the situation as one in which of necessity we ought to make a

virtue. It is true, as the old Chinese proverb runs, that "a wise man adapts himself to circumstances, as water shapes itself to the vessel that contains it." But personally I would not alter the circumstances. I confess I do not look forward with pleasure to the day when all men, subject to Canada's soil, climate, food, and the general aspects of Nature, will have the same habit of thought—if Buckle is right. Canada needs both mentalities, one to temper and strengthen the other. They are natural complements. The Provinces of Canada will gain, not lose, by protecting alike the culture of the descendants of the Old and the New Régimes. History does not justify Ontario's plea for repudiation on the ground of the inadequacy of State machinery. I cannot believe Lord Acton wrong in saying that "a State which is incompetent to satisfy different races condemns itself; a State which labours to neutralise, to absorb, or to expel them, destroys its own vitality; a State which does not include them is destitute of the chief basis of self-government." The existence of the French and English nationalities in Canada is the handiwork of Divine Providence, out of which, with mutual toleration, will come inestimable benefit to Canada, and it may be when both are bigger, older, and wiser, a substantial good to the whole world.

Those who would force an English mind upon the French-Canadian, who refuse to tolerate the "French pretensions to nationality" within Canada, have drawn great comfort from Lord Durham's report on the Affairs of British North America. Spending only five months in North America (and then the country had no expeditious travel by railway), Lord Durham became convinced of the necessity of homogeneity and blamed the British Government, as Sir C. P. Lucas, in his able review of Lord Durham's Report, says, "for not having steadily and with a whole heart, taken the British side and subordinated the French." Many English-Canadians share in this opinion, forgetting with Lord Durham that such a policy could have succeeded only, as Sir C. P. Lucas points out, on the hypothesis "that the home government had determined to run counter to the British instinct of fair-play and generosity to the conquered, which, after all, is nearly the *most valuable asset that a ruling race can possess.*" The italics are mine; but the words are those of one of England's able constitutional historians.

Lord Durham placed much of his case for submerging French-Canadian nationality, as do English-Canadians to-day, upon analogies taken from the United States. Professing no great regard for the integrity of American politics, there are men who are not above appealing to it on occasion for justification of their own conduct. But in this matter the analogy does not hold good. In our first chapter we found in the will to preserve a force which must be reckoned with in measuring the legitimacy of a claim for national recognition. This all-important factor was not sufficiently appreciated by Lord Durham. "He takes the case of Louisiana," says Sir C. P. Lucas, "but the French in the Province of Quebec held it by far greater numbers and by far longer tenure than they held Louisiana; while the Dutch in New York, to whom Lord Durham also refers, had only a fifty years' tenure of Manhattan Island and the Hudson valley before they were brought under British rule. He might have noted that the Dutch in South Africa absorbed the handful of Huguenots who settled among them, but this illustration also would not have been in point. From the dawn of colonisation in North America the valley of the St. Lawrence had been the home of the French, and the history of Canada had testified abundantly to their stubbornness and their strength. In the year 1838 or 1839 it was too late to talk of denationalising a people who had made the land their own; and it was hopeless to think that efforts to do so would extinguish the bitterness of race feeling."

If it was "too late" in 1838 to crush the national will of the French-Canadians, if then the French-Canadians had "made the land their own," how late is it in 1918 when the French-Canadians have grown by numbers and cultural achievement into full national consciousness. "It was left to Lord Elgin," continues Sir C. P. Lucas, "while carrying out in full Lord Durham's views of responsible government, and sharing Lord Durham's confidence that responsible government would make for loyalty and not for separation, to repudiate at

the same time his father-in-law's doctrine that the
French should be denationalised, and to advocate
free play for their language and their usages. Later
history has proved how far from the fact was Lord
Durham's estimate that the French-Canadian nationality must necessarily be absorbed; for, having
been left to its destiny under a system of popular
government, it has more than held its own within
and even beyond the province of Quebec."

But how are we to fit the casing around the
two nationalities? We are told there are so
many difficulties in the way—and there are a few.
It has been difficult to secure teachers who know
the two languages. Yes, and difficult to secure
teachers who know one. Securing teachers is, after
all, only a matter of money—and already enough
money has been poured out over litigation on our
bi-lingual school troubles to educate several generations of bi-lingual school teachers. There were
teachers, according to the government reports, in
the English-French schools that had not proper
certificates; and I am told there are a thousand or
more teachers in the English schools that have not
proper certificates. There will always be difficulty
in finding teachers for our schools until we are prepared to make teaching a permanent profession
paid in proportion to its importance. Where a
rural community is divided in such a way that it
is impossible to satisfy English and French require-
ments by a single school, then the State must step in
and satisfy both by two schools.   The situation

must be met, as in other countries, by a general levy. It is, if you like, a penalty for having obtained this land by conquest; a situation which must be met just as we meet our obligations to the aborigines. There are innumerable difficulties in the way of doing anything we do not want to do. When the will comes, then the way will follow. It was Napoleon who 113 years ago wrote to George III when on another occasion French and English differed, that "reason is sufficiently powerful to discover means of reconciling everything when the wish for reconciliation exists on both sides."

Across the Ottawa in the Province of Quebec there are 211 thousand Canadians of English and Scotch descent—or were when the census man went his rounds in 1911. On this side of the Ottawa in 1911, there were 202 thousand French-Canadians. In Quebec there were 244 thousand Protestants, and in Ontario 485 thousand Roman Catholics. If we really want to find a way to harmony in diversity, perhaps it is to be had no farther away than Quebec, where men neither as Englishmen nor as Protestants have reason to find fault in their school treatment. The "British Protestants," as they were named by the Fathers of Confederation, have a deputy minister or, as he is styled, Secretary of Education, in the State that is governed by French Roman Catholics. They have their inspectors, regulate their own course of studies, have, in fact, a school autonomy where they are a minority as one to eight.

22 c.

But in so controversial a matter I must be specific. At a meeting of the Dominion Educational Association, Mr. J. C. Sutherland, the Inspector-General of Protestant Schools in Quebec, was asked some questions by sceptical officials of the other Provinces, the answers to which are illuminative of the possibility of having harmony in diversity.

"Inspector Lang:—You are not really under an iron despotism, then?

"Mr. Sutherland:—No. We have wonderful freedom and whatever we want they give us; we never have any trouble. Agriculture and drawing are the only two compulsory subjects in the general school law, which says that those shall be taught in all public schools. The other course is decided by the Protestant Committee for the Protestant schools, and by the Catholic Committee for the Catholic schools. This committee is appointed for life. I was on the Protestant Committee for seven years before I was appointed in the Department.

"Dr. Carter: You are getting along very harmoniously, and you seem very optimistic.

"Mr. Sutherland:—We never have any trouble; we are happy as clams down there."

As "happy as clams in Quebec"—and clams are supposed to be extraordinarily chummy and happy —and all through tolerance. The French-Canadian Catholic majority has given the English-Canadian Protestant minority freedom, and both are satisfied. I cannot resist the temptation to re-quote

Bishop Creighton's apt sentence: "Practically we are tolerant because no harm comes of our being so."

Now let us have the situation west of the Ottawa. Here the French-Canadians have no deputy, no secretary, no committee, and no voice, as French-Canadians, in the education of their own children. The Province has taken fifteen of the sixteen ounces of flesh to which it is entitled under the British North America Act; Quebec has never drawn the knife. "Whatever we want, we Protestants there, we just say what we want and the Government wants to do it," Mr. Sutherland told the Ontario men at the ninth convention of the Dominion Educational Association—but without avail. Have the State loosen its control over the schools of the Province? Never! I hear some of my readers say with emphasis. But does it not all depend upon who is in control of the State. If the French-Canadian Catholics were in control in Ontario, as in Quebec, it might be a very good plan; in fact, it would probably be an exceedingly good plan. It may be that we are regarding these matters, not as of principle, but as of self-interest. But surely it is a poor rule that does not work both ways, or rather they are poor men who refuse to apply a rule both ways.

For the last time I ask: do we believe in freedom? Many of our English-speaking ancestors came to this country in search of it. They came not simply to be clothed and fed, to lay up bank

balances and die; but to make homes where they
and their children might live in free communion
with the thoughts and habits of life which were
dearer than others because they were their own.
Freedom in that sense, we, their descendants
have to-day.   Have we obtained it only by the
destruction of the freedom of others? Must
French-Canadians   pay   for· English-Canadian
freedom by the loss of their own? Is English culture to be built around the lakes and plains
of Ontario and Manitoba, even as Teutonic culture is being built around the mountains and val-
leys of Alsace and Lorraine—only when French
culture is smothered out? That may be Germany's
way, but it is not Britain's. There are signs
that even Germany is seeing the error of its way;
for since the war a German chancellor has declared
(on the authority of Mr. Asquith) in favour of
"giving the various races the chance of free evolution along the lines of their mother tongues and of
national individuality." Mr. Asquith in repeating
the remark, cynically suggested that "apparently
this principle is to be applied—I suppose on approved Prussian lines—both to Poland and to Belgium"; but even the declaration has value. It
means that Germany is at least awakening to a
realisation of the hopelessness and heartlessness of
the school crucible. But Germany will find it
difficult to acquire Britain's sense of freedom, for
it lies essentially in British spirit. Empires have
been built upon conquests of territories and States;

the British Empire as well as others. The difference lies in this: Britain after conquest removed the old casing and substituted for it her own; but the new casing, the British State, has been charged with protecting the encased; the national thoughts and national habits of mind have been preserved and left free for development within the land acquired. That is the distinction between "Britain's Way" and "The Other." That is the essence of Britain's sense of freedom. I would, if I could, write it indelibly in the minds of all who have inherited Britain's responsibilities.

Too seldom do we stop to analyse the real meaning of these things, too often do we play with the words "freedom" and "liberty" and their equivalents. For many they have become mere catchwords. But when men's liberties are in peril, these concepts are weighed in careful balances. General Smuts is one of the men who had reason to weigh. He was introduced to the Lords and Commoners of Great Britain, by General French, on the occasion to which I have before referred, "as a great commander and leader of men." Notwithstanding "the consummate bravery and ability" with which General Smuts commanded the Boer forces in the South African war, with—to use General French's words—"disadvantage in the way of numbers, arms, transport equipment, and supply," he was compelled to yield. The Boers lost freedom of State; and to-day are loyal to Britain. Why? By British hands the Boers lost State freedom, but by

British hands they retained freedom for the
thoughts and habits of life which were dearer than
others, because they were their own. That is the
secret of Britain's success in Imperialism. But let
us have General Smut's words, expressing his concept of the spirit which, animating the British Empire, compels the loyalty of those who have become
British by conquest. He told the Lords and Commoners of the United Kingdom: "What I feel in
regard to all the empires of the past, and even in
regard to the United States, is that the effort has
always been towards forming one nation. All the
empires we have known in the past and that exist
to-day are founded on the idea of assimilation, of
trying to force human material into one mould.
Your whole idea and basis is entirely different. You
do not want to standarise the nations of the British
Empire; you want to develop them towards
greater, fuller nationality."

After all, it is a very old principle which General Smuts admires; a very old principle which
the English-speaking British of Ontario and Manitoba have defied and the French-speaking British
of Quebec have applied. But let me state its
application to the clash of nationalities in Canada,
in words of another, W. S. Bullock, who at one
time was a Protestant clergyman, but on the
occasion referred to was, as representative of
Shefford, moving a rather famous resolution
in the Quebec Legislature protesting against
Ontario's action on the bi-lingual question.

Mr. Bullock is from the home of what has been named "The Tragedy of Quebec," the Eastern Townships, and ought to know its conditions as well as its tragedians. These are his words: "And speaking in my own name personally as a descendant of that noble band of Empire Loyalists, who left their homes in the New England States in order to remain under the British flag, and who came and united their lot in the Province of Quebec, with the French-Canadians of this province, speaking in this House as a representative of the Protestant minority in the Province of Quebec, and speaking in this House as a child of the bi-lingual school, and as a father of children who at this moment are attending bi-lingual schools, I simply wish to say to our friends in Ontario: Remember in all your legislation the greatest word that ever fell from the lips of the great Head of the Christian Church—'Whatsoever ye would that men should do unto you, do ye likewise unto them'—for this is the law, the spirit of all true law, the spirit of the law of the British Empire and the spirit of the law of the Dominion of Canada."

Mothers had pleaded that their children be not forced into an alien mould; strong men had cursed the humiliation to which they were subjected in a land which for 300 years had been the native land of their race; school-less children had stridently protested that come what may they would walk in their parent's national footsteps. Devout

clergy had sought the intervention of God on behalf of a people whose one sin was a desire to have
their children carry on what they in all conscience
believed to be the most desirable in human life.
And all had been in vain. Tighter still were drawn
the lines of restriction.   School trustees were
haled into court and fined $500 for the crime of
having permitted religious instruction in the
language of Bréboeuf and Lalement; and this in
the land where Bréboeuf and Lalement had laid
down their French lives for the cause of Christianity; as a last resort, the dire threat of the
confiscation of home, was held before a helpless
people.   Repression could go no further and
spare human life.   French-Canadian Catholic
entreaties and protests had failed to move
English-Canadian Protestant hearts.   And then
Bullock, an English-Canadian, a son of the
Loyalists, a former Baptist minister, a man living
in daily contact with the French-Canadian people,
raised his voice in the Quebec Legislature and
asked his co-religionists and compatriots of Ontario in Christ's name to give Christian charity.

Mr. Bullock's appeal was made many months
ago and—it was futile. If it caused twinges
of the Christian conscience of Ontario, they
were not visible in the words of its press and
hustings. God has many attributes from which
men have ever selected, according to their disposi-
tions. Differences in religion have become differences in emphasis. The learned Dean Inge tells

us that the exercise of "justice, mercy, and sympathy," are the distinguishing characteristics of the
Christian; but those directing the policy of Ontario against the French-Canadians—proceeding
ostensibly on religious lines—have chosen to
imitate God's power rather than God's love. Mr.
Bullock's plea for the application of the Golden
Rule, so far from being accepted, raised only a
raucous cry of protest against the interference of
Quebec. The press has persistently maintained
that there is no oppression in Ontario—and perhaps has believed it. "The great inlet by which
a coulour for oppression has entered into the world,
is by one man's pretending to determine concerning
the happiness of another," said Edmund Burke.
Men invariably fail to recognise their own tyran-
nies. Ever has the Golden Rule been accepted by
Christian and non-Christian men as a test of fair
conduct. Can we say *that if we English-Canadians were the minority in Ontario and French-Canadians the majority, we would have them do unto
us what we are doing unto them?* We have not
said so, nor are we likely to say so—and by the
Golden Rule stand convicted.

"The good old rule sufficeth us, the simple plan
That they should take who have the power, and they should
     keep who can."

It may not be considered too much to say that
Ontario's attitude on this question is summed up in
the following words: "The State is self-sufficient;
self-regard is its appointed duty." And yet these

are the words of Dr. Rumelin, Chancellor of the University of Tübingen, written in expression of Germany's policy. Surely the same idea was expressed by the "Toronto Star," when (May 9, 1916) it said: "There is no solution of the bi-lingual problem except the assertion and maintenance of complete Provincial control. Any attempt at dictation or interference from without can produce nothing but confusion and ill-feeling. The Province must be left free not only to enforce its own laws, but to apply them to special cases."

And this brings us to the second part of Mr. Bullock's plea—for it is two-fold—the appeal on British grounds. While each man is free to interpret Christian teachings for himself, free to reject them altogether, free to refuse to regulate his private and public conduct by them, British men in their corporate action may not deliberately refuse to apply Britain's cardinal principle of polity. "Here lies the difference between the British constitution and other forms of government, namely, that liberty is its end, its use, its designation, drift and scope as much as grinding corn is the use of a mill," said John Adams in 1766—and the test of liberty is, to repeat again the words of Lord Acton —"the amount of security enjoyed by minorities." We cannot be un-British in spirit and permanently remain a part of Britain. Our conduct has not yet gone before the world's review, and when it does, remembering Toynbee's words, "where a minority has clung to its native speech, it has been allowed to retain it," we cannot, in all conscience, have it added—except in Ontario and Manitoba.

Nor must we overlook the consequence of our refusal to abide by the arbitrament of the Golden Rule and the spirit of British justice. It is an immutable law that the majority as well as the minority, the strong as well as the weak (English-Canadians as well as French-Canadians), must each in its way suffer the violation of man's proper relation to man. As A. Maude Royden tells us in "Towards a Lasting Settlement": "To crush out all those who have the right to exist, but not the power to enforce that right, is to commend to one's own lips, not the 'choice wine' of humanity, but—

The bitter dregs of woe
Which ever from the oppressed to the oppressor flow."

BOOKS OF REFERENCE

Rt. Hon. J. C. Smuts, P.C., *War Time Speeches*. Hodder & Stoughton.

The Hon. N. A. Belcourt, *Canadian Club Address*. Quebec Telegraph Co.

Canada Year Book.

Vicount Bryce and Others, *The War of Democracy*. Doubleday, Page & Co.

Charles Langlois, *The Truth, Nothing but the Truth*, (pamphlet). "Le Devoir."

Warwick Bro's & Rutter, Limited,
Printers and Bookbinders, Toronto, Canada.